D0082730

Kuwait

Contemporary Issues in the Middle East

Kuwait

Social Change in
Historical Perspective

JACQUELINE S. ISMAEL

Syracuse University Press   1982

Copyright © 1982 by Syracuse University Press
Syracuse, New York 13210

All Rights Reserved

First Edition

Library of Congress Cataloging in Publication Data

Ismael, J. S.
    Kuwait, social change in historical perspective.

    (Contemporary issues in the Middle East)
    Bibliography: p.
    Includes index.
    1. Kuwait—Social conditions. 2. Kuwait—
Economic conditions. I. Title. II. Series.
HN669.A8I82   953'.67   81-21244
ISBN 0-8156-2254-6   AACR2

Manufactured in the United States of America

To
Abu Shereen

JACQUELINE S. ISMAEL received the B.A. and M.A. from the University of Calgary, and the Ph.D. from the University of Alberta, Edmonton. She is Assistant Professor on the Faculty of Social Welfare at the University of Calgary, Calgary, Alberta, Canada, and the author of articles in the *Middle East Journal, Arab Studies Quarterly,* and *Journal of Comparative Family Studies*.

Contents

List of Tables

List of Figures

ix

Preface

MY INTEREST IN KUWAIT was initiated in graduate school as a
deviant case focus for the theoretical study of modernization, development, and social change. This book represents the substantive outcome of theoretical and empirical investigations of the processes of social change and development in the capital-surplus, single-
resource–dependent societies.

The theoretical debate and issues have been an integral part of my
interest in these unique societies. However, this discussion has been
placed in the background in favor of the substantive empirical analysis of
Kuwait as a concrete case study. The utilization of dependency theory as
the analytical framework for this analysis represents, in effect, my
conclusions regarding the theoretical debate rather than the debate
itself. The introduction provides a summary of dependency theory to
place the subsequent analysis in theoretical perspective.

The remainder of the book is divided into two parts: Part I
examines the historical development of Kuwait in the pre-oil period;
Part II examines the post-oil period. Some comments on the sources
may be useful to the reader. Part I relies upon three basic sources for
historical data: (1) studies of the history of the Arab Gulf in English
(studies of Kuwait in English are limited); (2) studies of the Gulf in
general and Kuwait in particular in Arabic, and here the study of
Kuwait's history or specific aspects of it is more extensive and it is in
these works that documents pertaining to Kuwait's history have been
preserved; (3) British India Office (IOR) and Foreign Office (FOR)
records. Part II of the study relies primarily upon demographic and
economic data collected by the Kuwait Central Statistical Office, Central Bank of Kuwait, and the Planning Board of the Ministry of Planning.
These documents were made available to me by the Government of
Kuwait which kindly facilitated my field research.

The Library of Congress system of transliteration from Arabic was
utilized in the citation of Arabic sources with one modification: diacriti-
cal marks were dropped. In addition, the transformation of dates given

xi

in accordance with the Muslim lunar calendar was based on Hassubi Abdul Wahhab, *al-Taqwim al-Islami* (The Islamic Calendar) (Baghdad: al-Irshad Press, 1973).

To reduce cumbersome footnoting, in the initial citation of a source, the standard footnoting format was utilized, with the footnotes provided at the end of each chapter. In subsequent citations, the author is referenced directly in the text, and a bibliography is provided at the end of the book. References to the Kuwait Government Statistical Abstracts and Annual Statistical Abstracts has been abbreviated to ASA, year, and page, and have been incorporated in the text.

I am indebted to the many scholars, teachers, and friends who contributed so much to my research along the way. Although I cannot name all of them here, their contributions are reflected in the structure and substance of this study. I do, however, wish to acknowledge my special indebtedness to Dr. Baha Abu Laban of the University of Alberta whose guidance and encouragement brought this research to fruition, to the Canada Council which provided the funding that made this research possible, and to Dr. Len Richards, Dean of the Faculty of Social Welfare, The University of Calgary, who provided the time necessary to complete the present manuscript. Finally, I must acknowledge the "invisible hand" of my husband, Dr. T. Y. Ismael, manifest throughout the following pages.

Kuwait

Introduction

A GROUP OF SOCIETIES IN THE ARAB GULF HAS EMERGED onto the contemporary world scene that possesses a profound significance to the international political and economic order which is surprising in terms of its minute geographic and population dimensions. Because of their vast oil and financial resources, these small societies in effect impinge directly upon the jugular vein of the advanced industrial world. In spite of their significance to the contemporary world order, however, we understand little of the social dynamics that have shaped and are affecting them. This case analysis of social change in one of these societies—Kuwait—is an effort to provide a systematic analysis of the historical and contemporary processes of change in the region.

Contemporary Kuwait is one of the super-affluent, oil rich shaikh-doms of the Arab Gulf. These societies occupy an anomolous position in terms of theories of modernization, development, and dependency. Rather than reflecting the poverty and instability characteristic of other Third World societies, they are capital-surplus nations with the highest standards of living in the world. Under the impact of affluence from oil wealth, they have passed from traditional tribal shaikdoms subject to British colonial administration to independent urban-cosmopolitan centers of world finance and trade within a decade or two—and they have experienced these phenomenal transformations under relative sociopolitical stability.

Given the magnitude and rapidity of change, it appears that affluence itself is the primary explanatory variable of social change. A before affluence/after affluence framework does indeed describe the degree and rate of change, but does not explain the social dynamics—the people and events—that have shaped the trajectory of change in the region. The challenge of the analysis of social change is to identify and examine the patterns that emerge in the unfolding of history through people and events. These patterns are revealed by the characteristics of continuity as well as change. In this framework, affluence itself is only one of the characteristics. The relationship between past and present—between continuity and change—is the primary analytic problem.

1

For the social analyst, the problem must be approached from the perspective of a model that provides a set of interrelated analytic categories. The categories indicate the threads of history to be addressed—the kinds of people and events in the kaleidoscope of unfolding history—that pattern social change. The model itself, of course, constitutes the contours of a pattern, and in this respect superimposes an outline within which patterns are circumstantiated and through which the model itself can be refined. The patterns identified, then, are constrained by the model selected — just as any scientific endeavor is constrained by the tools available to it at the time.

The model utilized in this study of social change in Kuwait derives from dependency theory. The remainder of this chapter will be utilized to examine the analytic categories and inter-relationships of this model, the theoretical rationale behind it, and the theoretical questions it poses in analyzing social change.

THE DEVELOPMENT OF UNDERDEVELOPMENT: Dependency

Broadly stated, social change refers to the processes of alteration in the beliefs, values and institutions of people — changes in the way people think, act, and relate to others in the patterns of everyday life. Most theories of social change posit underlying sociological phenomena that encompass increasing complexity and structural differentiation. Indeed, this has been identified as a basic evolutionary trend in human history.

Social change in Third World countries has been viewed as a special case of this process; specifically, as the reaction of traditional societies to the unprecedented growth in material culture of modern societies. The process of modernization or development has been conceptualized as the transition from static tradition-bound structures to the dynamic, continuous growth structures of modern industrial societies. Most definitions of development or modernization, as this process has been called, are based on the technological correlates of industrialization. The implicit or explicit sociological questions have centered on the social and political hindrances to or imperatives of achieving economic takeoff (the stage where a society achieves a self-sustaining rate of economic growth). The assumption has been that traditional institutions and values offer resistance to social change and thus hamper economic development. Thus, traditional/modern and undeveloped/developed dichotomies have been fundamental to most of the literature on modernization.

Dependency theory emerged as a critique of neo-classical development and modernization theories. It has identified the essential unity of the development/underdevelopment dichotomy of nations. Both are part of the same historical process of capital accumulation and expansion and are integrally related in terms of production, distribution, exchange, and consumption. As a historical process, the development of underdevelopment is integrally related to the deepening of the capitalist mode of production in the central capitalist nations through its expansion to pre-capitalist nations as peripheral formations for capitalist exploitation. Samir Amin has identified the dynamic of the deepening-expansion process as the means by which capitalism checks the tendency of the rate of profit to fall: (1) increasing the rate of surplus value; (2) spreading the capitalist mode of production to new regions where the rate of surplus value is higher; and (3) developing various forms of waste.[1] The era that hindsight now calls the stage of imperialism reflected the dominance of the second mechanism when a main thrust of capitalist development (deepening-expansion of the capitalist mode of production) was "toward the territorial division of the world among the leading capitalist countries."[2] According to Nicos Poulantzas, this era marked the transition from dominance of the periphery by means of simple commodity export to dominance by means of the export of capitals, corresponding to the transition of capitalism in the center from competitive to monopoly capital.[3] The expansion of this era, achieved through force of varying degrees, induced the articulation of the peripheral pre-capitalist societies with the demands of the central capitalist nations and their integration into the evolving world division of labor.

Ignoring this historical role of imperialism, the neo-classical view of economic development views pre-capitalist societies as essentially static entities that are recently embarking upon the road to economic development. According to this essentially unilineal view, economic development is initiated when production in some sector or industry becomes oriented to larger markets—regional, national, or international. Orientation to the larger market stimulates capital investment, centralization of production and specialization of function to increase per capita productivity. Centralization and specialization increase the demand for supportive goods and services as production and consumption become differentiated. While the application of capital displaces nonspecialized labor, the market for new goods and services generates a demand for specialized labor. This new market stimulates capital investment and specialization. And so, through a series of stages of growth generally marked by the level of capital investment, the cycle becomes self-generating, gradually enveloping larger and larger segments of the society into integrated, interdependent markets on a regional, national, and international scale. Thus, the traditional, localized exchange activities and relationships of underdeveloped societies are gradually displaced by differentiated, centralized activities. This is accompanied by structural shifts in the distribution of labor as labor markets expand and diversify in conjunction with markets for goods and services. It is through the labor market that the wealth generated by increased output is distributed to the population in the form of income. Increasing incomes associated with higher levels of productivity generate demand for consumer goods and services, thus contributing to the growth of markets and the rising standard of living of the population.

This broad summary of the neo-classical view of the process of economic development and growth points up the important factors that have been stressed in the literature: capital investment, specialization of labor, and the expansion and diversification of markets. Capital investment, either at the level of the individual entrepreneur or at the level of the national economy, is generated from the level of surplus (or the profit margin for the individual entrepreneur). The level of surplus, as a measure of wealth in an economy, is related to the level of demand for goods and services and also to the amount available for further capital investment. The continuing process of development, then, is directly related to the rate of growth of surplus because of the capital investment it permits and the new markets it generates. The level of complexity and the rate of increasing complexity of the division of labor are thus directly dependent upon the rate of growth of surplus; and the distribution of wealth in the form of income is directly related to the rate of labor specialization and hence the rate of growth.

However, dependency theorists such as André Gunder Frank argue that creation of a primary commodity export economy dependent upon the importation of foreign capital equipment created and perpetuates a situation of underdevelopment. In effect, such policies maintain the imperialist relationship of Third World nations as sources for cheap raw materials and labor, and markets for the capital equipment and consumer goods of industrialized nations, thus restricting the development of internal markets and industries. Under this circumstance, the capital investment and specialization of labor that occur are limited and are related to and dependent upon the mode of production of other (metropole) nations, while the capital accumulated is transferred out of the nation.

In terms of the neo-classical view, then, economic development is based upon capital as a prime factor of production. It is the rate of capital accumulation that affects the level of capital investment and hence the rate of specialization of labor. The demands for supportive and consumer goods and services generated by what centralization of production and specialization of labor that have occurred cannot be satisifed internally. These demands then must be satisfied by external markets, in effect creating a further drain on capital resources. Dependency theorists like Frank argue that this creates a vicious circle with the goal of achieving a self-sustaining rate of growth ever elusive.

The result of integration into the world market and the application of foreign capital is the creation of the so-called dual economy—a small enclave of a high productivity economic sector based upon imported technologies and oriented to external markets (in terms of both production and consumption), in the midst of a low productivity sector oriented to subsistence. The social structural counterpart of the dual economy is the co-existence of an urban-based modern highly specialized occupational structure oriented to modern modes of production and consumption and a rural-based unspecialized structure oriented to subsistence.

The linkage between the two sectors is the rate of transfer of capital and labor from one sector to the other. In effect, the dependency relationship that exists between the metropole and satellite nations is duplicated internally in the relationship between the dominant modern sector and the subordinate traditional sector (Frank's metropole-satellite chain of exploitation).[4] Value expropriated from the subordinate (rural) sectors is concentrated in the dominant (urban) sectors. Rather than being re-invested internally, however, and hence providing urban jobs for labor displaced in the subordinate sector, the capital is expropriated to the metropole. The result is the more or less rapid transfer of capital and the dislocation of labor.

Working from the theoretical perspective of imperialism, dependency theorists have identified the contradictions between the forces of production and the relations of production inherent in the capitalist mode of production that are manifested internationally in the relations between developed and "developing" nations. André Gunder Frank identified three contradictions in the development of capitalism as a world system that form the context of underdevelopment: (1) the contradiction of expropriation/appropriation of economic surplus; (2) the contradiction of metropolis-satellite polarization; and (3) the contradiction of continuity in change—referring to the maintenance of the essential structure of capitalism through the process of change in its configuration.[5] Development and underdevelopment, imperialism and dependency, in other words, cannot be viewed in isolation. In the words of T. Dos Santos:

To understand dependence as a conditioning context of certain kinds of internal structure is to understand development as a world-wide historical phenomenon, as a consequence of the formation, expansion and consolidation of the capitalist system. This approach implies the need to integrate into one single historical account the capitalist expansion of the developed countries and the consequences of that expansion in the countries which are today adversely affected by it. These consequences are not "effects" of capitalist development in a simplistic sense, but rather they are integral and determinant parts thereof.[6]

THE SOCIAL STRUCTURE OF DEPENDENCY: The Dependency Syndrome

The corollary processes of the transfer of capital out of the nation and the dislocation (proletarianization) of labor are the progressive marginalization of the masses and the integration of the elite into a supranational economic, political, and/or social order. These processes have been of more recent focal concern to dependency theorists who have come to recognize that the essentially external explanation of dependency in terms of world capitalism is no longer adequate to explain the dynamics of dependency. According to Fernando Cardoso:

> as the process of internationalization of dependent nations progresses, it becomes difficult to perceive the political process in terms of a struggle between the Nation and the anti-Nation, the latter conceived as the Foreign Power of Imperialism. The anti-Nation will be inside the "Nation" — so to speak, among the local people in different social strata. Furthermore, to perceive that, in these terms, the Nation is an occupied one, is not an easy process: there are very few "others" in cultural and national terms physically representing the presence of "the enemy" (p. 93).

Dependency exists, in other words, no longer primarily in terms of external exploitation, but in the very structure of social life within the society. This structure is characterized by fragmentation—i.e., by the progressive disarticulation of the forces of production in terms of productive levels, and by the progressive disarticulation of the relations of production across various sectors of economic activity at different productive levels. This segmentation within the society is a result of the articulation of selected socioeconomic sectors with central capitalist economies and subordination of other sectors to the demands of accumulation in the dominant sector (Frank's metropolis-satellite chain of exploitation in social space as well as spatial space).

Whereas capital expansion in central capitalist nations presupposed the elimination of all other modes of production through the progressive capitalization of all the forces of production due to the deepening of the internal market, in peripheral nations capital expansion appears to presuppose the subordination (as opposed to elimination) of other modes. If this is the case, then what appears to be structural disarticulation may actually be a mode of articulation among forces that sustains primitive accumulation while obviating expanded reproduction. This is essentially Amin's point in *Accumulation on a World Scale*, where he analyzes the complex "mechanisms of primitive accumulation for the benefit of metropolitan capital" (p. 11). Within this context, Frank's argument that the penetration of capitalism eliminates pre-capitalist elements by their integration into a single capitalist system gains perspective.[7] We may speak of non-capitalized or undercapitalized forces of production, but non pre-capitalist modes, and in particular not pre-capitalist relations of production. C. Meillassoux makes a similar point when he notes that the apparent "survival" of the rural community in developing nations is really "an organic component of capitalist production." He explains that "the agricultural self-sustaining communities . . . fulfill functions that capitalism prefers not to assume in the underdeveloped countries: the functions of social security. The cheap cost of labor in these countries comes from the super-exploitation, not only of the labor from the wage-earner himself but also of the labor of his kin-group." Thus, he concludes, "because of this process of absorption within the capitalist economy, the agricultural communities, maintained as reserves of cheap labor, are being both undermined and perpetuated at the same time, undergoing a prolonged crisis and not a smooth transition to capitalism."[8] The result of this parasitic relationship of socioeconomic sectors at different levels of productivity is growth without development, expansion without deepening.

The dynamic of capitalist expansion thus appears different in peripheral societies from its dynamism in central capitalist societies, although the theoretical framework for specifying this difference has not yet been adequately developed. This problem will be discussed again in the following section. The point to be made here is that the social structures of dependent societies are characterized by a syndrome of segmentation. The features of this syndrome are: (1) the progressive subordination of all sectors of the socioeconomic infrastructure to the demands of a limited primary commodity export economy; (2) dependence of the productive sector upon the importation of the products of

Western technologies; (3) dependence of the internal market on the importation of essential consumer goods; (4) proletarianization of labor; (5) low levels of employment in the productive economic sector (marginalization of labor); (6) rapid growth of the tertiary sector; (7) increasing concentration of wealth and power.

DEPENDENCE AND SOCIAL CLASS

Colin Leys has pointed out the limitations of dependency theory. In particular, he notes its "economistic character" and the rather abstract role the concept social class plays.[9] Working from the theoretical perspective of imperialism, dependency theorists have focused on the role of capital as a primary contradiction negating the development thesis. However, while dependency theory has demonstrated effectively that the external relations of domination inhibit the development of the forces of production within dependent societies, it has not demonstrated why these relations are continually reproduced in the structures of dependent societies, nor, indeed, why the structures of dependency have actually deepened in most Third World nations in spite of the national liberation movements which swept across Latin America, Asia and Africa, freeing these nations from overt colonial domination. Philip O'Brien in this regard points out the circular argument of dependency theory: "dependent countries are those which lack the capacity for autonomous growth and they lack this because their structures are dependent ones."[10]

Given the removal of the overt structures of imperialist domination, Ian Roxborough[11] has posed the problem directly in asking why the value extracted from the subordinate internal sector flows abroad rather than initiating a process of internal capital accumulation. This raises directly a fundamental question posed by Amin as to whether autonomous capitalist development is possible in Third World countries.[12] Indeed, the concentration on capital flows does suggest this possibility, but only if capital itself is narrowly interpreted in an "economistic" way.

In its fundamental meaning, the concept of capital, as conceived in social class theory, embodies an objective relation between constituted labor and living labor. This relation is manifest in the objective social opposition between the expropriators of constituted labor (i.e., capital) and the owners of living labor (that is, labor power). Class analysis is posited on the proposition that in the capitalist mode of production there is a necessary link between the rate of surplus value and the level of development of productive forces. In other words, the level of development of the capitalist mode is dependent upon the rate of exploitation of labor. This is the dialectic of social class in the capitalist mode of production. It is this objective opposition of social classes that constitutes the dynamics of advanced capitalist society.

What has to be demonstrated in dependency theory is that the flow of capital out of the nation and other features of the social structure of dependency are the result of objective class relations within a dependent society. One of the problems posed in forwarding the class analysis of so-called dependent societies is their heterogeneous character. The question arises as to whether they constitute a homogeneous category in terms of the fundamental concept of mode of production. While the linkage fostered by imperialism between the capitalist mode of production and a pre-capitalist mode of production has been the historical process for the creation of dependency, how this actually changed the nature of the pre-capitalist mode of production varies from society to society depending upon:

1. the level of development of the capitalist mode of production at the time of imperialist penetration into the pre-capitalist society; and, correlatively,

2. the point of integration into the evolving world division of labor;

3. the nature of the pre-capitalist social structure at the time of imperialist penetration;

4. the way and extent this structure was modified by imperialism;

5. the subsequent changes in the world capitalist system and their effect upon the particular history of each society since imperialist penetration.

One result of the wide range of variability in the structures of dependent societies is the inability to generalize about objective class dynamics within them. The theory remains fundamentally rooted at the level of dynamics of the international system rather than at the level of social class dynamics. While it is empirically demonstrable that capital accumulated at the national level is expropriated out of the nation, and that this is explainable in terms of an international division of labor, unequal development of productive forces, and the consequent assymetrical exchange relations thus fostered, aside from instances of overt coercion by international powers it is not theoretically deducible why Third World nations have continued to participate in this disadvantageous system—that is, why the relations of dependency continue to be reproduced in these societies in spite of the widening rift between developed and underdeveloped nations on most of the standard measures of development.

A theory of the reproduction of the relations of dependency requires an analysis of the dynamics of social class structure of the society. If we are to understand dependency as something more than neo-imperialist coercion, we must begin to analyze the objective opposition between social classes that constitutes its dynamic. Here the analysis immediately founders on the fundamental concept of mode of production. Third World nations exhibit such a variable array of capitalist and pre-capitalist or non-capitalist elements that application of the categories of class analysis, developed in terms of the pure capitalist mode of production, results in considerable modification (evidenced by the veritable proliferation of class nomenclature) of this analytical model.

As indicated earlier, the dominant conceptualization of the variable mix in Third World nations of capitalist and non-capitalist elements is that capitalism in dependent societies operates by a different dynamic than capitalism in advanced capitalist nations, and this difference is signified by the neologism "peripheral" capitalism. Here the conception (explicit or implicit) is that we are dealing with the capitalist mode of production but that it operates by a different dynamic than central capitalism. This difference is described by the external orientation of peripheral capitalism (as opposed to the internal orientation of central capitalism) and by the dependent relationship that exists between peripheral and central capitalist economies (as opposed to the interdependent relations between advanced capitalist economies). Presumably, however, the objective class relations operate differently in each society depending upon the particular mode of articulation of capitalist and pre-capitalist elements. We are not, then, dealing with one dependent or peripheral capitalist mode of production but with an array of modes whose common characteristic is the limitation on autonomous capitalist development imposed in one way or another by a relationship with central capitalism.

Again, however, we arrive at the persistent dilemma of dependency theorists as to whether autonomous capitalist development is possible if the domination of central capitalist powers is overcome—that is, if the capital accumulated internally is reinvested rather than expropriated out of the nation. While reference to the international division of labor, unequal development of productive forces and assymetrical exchange address the probabilities of autonomous capitalist development, nevertheless they do not rule out the possibility. This question can ultimately be answered only by reference to the objective dynamics of social classes. This must be the point of reference of mode of production and not vice versa.

DEPENDENCY IN PERSPECTIVE

Dependency theory, it must be recalled, emerged in terms of an analysis of the relations between nations, not social classes. It takes its point of departure from the fact that the relations of production on a world scale are constituted in a particular political structure, and that the historical development of political structures in Third World nations is explained by the imperialism/dependency dialectic. It is not social classes that are the historical actors but capitalist nations. While this perspective has identified the historical process of the development of underdevelopment, nevertheless it remains one level of analysis above the question of the reproduction of dependency. To bridge this level of analysis, we must take the central clue offered by dependency theory — that there is a necessary (objective) link between an expropriating class (peripheral capitalists) in the dependent nation and central capitalism—and subject it to intensive empirical investigation from the level of analysis of social classes to define its nature and dynamics (internal as well as external).

Such an analysis must begin with the organization of social labor in a society to determine empirically the historical structuring of alienation and expropriation, and the nature of the dialectic between substructure and superstructure, that constitutes the mode of production. Modes of production cannot be theoretically deduced but must be empirically determined from the concrete material history of a society. Only in this way can we begin to determine whether dependency constitutes a distinct mode of production—i.e., whether these societies are subject to the same laws of motion — or whether they constitute an array of different modes collectively subordinated to the dynamic of central capitalism.

THIS STUDY

This perspective defines the framework of the present study of Kuwait. Beginning with the organization of social labor in Kuwait prior to its integration into the world division of labor, the study seeks to delineate the social structure of that period. This investigation focuses on the question of whether or not Kuwait in this period was a class-structured society—i.e., a society based upon antagonistic relations of production —and if so, what was the dynamic of class relations in early Kuwait. This analysis, then, constitutes the delineation of early Kuwait's mode of production.

In 1899, Kuwait became a British protectorate, and did not receive formal independence until 1961. The analysis of the establishment of Kuwait as a protectorate will focus upon the issue of how this affected the social structure of Kuwait. It is in this respect, then, that an understanding of Kuwait's mode of production prior to the period of British penetration is important.

This analysis will also address the issue of whether or not the establishment of Kuwait as a British protectorate initiated within Kuwait the historical process of the development of underdevelopment. In 1936, Kuwait signed an oil concession covering the whole of Kuwait with a British-American consortium. While clearly this was the initiation of Kuwait's contemporary integration into the world division of labor as a major oil exporter, nevertheless this role did not materialize until the early fifties. What were the structural dynamics within Kuwait prior to its emergence as a major oil producer? There is an apparent hard and fast break between the social structure of pre-oil Kuwait and that of affluent Kuwait. With the emergence of oil as the principal source of wealth, the forces of production within Kuwait underwent a sudden and radical transformation. Yet underpinning this apparent discontinuity marking Kuwait's rapid transition from rags to riches is considerable continuity in the relations of production. In order to understand both the aspects of change and continuity an examination of the structural dynamics of the period from 1899 to the early fifties is crucial.

All of the above, of course, is historical research to provide the basis for understanding the dialectic between the forces of production and the relations of production within contemporary Kuwait. Unlike most Third World nations, contemporary Kuwait is a capital surplus nation. If capital shortage *per se* is not the origin of either underdevelopment or dependency, as dependency theorists maintain, then can Kuwait be characterized as an underdeveloped and dependent nation? It bears the historical characteristics of the process identified by dependency theorists: a pre-capitalist society penetrated by a Western capitalist nation in the historic era of imperialism and integrated into the contemporary world division of labor as a primary commodity export economy. Does Kuwait also reflect the structural characteristics of dependency, the dependency syndrome?

All of these questions ultimately bear upon the central theoretical dilemma of dependency theory — that is, is autonomous capitalist development possible in a dependent nation. While this issue may not be resolved by a case study of Kuwait, the related and logically prior question (from the perspective of social class analysis) will be a central issue of this study—that is, is there a necessary (objective) link between an expropriating class in the dependent nation and central capitalism, and does this link define the structural dynamics of dependency. It is hoped that an answer to this question in the case of Kuwait will contribute to the theoretical development of dependency theory.

Dependency theory, then, provides the framework of this analysis. As used in this study, dependency refers to the perpetuation of underdevelopment. It is a central proposition of dependency theory that it is the relations of production of capitalism as a world system that inhibit the possibility of autonomous capitalist development in underdeveloped societies integrated into the world capitalist division of labor. Dependency, then, refers to a specification of the relations of production. Underdevelopment, on the other hand, refers to the forces of production specified relatively on two dimensions: historically, i.e., a society was at a higher level of development of productive forces prior to capitalist penetration; comparatively, i.e., a society sustains functioning at a level of primitive accumulation subsequent to capitalist penetration, in contrast to expanded capital accumulation in classical capitalist development. Primitive accumulation is the process of divorcing the producers from the means of production—the process of the proletarianization of labor—resulting from the expropriation and concentration of the means of production. Capital accumulation is the process of the expansion and centralization of capitalist production resulting from the expropriation and concentration of already formed capitals. In primitive accumulation, the volume of social capital increases relative to the rate at which the means of production are brought into capitalist production; it is directly associated, then, with the rate at which labor is proletarianized. This is the process of the expansion of capitalism referred to earlier. In capital accumulation, the magnitude of social capital increases relative to the rate at which the volume of constant capital expands; it is associated with the rate at which labor is marginalized by the increase in constant capital at the expense of variable capital. This is the process of the deepening of capitalism referred to earlier.

Rather than viewing the problem from the outside in — from the perspective of nations as historical actors—the analysis begins from the inside out—from the perspective of the historical organization of social labor, the class dialectics generated from this organization, the changes wrought in this organization by imperialist penetration, and integration into the world division of labor.

The above discussion provides the general framework for the organization of this study. Part I encompasses the pre-affluent era, examining the structure of Kuwaiti society prior to the establishment of the British protectorate (1899), and the period subsequent to it until the emergence of Kuwait as a major oil exporter (circa 1952). Part II encompasses the affluent era to the present, examining both the themes of change and continuity in Kuwaiti society.

PART I
Pre-Oil Kuwait

1

The Origins and Structural Development of Kuwait

*K*UWAIT IS A TINY SHAIKHDOM situated on the western shore of the Arabian Gulf. Isolated on three sides by vast expanses of desert and on the fourth by the Arabian Gulf, Kuwait society in the pre-oil era was shaped by the counterpoint of the two dominant themes of its environment—the desert and the sea. The geography of the Middle East outlines broadly the interplay of social forces that shaped early Kuwait. The juxtaposition of arid desert, sea coasts, and fertile river valleys delineates three distinct life styles: nomadic, maritime, and agricultural. While the influence of agriculture is indirect in Kuwait, the desert and the sea come together there to provide both the stage and plot of early Kuwaiti society. How each influenced its structure, and how each was modified by the other in a continuous interplay of essentially antagonistic patterns is the subject of this chapter.

THE BEDOUIN BASIS OF SOCIAL STRUCTURE

The influence of the desert on early Kuwait society relates intimately to the great bedouin tribes of the Arabian desert. To these tribes Kuwait traces the origins of its founding fathers, and from the tribes Kuwait inherited and modified the structural foundations of the society.

Communal in character, the pure nomadic life of the Arabian tribes as exhibited in the heart of the desert was organized around pastoral wanderings as the basic means of subsistence within the harsh desert environment. There existed within Arabia's arid ecological zones two distinct patterns of socioeconomic activity—sheep herding and camel herding. The articulation of the two patterns took the sociopolitical form of tribal organization. More mobile than sheep herders (in terms of distance, speed, and range in the continuous search and competition for pasture land and water), camel herders achieved hegemony in the desert and assumed aristocratic origins as a legitimation (known as sharif bedouin tribes). They maintained their exclusiveness through rules of marital exchange that precluded intermarriage with tribes of non-sharif origins. The less mobile sheep herders evolved as a class of producers organized along client tribal lines in a serf-like position tending the flocks owned by the sharif tribes, or tending the flocks of wealthy town-dwellers on the periphery of the desert, or as owners of their own flocks and organized as independent tribes, but generally allied to one of the powerful bedouin tribes.

This articulation took the normative form of descent lineages. Segmented lineage systems served as the basis of social organization, with lineages organized in terms of *ashira* (descendants from a common ancester, real or mythical), and subdivided in terms of *fakhths* (segmented lineages) and families. These segments were related by the degree of kinship between them. The *ashira* defined the broadest level of effective kinship, and the degree of kinship delimited the sphere of cooperative social labor—the way people were joined together in group endeavors. Outside these limits the expectation of hostility was the norm, while within them the closeness of the kinship tie moderated the incessant competition between groups over the use of pasture lands and wells, and the possession of camels and horses—the means of subsistence of nomadic life.

The *ashira,* then, defined a kin relation through time, while the relation between *fakhths* and families was continuously shifting over time in a kaleidoscopic fashion. In the constantly shifting alliances, segmentation, and reorganization of tribal segments that constituted the political history of the desert, kinship ideology served as both the legitimation of cohesion and cleavage in the continuous competition for scarce resources. In the long view, tribal genealogies served as the dogma of the powerful tribes and the ideology of ascendant tribes. Knowledge of the complex genealogies was the epistemology of the Arabian desert.

Corresponding to the kinship form of social organization was a patriarchal form of political organization, with allegiances organized in a hierarchical order around the male elders of the family, the *fakhth* and *ashira*. Each *fakhth* had a shaikh, while the *ashira* had a paramount shaikh (*shaikh mashaykh*—shaikh of the shaikhs). While the position of shaikh was hereditary to a family, the order of succession was arbitrary, depending essentially upon tribal consensus of the most able of the potential successors, and the issue of succession itself was often a catalyst to tribal segmentation. In addition, the shaikh had no mystified or special powers over tribal affairs. He was merely an equal among equals, and his ability to lead depended upon his ability to maintain the confidence of tribal elders, whom he was obliged to consult in all matters. This essentially egalitarian structure of political organization is reflected in a poem of a tribal elder:

> We are friends of his highness the shaikh,
> But we shall reject him if we see evil intentions.
>
> If you accept advice, we will advise you.
> And if you do not accept advice,
> We will banish you to hell.[1]

As a mode of production, camel pastoralism was a self-sufficient, self-perpetuating form of economic appropriation that required geographic mobility and group elasticity and autonomy. These were reflected in the elastic kinship structure and decentralized authority structures. The camel alone could provide all the basic means of appropriation from the arid environment and was the fundamental form of wealth in the nomadic culture. From the camel came all the means of survival and artifacts of private ownership—shelter, clothing, and food. Sheep, goats, and horses, where they were incorporated, were supplementary to the camel, not substitutive among sharif tribes.

Corresponding to the segmented lineage system, stocks were privately owned, with families representing corporate units of ownership. In contrast, wells, pasture, and tribal range were tribally possessed. Intertribal raiding was a chief means of expropriation and one of the sole means of surplus appropriation within the desert, although it did not raise the meagre level of surplus available. According to the eminent historian, Philip Hitti, the raid "otherwise considered a form of brigandage, is raised by the economic and social conditions of desert life to the rank of a national institution. It lies at the base of the economic structure of Bedouin pastoral society."[2]

Around these central activities of appropriation-expropriation revolved the tribal culture, history, and lore of bedouin life. Tribes flourished and languished in terms of their fortunes with camel herding and raiding — the cooperative and competitive aspects of camel pastoralism. And the maximum mobility and autonomy that camel pastoralism provided made it a fiercely independent, maurauding life style antagonistic to the settled and civilized ways of agriculture and trade. Around camel pastoralism developed the mystique of haughty indepen- dence, kinship fealty, and personal integrity that were the characteristics of a communal life style contemptuous of property, intransigent to organized authority, and independent of exploitable resources or surpluses (save camels).

To the aristocrats of the desert, all other patterns of socioeconomic organization were dialectically related. Other nomadic or semi-nomadic groups, organized and specialized along tribal lines — sheep herding, smiths, camel merchants, etc. — lived in a subordinate symbiosis with them. Urban centers established alliances with them to establish and protect trade routes, at the same time, living in trepidation of their occasional maurauding outbursts from the desert; and governments cajoled and coopted their leaders into the aristocracy of the cities. The history of the entire Middle East is intimately connected with the ebb and flow of the bedouin tribes who were both the scourge to and the well-spring of the great urban civilizations that dominate its history since antiquity.

From this turbulent background of nomadic tribal life emerges the origins of Kuwait's history. According to traditions related by Kuwaiti historians,[3] in the late seventeenth century intra-tribal conflict within the Anizah tribe (one of the largest bedouin tribes inhabiting Najd and North Arabia) resulted in the expulsion from the area of Hidar (in the district of Aflaj in the southwestern part of Najd) of a federation of families.[4] The Bani Utub (sons of the trekkers, as the emigres were subsequently called) embarked upon emigration northeastward, first seeking refuge in Qatar, where they spent about fifty years. According to Khazal:

> Ahl Hasan conquered Ahl Hidar and expelled their enemies. Among them were al-Sabah. They were forced to leave to Qatar, seeking refuge under Ahl Musallam, the rulers of Qatar at the time. After they were there for some time, however, the Ahl Musallam became worried and were afraid of their strength and forced them to leave Qatar. They [the émigrés] rode dhows [Arab Gulf sailing vessels] and took to the sea. This was the year 1086 hijari [1676].[5]

The Ahl Musallam followed the Bani Utub, and in Ras al-Tanurra (between Bahrein and Hasa) a battle between the two tribal groups occurred. The Bani Utub, victorious, continued their march, arrived in the area of al-Mukhraq and dispersed from there. According to Khazal:

Some of them lived in Subiyah. One lived in Abbadan and some stayed in Mukhraq. As for al-Sabah, al-Khalifah, al-Zayyid, al-Jalaahmen, and the Maawdah, they settled closer to the Shatt al-Arab in today's Um Qasir. They remained there, working in piracy. ... That kind of work was accepted and common in Basra and is similar to the raiding inland among the Arab tribes. (pp. 41–42)

The Ottoman Government, however, forced them to leave. Regrouping in Subiyah, the domain of the Dhfur tribe, the Bani Utub were threatened by the Dhfur and forced to leave.

Sometime in the early seventeenth century, they began arriving at the site of modern Kuwait City. According to al-Qinaie: "Their migration to Kuwait was gradual because after leaving Qatar, they were dispersed in different lands.... They then began arriving in Kuwait and were followed by a lot of other people, Arabs and Persians."[6]

Kuwait was in the domain of the Bani Khalid, a powerful bedouin tribe which dominated northeast Arabia. Here there was a supply of sweet water and a splendid natural landlocked harbor. The shaikh of the Bani Khalid maintained a small fort *(Kut)* for storage of food and ammunition. He afforded protection to the Bani Utub and gave them the fort and surrounding area.

The Bani Utub's tribulations in the period reflect the intimate relationship between the tribe and its *dirah* (tribal range). Alienated from their *dirah,* the Bani Utub were alienated from the dominion of their tribe—its traditional pastures as well as cooperative kinship structures. In the domain of other tribes, the Bani Utub were suspect and vulnerable intruders. The story of their steady progression northeastward reflects their move away from camel pastoralism. Unable to follow the regular migration paths in the search for pastureland that was the essential pattern of camel pastoralism, the Bani Utub were probably forced to diversify their productive means, attaching to them segments of other pastoral and non-pastoral groups along the way.[7] In Qatar and other ports of the Gulf to which they dispersed they were exposed to the maritime, merchant, pearling, and other activities. The point to be made here is that by the time they arrived in Kuwait, the Bani Utub had moved significantly away from camel pastoralism, acquired a cohesive tribal identity of their own and were accompanied by a diverse cross-section of economic groups attached to them in a client-tribal relationship.

The alienation of the Bani Utub from their tribal domain, however, must be placed in the larger context of the great transformations nascent in Central Arabia at the time of their departure. Bordered by the declining Ottoman Empire on one side and an emerging Persia on the other, the bedouin tribes of Central Arabia nevertheless remained outside the control of either power. Camel pastoralism and the isolation of the desert rendered them largely independent and impervious to foreign interference. However, the caravan trade routes which began withering with the shift from Mediterranean to Atlantic trade in the fifteenth and sixteenth centuries were enjoying a renaissance as a result of the imperialist competition between the expansive mercantile powers of Western Europe. With the resurgence of trade through the area, the bedouin tribes were again being drawn out of their desert isolation and into the mainstream of world history. Some of the powerful bedouin families were already shifting their attention from the pastures of the desert to the trade routes and urban centers of trade that were emerging in the area, precipitating inter- and intra-tribal conflicts as expropriation from trade became a real alternative to appropriation from camel pastoralism. Occurring on the eve of the Wahabi unification of Central Arabia, the Bani Utub migration must be understood in the context of the substantial changes already underway in the area. Their transition from nomadic pastoralism to a maritime mode of production is one aspect of these changes.

THE STRUCTURAL BASIS OF KUWAITI SETTLEMENT

At the time of the arrival of the Bani Utub at the site of Kuwait City, al-Rushaid (p. 31) reports that the area had no permanent settlement, but according to al-Qinaie (p. 9) was inhabited by groups of bedouin and fishermen. The area could support no agriculture at all, hardly even a kitchen garden, but the Gulf offered abundant supplies of fish. Little is known about the Bani Utub in their initial settlement of the site; it appears that they did not constitute more than 10–15 percent of the subsequently settled population.[8] Among the earliest tribal sections or families of the Bani Utub to settle in Kuwait were al-Jalaahmeh, al-Sabah, al-Khalifah, and al-Maawdah.[9]

The transition from nomadic to sedentary settlement was already well underway by mid-century. "In the first fifty years after its foundation," noted Lorimer (vol. 1, pt. 18, p.1001), "the town of Kuwait grew rapidly in wealth and importance." In 1760, the German traveller Carsten Niebuhr visited Kuwait and noted that it was a thriving commercial port of about 10,000 population which sustained itself on pearling, trading, and fishing and had some 800 boats.[10]

From the beginning, the transition from nomadic to sedentary life was based upon the industries of fishing, pearling, and commerce with desert and coastal tribes. The Arab Gulf has been an important sea route between India, the Middle East, and Africa since ancient times. "The Gulf," observed Arnold T. Wilson in his definitive history of the sea, "has a place in the written history of mankind older than that of any other inland sea."[11] Ship-building, sea-faring, and pearling were age-old productive means of the many scattered communities along its coast. These groups—whether they accompanied the Bani Utub to Kuwait or arrived subsequently — were likely the productive basis of the sea-oriented industries that were flourishing when Niebuhr visited Kuwait City in 1760.

From the beginning, however, control of the productive forces remained in the hands of the Bani Utub—the aristocrats of the desert transformed into the ruling class of the town. It is reported in the traditions of Kuwaiti historians that a tripartite pact among three of the original Anizah families that settled in Kuwait was made in 1716, in effect dividing control of the productive means among themselves. According to Khazal (p. 42):

> In the year 1129 hijari [1716], the chiefs of the most important three tribes that inhabited Kuwait entered into an alliance. These were Sabah bin Jabar bin Salman bin Ahmad, Khalifah bin Mohammed and Jabar bin Rahmat al'iIbi (the chief of the Jalaahmeh). The conditions [of the alliance provided that] Sabah will have leadership in the affairs of government, in consultation with them [i.e., the other two chiefs]; Khalifah will have leadership of the financial affairs in commerce; and Jabar will control the affairs of work on the sea. All profits were to be equally divided among them.[12]

Whether the tradition is valid or not, it reflects the bedouin structure transferred to the Kuwait community. The heritage of power that differentiated camel pastoralists from other classes of producers in the desert, in the sedentary community became the basis of differentiation between appropriators and expropriators. In the sedentary community, the nomadic tribal structure of classes of producers became the basis of a nascent social class structure articulated in a tribal context. In effect, the Bani Utub became a class in themselves by their asserted right of control over the factors of production—fishing, pearling, and commerce.

In early Kuwait, however, this was only nascent. The generation and distribution of a meagre social product appropriated from the desert and the sea did not really represent a new development of the forces of production; rather, it represented a new articulation of already existing forces. Early Kuwait was a subsistence economy, albeit relatively prosperous, and the character of production relations still essentially communal. The productive forces maintained the tribal character of the desert, providing a tribal pattern to the organization of labor and politics.

Economic Organization

The boats Niebuhr observed were the pearling and fishing fleets. From the beginning, the basis of Kuwait's settlement was the sea, and boat construction must have been one of the initial industries of the settlement. According to Winstone and Freeth:

> The development of the intense maritime activity upon which Niebuhr later commented must have depended upon an early influx of Baharina people, for this special group have always been the master shipwrights of the Gulf. ... Within their close-knit community the traditional skills of boat-building were passed from father to son; the Baharina has a virtual monopoly in this trade.[13]

However, neither Kuwait nor any of the Gulf area for that matter has timber. Most of the timber supply for the Gulf came from India; but in this early period of settlement the level of development of the Kuwaiti boat construction industry was primitive. According to al-Rushaid (p.36), the small boats built there were confined to the Gulf, and Kuwait must have picked up the timber from other ports within the Gulf supplied with timber from India.

What this reflects is the close association between commerce and all aspects of production in early Kuwait. In fact, its mode of production was based on two pillars — pearling and commerce. Pearls harvested from the rich pearl banks of the Gulf for the luxury markets of the world were exchanged for basic consumption necessities. Lacking any agricultural production of its own and with fishing and some sheep herding as the only means of subsistence production, Kuwait not only lacked a surplus product; it lacked most of the necessities and depended almost entirely on trade for its subsistence. Pearl production provided the means of acquiring the surplus product and commodities from centers all over the Gulf, either for consumption in Kuwait or for exchange with the nomadic and semi-nomadic tribes who stopped in Kuwait on their annual migrations to exchange their surplus product. Thus, pearling and commerce were the economic basis of settlement.

There was, then, a direct relationship between capital accumulation from pearling and the development of commerce. Pearling provided the capital for commerce, and commerce in turn provided the basis for perpetuation of the pearling industry — the material subsistence of the community as well as the material needs of the pearling industry. For both pearling and commerce the source of supply was external. The markets for pearls were also external. For commerce, however, the market was both internal and external. The viability of the internal market depended upon the rate of exploitation of pearls — in terms of both their appropriation and marketing. But the development of the pearling industry depended upon the commerce that provided the timber and other material resources for development of the fleet, as well as the subsistence requirements of the community. It was toward this subsistence-oriented market that Kuwaiti commerce was directed, and it was the needs of this market that propelled the initial development of both pearling and commerce.

Thus, the technical and social organization of pearling and commerce were dynamically interlinked, providing the basis for a rapid development of productive forces. This development took the form of tribal organization articulated in Kuwait as nomadic, semi-nomadic, and sedentary labor. While the nomadic tribes still represented independent producers exchanging their surplus product as autonomous producers, the new articulation of the semi-nomadic and sedentary groups surmounted the boundaries of the tribe as a division of labor. The labor of this production was differentiated along tribal lines. The al-Awazim and al-Rashaida tribes supplied the products from agriculture and fishing. The limited amount of agriculture that could be pursued in the desert occurred around oases and wells, and semi-nomadic groups followed the rains to exploit the agriculture where it existed. They traded their products with Kuwait for supplies, and settled in and around Kuwait during the dry season and sustained themselves through fishing and pearl-diving. The semi-nomadic shepherd tribes provided the products of sheep and wool for the community, also following the rains for the essential grazing land and centering their trading activities around Kuwait. The al-Sulb tribe provided the iron-mongers and smiths for the community. The products of camels (from food, clothing, and fuel to beauty aids) were supplied by the noble sharif tribes who made Kuwait their supply center on their annual migrations.[14]

Thus, the tribal framework of organization was maintained, but within Kuwait the tribe ceased to exist as a self-sufficient, self-perpetuating unit of production. Within the new articulation, it was transformed into a unit of occupational stratification and a mode for the reproduction of different kinds of labor. [15]

Sea-faring and pearl-diving represented the essential labor of Kuwait's mode of production, and ships the socially-produced means of production. The labor for both sea-faring and pearl-diving was derived principally from semi-nomadic tribes, while the Baharina produced the boats. The Bani Utub emerged as a class of independent captains of their own boats, engaged directly in appropriation from the sea, marketing, and commerce.

In this early period, then, the boat represented the unit of production, independently owned by the captain. The product of pearling boats represented commodities produced for exchange to merchants of the international markets. Petty pearl merchants in Kuwait *(tawawish)* purchased pearls directly from the captains either in the diving areas or city markets and resold them to the wholesale merchants *(tujjar)* of Bombay who channelled them to the world markets. These petty merchants constituted the financial class in Kuwait. The crew worked for pre-arranged shares of the ship's earnings.

In commerce, the distribution between capital and labor was similarly organized, though its basis was not commodity production *per se,* but the transformation through commerce of surplus product produced elsewhere into commodities for exchange in local and regional markets. Basra was one of the first ports of supply for Kuwaiti commerce. Located only 80 miles from Kuwait, it was accessible by both sea and desert routes. As one of the busiest ports on the Gulf serving as the transfer point between Gulf and caravan commerce from India, the Arabian Peninsula, and for Ottoman and European commerce, Basra was the emporium of the Gulf.

So long as the owners and laborers were intimately related in the production-exchange-consumption cycle and the character of the exchange of labor, the tools of labor and the products of labor was generally symmetrical, the communal character of tribal relations over-rode the class character of production relations. The cycle was subsistence, not accumulation oriented, and the only effective distinction between labor and capital was the distinction between captains and crew — a tribally delineated distinction. Capital had no independent existence but was merely an integral part of a subsistence cycle. Nevertheless, within the new articulation was a fundamental division in terms of the generation and distribution of the social product that was class, not tribal, in nature.

Political Organization

In its formation, Kuwait served as a trading center for the tribes of the Bani Khalid. It remained under the suzerainty and protection of the amir of the Bani Khalid, but throughout the eighteenth century intra-tribal strife and growing Wahabi power in Central Arabia gradually weakened the tribe's authority in the area. The Bani Utub were able to establish their independence and sometime in the seventeen fifties elected Sabah I as shaikh.

There are many different traditions explaining why Sabah I was selected as shaikh. Irrespective of the personal qualities attributed to him, however, the importance of relations with the tribes in the area must be considered as primary in the light of the eclipsing role of the Bani Khalid. The very survival of Kuwait depended upon relations with the tribes. First, the community depended upon the tribesmen for the production of basic necessities. Second, Kuwait required protection against perennial tribal raiding. No longer protected by Bani Khalid power, Kuwait required a shaikh both respected and feared for the number of tribesmen he could call into arms in an emergency. Third, the labor for pearling, fishing, and commerce was supplied by the tribes.

Apparently, unlike many of the Utbi families whose interests turned toward the sea (and whose ties with the bedouins consequently diminished), the Sabah family remained oriented toward the desert, apparently based on their interest in the active caravan trade between Aleppo and the Gulf. [16] They continued an active relationship with the bedouin tribes, camping out with them regularly and marrying from among them. In the desert, the tribes paid *zakat* (tribute) to the paramount shaikh of their area, and very early in the process of settlement, the Sabah house, because of its apparent interest in the caravan trade, had achieved this role, "partly by means of matrimonial alliances with other tribes in the neighborhood," according to Lorimer (vol. 1, pt. 1B, p. 1001). *Zakat,* in fact, was an important source of income for the Sabah family. [17] Sabah was selected as shaikh, then, because, according to al-Shamlan:

Sabah all year around remained in Kuwait or around it as his work was on the land. As for the majority, their work was on the sea with navigation, fishing, pearling and such. So they were absent from Kuwait for periods. (p.116)

Thus, Sabah power was based upon the family's relationship to the desert, and consequently their interests were closely allied to the nomadic mode of production, while the economic life of the community was more closely tied to the maritime mode. This separation of interests within the Utbi class was merely a functional division of power in a social equilibrium between modes of production. But the equilibrium was momentary, and its disintegration led to a changing balance of power.

THE CHANGING BALANCE OF POWER:
1762–1896

Both pearling and commerce were related to sets of external factors in such a way as to disturb the momentary equilibrium of interests differentially coalesced around them. Three factors uniformly affected all pearl-diving units of production: access to the pearl banks, level of development of the diving industry, and access to the pearl markets. Commerce, on the other hand, could be distinguished between desert and sea commerce. While the development of desert commerce was principally affected by relationships with the tribes of the area, sea commerce was principally affected by the level of development of the transport industry, access to supplies of marketable products, and access to external markets (a factor related to desert commerce in the case of inland or overland markets). In its initiation, both desert and sea commerce were oriented to the subsistence requirements of the internal market, and this was directly dependent upon pearling. The interests of pearling (which in effect represented the financial interests of Kuwait) were, not surprisingly, the first to emerge as a class of self-conscious interests.

The Emigration of al-Khalifah, 1766

The pearl banks were located in an almost continuous chain along the Arab side of the Gulf's coast, but the richest banks were in the area of Bahrain, some 300 to 400 kilometers from Kuwait. Access to these banks was a primary concern of the pearl merchants and diving captains (who were primarily of the al-Khalifah and al-Jalaahmeh branches).

In 1766, the whole of al-Khalifah (and shortly thereafter a major section of al-Jalaahmeh branch) left Kuwait with the intention of settling in Bahrein, but the rulers of Bahrein (the Shaikh of the Abu Shahr tribe which had suzerainty over the island and paid tribute to the Shah of

Persia) did not permit them to settle there. From there they proceeded to Qatar, not 50 kilometers southwest of Bahrein, and settled at Zubara. This settlement rapidly developed as an important Gulf port because of its participation in the rich Bahrein pearl fisheries. In 1783, with the assistance of Kuwait, al-Khalifah conquered Bahrein and made it the center of their authority.

Various reasons for the migration of al-Khalifah and al-Jalaahmeh from Kuwait have been advanced in local tradition. Whatever the case, their self-conscious direction toward the Bahrein pearl fisheries — an area well known to them from their earlier settlement in Qatar before arriving at Kuwait — gives credibility to the explanation of Francis Warden in one of the earliest studies of the Utbi tribe in English (1856). He states that "the accumulation of wealth rendered the mercantile branch desirous of seceding from the original league, that they might singly enjoy to add to their acquired riches" (pp. 158–59) by participating directly in the lucrative pearl fisheries.

The migration of al-Khalifah had two major effects upon Kuwait. First, it consolidated the leadership role of the Sabah family in the community. In 1762, Abdullah had succeeded his father Sabah I as Shaikh, and with the exodus of al-Khalifah and al-Jalaahmeh, there was no serious challenge left in Kuwait to Sabah authority.[18]

Second, it gave Sabah a tribal ally on the coast in the important area of the pearl fisheries. Whether the migration materially diminished the pearling industry in Kuwait in the short-run is not known. Even if it did, however, the transfer of merchant capital from Basra to Baghdad in 1775, discussed below, facilitated the rapid recovery of the industry; the Utub settlement at Zubara provided a secure channel of access facilitating the expansion of this capital, and with the conquest of Bahrein in 1783, a direct access to Manama, one of the busiest ports for commerce and pearl marketing in the Gulf. There was apparently no major rupture of relations between al-Khalifah and al-Sabah as a result of the migration, for in 1776 many of the notables of Kuwait (including members of the Sabah family) took refuge in Zubara as a result of the Persian occupation of Basra, and in 1783, Kuwait aided al-Khalifah in the conquest of Bahrein.

The Persian Siege of Basra, 1775

In March 1775, the forces of the Persian ruler, Karim Khan, began a siege of Basra which finally ended in the city's occupation in April 1776. While Kuwait remained aloof from the Persian-Ottoman conflict, the occupation of Basra had several major effects upon Kuwait. First of all, as the major port in the Gulf for the land-sea transfer of goods in east-west and north-south commerce passing through the Middle East, Basra was a major entrepot of world commerce. From its beginning, Kuwait had enjoyed the benefits of siphoning off the fringe of this commerce because of its proximity to Basra and its natural harbor. However, as explained by Lorimer:

> Kuwait, of which the prosperity was at this time considered to stand necessarily in an inverse ratio to that of Basra, benefited greatly through the occupation of the latter town by the Persians, in consequence of which the whole Indian trade with Baghdad, Aleppo, Smyrna and Constantinople was between 1775 and 1779 diverted to it. Even after this, until 1781, merchandise for Aleppo was sometimes forwarded by direct caravan from Kuwait, thus escaping the duties levied by the Pasha of Baghdad on goods forwarded through Basra. By 1790 Kuwait had begun to share in the commercial prosperity which the seizure of Bahrain had brought to the whole Utub tribe by drawing them into the carrying trade; and goods were imported from Masqat, Zubarah, Bahrain and Qatif. Merchants were efficiently protected at Kuwait, and the duty on imported goods was levied at the low rate of 1 per cent, *ad valorem*. (vol. 1, pt. 1B, pp. 1003–1004)

The shift of commerce from Basra to Kuwait was accompanied by the migration of merchants. Lorimer observed that:

> A noteworthy consequence of the Persian occupation of Basra was the migration of a number of merchants to Kuwait and the removal of others, who did not feel themselves secure even there, from Kuwait to Zubarah in Qatar. The trade and general growth of both Arab seaports were strongly stimulated by these events. (vol. 1, pt. 1A, pp. 146–47)

Development of the Boat Construction Industry

The transfer of externally oriented commerce (transit trade) and merchant capital to Kuwait provided both the incentive and surplus capital necessary for the development of the boat construction industry upon which depended both the pearling industry and sea commerce. According to Abu Hakima (p. 175), by 1780, Kuwait had already acquired ships—probably imported from India—large enough to make the sea voyage to India, giving Kuwaiti merchants direct access not only to Indian goods but also to the timber necessary for Kuwaiti ship construction. Although there are no statistics available, it is reported that this industry developed to such a level that Kuwait became an exporter of ships to the entire Gulf. In 1905, Lorimer (vol. 1, pt. 2, p. 2321) observed that "Kuwait appears to be the principal place where native craft are built." He reported (vol. 2, pt. 2B, p. 1054) that 20–25 vessels were turned out annually and about 300 carpenters gained their livelihood by boat-building. The migration to Kuwait of merchant capital was an important stimulus to the development of this industry.

But the development of this industry was not important in itself in Kuwait's mode of production. Most significant was its relationship to the development of the commercial and pearling fleets. Here again, statistics are wanting because of the lack of records at the time. Nevertheless, there is sufficient evidence to indicate the continuous growth of the fleets over the period and the changing relationship between small and large cargo vessels. As early as 1790, an official report to the British Government in India on the commerce of Arabia and Persia noted that the tribes of the Bani Utub (including Kuwait, Zubarra, and Bahrein at that time) had become the most powerful tribes navigating the Gulf:

> Their gallivats, the Boats are numerous and large, and they have engrossed the whole of the Freight Trade carried on between Muscat and the Ports on the Arabian shore, of the Persian Gulf, and a principal part of the Freight Trade, carried on between Muscat and Bussora.[19]

Lorimer noted (vol. 1, pt. 1B, p. 1006) that in 1829 Kuwait was credited with having a mercantile fleet of fifteen Baghlahs (a sea-going vessel) with a cargo capacity of from 450 to 100 tons, twenty Batifs and Baghlahs (vessels used chiefly in Gulf commerce) with cargo capacities from 120 to 50 tons, and 150 other boats used chiefly in Gulf and Shatt al-Arab commerce with cargo capacities of from 150 to 15 tons. Furthermore, he reported (vol. 2, pt. 2B, pp. 1053–54) that by 1905 the mercantile fleet included 36 sea-going cargo vessels, 50 coastal cargo vessels, and 50 Ballams engaged chiefly in trade from the Shatt al-Arab.

The growth of the pearling fleet over the period was similar. There was a steady transition from the small pearling boats with crews of five to the larger ships with crews of up to 70,[20] reflecting the development of the boat construction industry in terms of more sophisticated and complex vessels able to carry larger crews longer distances. In fact, there was a great deal of overlap between the commercial and pearling fleets. Many of the boats that engaged in commerce in the winter months shifted their operations to pearling in the summer months. Although the

actual estimates of the size of the fleet engaged in pearling vary considerably,[21] nevertheless by about 1890 Kuwaiti pearling ships were engag-
ing in pearling operations off the Ceylon coast in the winter months when
the season for pearling in the Gulf had passed. Lorimer (vol. 2, pt. 2B, p.
1053) noted that by 1905 "no less than 3,000" pearl fishers from Kuwait
pearled in Ceylon waters regularly.

The Kuwaiti historian Abd al-Aziz Husayn summarized the development of the boat construction industry in Kuwait accordingly:

Kuwaitis imported their first ships from other ports in the Gulf or from
India. Then they began building ships themselves and became experts in
this industry until it became one of the most important industries in
Kuwait. The Kuwaiti ships had a great reputation at sea. They began
innovating in this industry and created the well known kind [of ship] called
Bom which is purely from the experiences of the Kuwaitis at sea and
proved to be the best in passing the oceans to India and the eastern coast of
Africa. All the wood which was used in building ships and all the instruments that were needed were imported from India. Ships for fishing, ships
for pearling and ships for long distance travel were all built in Kuwait.
Each one of these professions had its special ships. The year was divided
into two parts: in the summer people worked in diving for four months;
and in the winter they travelled on the big commercial ships for five
months. (pp. 44–45)

Commerce: The Transition to External Markets

While the siege and occupation of Basra in 1775 by the Persians
shifted the route of long-distance trade to Kuwait, nevertheless this was
temporary and by 1781 the major portion of this trade had shifted back to
Basra. What this period left in Kuwait was a realization among Kuwait's
merchant captain community of the huge profits to be made in transit
trade and a small group of wealthy merchant emigres from Basra with
sufficient capital accumulated to finance the development of the
maritime fleets. Thereafter, Kuwait became very active in the carrying
trade between Masqat and Basra—the two principal ports of the Gulf
through one or the other of which passed the great bulk of the goods that
either entered or left the Gulf. Lorimer summarized the nature of Gulf
commerce between 1779 and 1797 accordingly:

The leading articles imported by way of the Gulf into both Persia and
Turkish 'Iraq were Bengal piece-goods, Coromandel chintzes, Madras

long-cloth, cotton yarn, and various cotton manufactures of Malabar, Broach, Cambay, Surat and Gujarat; English woolen goods; silks, Arabian coffee; sugar and sugar candy; spices, condiments and perfumes; indigo; drugs; chinaware; and metals. ... The trade in coffee was one of great volume and importance; half the produce of Yaman, it was estimated, found its way to the Gulf; and from the Gulf not only the whole of the surrounding countries, but even parts of Europe, were supplied with the berry. (vol. 1, pt. 1A, p. 165)

About this time, too, the Qawasim tribe of Ras-al-Khaimah began indulging in large scale piracy; and although piracy was not a characteristic of Kuwait, by 1817, Lorimer (vol. 1, pt. 1B, p. 1007), "vessels from Kuwait frequented the ports of Bahrein and were the chief means by which plunder brought to Bahrein by Qasimi pirates was conveyed across the Gulf for disposal in Persia." In this period, too, Kuwait became one of the principal centers through which Indian merchandise reached the Central Arabian interior, and became a center for the smuggling of goods across the desert to Baghdad and Aleppo. Based upon a careful examination of the records available for the period to 1800, Abu Hakima concluded:

The Utub's share in this prosperous trade was enormous, for they participated in its conveyance both by sea and caravan. They seem to have made use of all legal and illegal means to benefit from that flow of trade. They did not hesitate to smuggle goods from Kuwait to the markets of Baghdad and Aleppo, to avoid the Basra customs. Their mercantile activities increased enormously after their conquest of Bahrain.[22]

Production: The Transition to Units of Scale

This participation in externally oriented transit trade brought comparatively huge profits to Kuwait, but these profits accrued to private interests that consequently accumulated large fortunes, in contrast to the petty merchants who dealt in trade with the internal market. It also benefitted the pearl merchants by giving them direct access to the international pearl markets of Lingeh, Manama, and India. Since the returns to labor in the pearling industry of Kuwait were set by a market price in Kuwait in the exchange between pearling captains and merchants, those pearling merchants who could eliminate the middlemen and deal directly in the international pearling markets realized huge profits. They, too, accumulated relatively large fortunes.[23] These fortunes were used in financing the development of Kuwaiti commercial and pearling fleets, discussed earlier.

The social equivalent of the development of larger ships that could travel longer distances and accommodate larger crews was the proletarianization of independent labor: in commerce, the independent boats engaged in petty commerce between Kuwait and the Shatt al-Arab were gradually displaced by larger ships working on markets of scale; in pearling, the independent divers working nearby waters were proletarianized by the larger pearling ships working the distant but more lucrative fisheries. Over the period, then, the unit of production was gradually shifting from the small independent boats to the larger ships, and labor was gradually losing its autonomous and semi-nomadic character as occupations in sea-pearling in the summer and maritime commerce in the winter provided year around employment.

Nevertheless, the competition for skilled divers and crew and the higher returns being made in the exploitation of external markets no doubt brought higher returns to labor during this period of rapid expansion of commerce, and the divers and crew on the larger ships were materially better off in the transition. Although there are no actual statistics available on income because of the lack of records in Kuwait over the period, the higher standard of living is indicated by Lorimer's quotation (vol. 1, pt. 1B, p. 1006) of the estimated annual imports of Kuwait in 1829 at $500,000 and the exports at about $100,000. The deficit in the balance of trade must be assumed to have been made up by Kuwait's participation in the coastal transit traffic. Al-Qanie provides a lively description of the material improvement in the diver's condition:

> The condition of the diver was very weak in the beginning of Kuwait. His income was limited and his life difficult. His staple diet was year old dates, called al-hawil, fish and only two meals of rice a week. He did not use dishes but spread his food on sifrah. On that dirt was piled up and he would wash his sifrah only once a week. Then his life began to improve because of the increase in the prices of pearls. He could use dishes to eat instead of sifrah and began to eat rice for dinner with some butter. Diving continued to improve until most of Kuwait's wealth was earned from it and the number of diving dhows in the days of Mubarak al-Sabah [1896–1915] reached 812. The income from diving reached 6 million rupees in the diving season alone, which is only four months a year. (p.79)

A corollary of the shift of the unit of production to larger ships was the necessity of financing the voyage. Not only did the ships have to be outfitted with equipment and supplies, but the crew had to provide their families with adequate provisions during their longer absences. In this period a system of financing began to emerge—a system that was based upon the financing of voyages by the small group of merchants with sufficient capital accumulated. In return for financing the voyage, the merchant, in the commercial case, took a percentage of the ship's earnings; and in the case of pearling, the captain was committed to sell his pearls to the merchant. This system strengthened the accumulation of wealth in a small segment of the population. Through this method not only did the financial-commercial interests consolidate their hold on the exchange process where surplus was realized, but they also expropriated a portion of the product.

Politics: The Transition of Power

As pointed out earlier, Sabah interests lay in the desert, and pearling and maritime commerce were only tangential to this. The caravan trade and tribal relations were its primary concern. From Sabah I's death in 1762, there were five Amirs in a direct line of descent from him who were selected in the traditional tribal manner: Abdullah, 1762–1812; Jabir, 1812–1859; Sabah II, 1859–1866; Abdullah, 1866–1892; Mohammad, 1892–1896. Of these rulers, al-Shamlan observed:

> [They] were not privileged from most of the Kuwaiti population in any way. They were similar to the shaikh of a tribe. There was no distinction between the shaikh and members of his tribe. The power of the ruler was limited, and there were some Kuwaiti leaders who had more authority than the ruler himself. (p. 117)

Nevertheless, the community had in fact surpassed the subsistence character of tribal relations, and this was based upon the sea, not the desert. Furthermore, the traditional tribal character of desert politics that was the arena of power of the Sabah house was being rendered obsolete. This was indicated by the rise and decline of the Wahabi movement in the nineteenth century. Sabah authority over the tribes in the area was progressively weakening, while its relations with the Ottoman Empire progressively increased in the nineteenth century.

In fact, the substructure of productive forces in Kuwait had over the period developed well beyond the political superstructure of a tribal shaikhdom, and the Sabah house had only a very peripheral relationship to this development. The real power in the community resided in the financial-commercial class that in effect controlled the development of productive forces. The Sabah house over the period had become financially dependent upon this class and politically subordinate to it.[24]

But there were developing within the region counterforces. These forces were brought to the fore in 1898 when Mubarak, half-brother of the ruling Shaikh Mohammed, assasinated Shaikh Mohammed and his brother Jarrah, seizing for himself the title of Amir. Thus, the first period of Kuwait's development was brought to an abrupt end. The significance of Mubarak's coup d'etat, considered by the Kuwaiti historian Abd al-Aziz Husayn (p. 92) as "the beginning of a new development in Kuwaiti life and its modern history," must be examined in the broader context of regional and international forces impacting on Kuwait. Before examining the development of Kuwaiti society following Mubarak's seizure of power, these events will be placed in their regional and international context.

2

British Gulf Policy and Kuwait in the Nineteenth Century

*I*N HIS DEFINITIVE HISTORY OF KUWAIT to 1800, Abu Hakima identified "the confused internal state and consequent lack of centralised power in Persia, Ottoman 'Iraq and Arabia"[1] as one of the main factors allowing the establishment of the Utub at Kuwait. Throughout the eighteenth century, the main external impact on Kuwait was tribal, not state. By the nineteenth century, however, this was rapidly changing, and Kuwait was increasingly drawn into the vortex of the region's international politics. The impact of this on Kuwait will be examined in terms of the growth of British imperialism in the Gulf.

BRITAIN IN THE ARAB GULF

Britain's role in the Gulf was initiated in the seventeenth century through the activities of the British East India Company. Incorporated on the last day of 1600 as the "Governor and Company of Merchants of London trading into the East Indies,"[2] between 1616 and 1617 the company established the first British Factories in Persia, and by 1623 had factories in the Persian ports of Jask and Bandar Abbas.

Prior to the arrival of the British, the Portuguese were the only European nation operating in the Gulf. Having established themselves there in 1507, by the time of the arrival of the British, the Portuguese had fortified stations at Hormuz (commanding the eastern entrance into the Gulf), Bahrein, Qishm, and Musqat, and enjoyed a virtual monopoly on European trade with the region. From the arrival of the British there was

37

intense rivalry between the two European powers in the Gulf. The British successfully allied themselves with the Persians, who were the major power in the area at the time, and by 1622, the Portuguese were all but routed from participation in the Gulf.

However, the withdrawal of the Portuguese did not leave the British East India Company unchallenged in Gulf commerce. The Dutch, already a powerful mercantile rival to the British in the east, arrived in the Gulf in 1623, and throughout the seventeenth century proved a scourge to British commerce. In consequence of Dutch activities in Persia, in 1645 the British temporarily removed their factory at Bandar Abbas to Basra. The history of British East India Company activities in the Gulf in the eighteenth century is dominated by rivalry with the Dutch, and the declining importance of trade with Persia (partly caused by Dutch success and partly by the increasing instability of Persia). In 1763, the company permanently removed its factor at Bandar Abbas to Basra, which thereafter became the principal British establishment in the Gulf.

Throughout the eighteenth century, however, the company's mercantile role in India was gradually changing, and by the end of the century had assumed a distinctly political character. In consequence of this, the company's position in the Middle East, as the gateway to India, took on increasing significance. By the turn of the century, the British were approaching the area more from a political than mercantile perspective.[3]

The strategic importance of the Middle East came to the fore from the time of Bonaparte's invasion of Egypt in 1798. The French, systematically harassing British seaborne commerce in eastern waters from their base on the island of Mauritius and actively seeking a foothold in Persia and Oman, began raiding British commerce in the Gulf in 1799. In 1810, a British military force dispatched from India routed the French from Mauritius, bringing to an end French harassment of British commerce in the east.

More important in terms of the expansion of British policy in the Middle East, including the Gulf, were fears of French designs in the area. British diplomatic activities in both Ottoman Iraq and Persia greatly increased during the period, beginning with the establishment of a British Residency at Baghdad in 1798 and culminating in an exclusive treaty with Persia in 1809. This period, in fact, witnessed the initiation of British imperialism in the Middle East.

Within the Gulf in this period, Britain not only sought to exclude European powers that might threaten its growing empire in India, but also to work the area into the British division of labor. The suppression of Indian handicrafts industry and its transformation into a source of raw materials and market for British industry had already begun in 1700. And by 1800, the British were seeking to secure the Gulf markets for British goods. India had been a principal trading partner of the Gulf since time immemorial, and it was the British object to substitute British goods for Indian merchandise. It was in this period that the British sent several missions to the Gulf to investigate the prospects for British commerce. An extensive report prepared by Messrs. Manesty and Jones of the Basra Residency in 1790 provided an extensive review of commerce in the region. With respect to the Port of Basra, the report noted that ... "although essential Advantage is known to have accrued to British Individuals from the prosecution of a rather extensive commerce with that country that little Benefit has arisen to the Hon'ble Company from the disposal of their consignments thither, which have principally consisted of woollens, and which have seldom met either a speedy or advantageous Vend."[4] The report concluded with a list of recommendations for improving the East India Company's commercial position in the area.

The first priority Britain took was to establish its naval power in the Gulf. Fear of growing Wahabi power in Arabia, the Wahabi capture of the port of Qatif in 1800, and by 1803 their control of the Arab coast from Qatif to the Trucial coast, and increasing tension between Britain and Turkey were the prime motivations to British naval action in the Gulf, although the pretext was piracy. In 1805, the first British expedition entered the Gulf and participated with the Sultan of Oman in naval action in the Gulf against the Persian port of Bandar Abbas and Qasimi ships in anchorage at Qishm. Between 1807–08, a British squadron was stationed in the Gulf. And in 1809, the British sent a major naval and military expedition to the Gulf that wiped out Arab fleets all along the Persian and Trucial coasts and captured Ras al-Khaima, the Qasimi stronghold.

Between 1811 and 1818, the British were absorbed in consolidating their hold on India. The Wahabi threat in that period was substantially diminished by the forces of Mohammed Ali, Pasha of Egypt, who initiated a campaign in 1811 to recapture Ottoman Red Sea districts lost to the Wahabis, and by 1818 had destroyed the Wahabi capital at Daraiya and annexed to the Ottoman empire the districts of Hasa and Najd. Egyptian forces withdrew from Arabia in 1819; and the British again turned their full attention to the area, determining to consolidate their hold on the Gulf.

To effect this, a major British military expedition left India for the Gulf in November 1819. Lorimer observed that by January 1820:

> a fort having been constructed and a British garrison established at Ras-al-Khaimah, the other ports of the Pirate Coast were visited, and a clean sweep was made of their military defences and of their larger war vessels. A squadron also repaired to Bahrain and obtained the surrender and destruction of several piratical craft which had found refuge there; and similar measures were taken at Lingeh, Mughu, Asalu and Kangun upon the Persian side. (vol. 1, pt. 14, p. 198)

The culmination of this operation was the Treaty of Peace concluded in 1820 with all the principal Arab shaikhs of the Trucial Coast and Bahrein (ten signatories in all). While the terms of the treaty[5] prohibited acts of piracy in the Gulf and conferred upon the British the right to punish such acts, and introduced a system of ship registration, the effective result of the treaty was to pacify the petty principalities of the eastern half of the Arab littoral and bring the coast under the complete domain of British hegemony. According to Philip Ireland, the treaty marked the "beginnings of the political supremacy of Great Britain over the Arabs on the Gulf."[6] Its commercial impact was to enhance British commerce by fully protecting it against piracy, while leaving the commerce carried on Arab vessels fully at risk. Furthermore, the registration system gave Britain an effective way of monitoring all sea traffic on the Gulf. The vessels of signatories to the treaty had to carry papers of "Register and Clearance," to be produced on demand by British vessels they met. The papers were to include such vital information as the point of departure of the vessel, its destination, its arms, its capacity, and the number of crew.

While the treaty brought the eastern entrances of the Gulf and the ports of Muscat and Manama under effective British control (a control that continued to tighten throughout the century), it still left the Persian and Ottoman areas, and the most lucrative ports of entry to their markets (Basra and Bushire) outside their domination. Ottoman Iraq and Persia represented state powers as opposed to the petty tribes brought under British dominion by the treaty, and they possessed the real wealth to be expropriated from the area and the key areas of imperialist competition. The imperialist penetration of Ottoman Iraq and Persia, however, presented a far more complex matter than the subjugation of some petty tribal principalities, and the Gulf represented only one avenue of this penetration. Furthermore, so long as these powers were not under

British control, Britain's role in the Gulf was also vulnerable. These fears were manifest in Anglo-Russian rivalry in Iraq and Persia that began about 1830 and was the principal theme of British policy in the area for the remainder of the century. By the end of the century, German rivalry in the Gulf and the Ottoman Empire expanded the context of imperialist competition.[7] Lord Curzon, Viceroy of India from 1899 to 1905 (and one of the main architects of British policy in the Middle East), clearly resounded the imperialist tenet when he observed that the lands of the Middle East "are the pieces on a chessboard upon which is being played out a game for the dominion of the world."[8] Zaki Saleh summarized the thrust of British imperialism in Iraq from 1830 onward accordingly:

> To dominate the region was highly desirable for the British, but to be in a position to thwart any possible Russian thrust in that direction seemed of absolute necessity for them. Their priority in the Ottaman [sic] Empire, their interests in the Persian Gulf, and, above all, the very existence of their Indian Empire, would be gravely menaced, if Russia were allowed to gain a foothold on the banks of the two rivers. This conception, originating with the British about the year 1830, and developing during the ensuing four decades, was firmly established by the year 1878.

Reviewing the means of British penetration of Iraq over these decades, Saleh concluded:

> Through these activities and attendant circumstances, Mesopotamia was virtually turned into a British sphere of influence, with the usually defined status of such a sphere: interests, privileges, and priority, enjoyed by a certain power in a so-called backward region.[9]

BRITAIN AND KUWAIT

It is in this larger context of British imperialism in the Middle East in general, and the Gulf in particular, that Britain's relationship to Kuwait must be placed. In its beginnings, Kuwait was an insignificant, relatively peaceful port that the British regarded as a dependency of Basra. Khazal (p.55) observed that "despite the expiration of 50 years since the establishment of Kuwait, relations between the British East India Company and Amir Sabah I did not materialize."

From the beginning, it appears that Kuwait paid nominal recognition to Ottoman authority in Iraq, though in fact it pursued an independent policy. In 1789, for example, the resident of the British East India Company at Basra communicated to the Shaikh of Kuwait the Pasha of Baghdad's threat to "proceed on an Expedition against" Kuwait unless asylum was denied to political expatriates seeking refuge in Kuwait.[10] Shaikh Abdullah replied that "the Town of Grain [Kuwait] belongs to the Bacha, the Inhabitants of it are his Servants," and firmly denied the request.[11] No expedition was ever carried out, and the issue seems not to have caused more than momentary irritation. Nevertheless, the incident reflects the basic autonomy of Kuwait.

British records at the time generally identified Kuwait as a dependency of Basra. However, Kuwait's close relationship to Basra was based upon commercial, not political ties. Basra was Kuwait's main trading partner, even after the period of Persian occupation of Basra and the subsequent rise of Kuwait's maritime power.

During this early period, in fact, Ottoman authorities in Iraq had no Gulf policy *per se* and were not interested in asserting effective control over Kuwait. They were hard-pressed to maintain control over the tribes of Iraq and embroiled in continuous competition and intermittent wars with Persia. So long as Kuwait gave nominal recognition to Ottoman authority, then, and did not become allied to hostile powers, Kuwait was in fact not threatened by interferences in its internal affairs.

Kuwait's first recorded contact with the British occurred in 1775 when Basra was under siege by the Persians. At that time, the British transferred to Kuwait the dispatch of their Gulf to Aleppo mail. According to Lorimer (vol. 1, pt. 1B, p. 1002), "This arrangement was continued during the Persian occupation of Basra until 1779." During this period, as pointed out earlier, the bulk of caravan trade to Baghdad and Aleppo was transferred from Basra to Kuwait, and this included the merchandise of the British East India Company coming from Bombay. Furthermore, there was consideration among the company's directors of establishing a factory at Kuwait. However, because of fear the Persians would take possession of Kuwait, this was dropped. Nevertheless, the excellent harbor of Kuwait and the advantages of shipping from there were noted.[12]

From that time, at least, members of the British Factory at Basra appear to have maintained very friendly relations with the ruler of Kuwait and, as was the company policy in the area, to have extended presents to the Shaikh from time to time "for the security of the Company's Dispatches, of the English Trade, and of English Travellers passing between Bussora, Aleppo and Baghdat. Timely Presents are often of great Use in preserving this good Understanding."[13] Abu Hakima observed that the friendship was natural "because of the benefit to both. For some time past the Company had depended on Kuwait for her dispatches. The Shaikh derived substantial benefit from the traffic."[14]

In 1793, when difficulties arose between the Pasha of Baghdad and British Factory officials at Basra, the factory was removed to Kuwait, where it remained until August 1795. This, for the period, renewed Kuwait as a center for caravan traffic as British goods were dispatched from Kuwait instead of Basra. And by that period, as observed earlier, Kuwait was already well established in the carrying trade of the Gulf. Also, it reflects the company's recognition of Kuwait's independent status. According to Lorimer:

> From the selection of Kuwait as a place of retreat from the Turks, it is clear that, whatever may have been the case in 1775, it was not in any real sense a Turkish dependency in 1793.... For the protection of the British Factory at Kuwait a small cruiser was kept anchored in the bay, and a guard of sepoys under a native officer was stationed on shore. (vol. 1, pt. 1B, p. 1004)

Kuwait was under attack by the Wahabis during this period, and Lorimer (vol. 1, pt. 1B, p. 1005) suggests that the British Factors (in spite of an official position of neutrality) may have employed two guns from the British cruiser and the sepoy guard to help Kuwait repel one serious attack. Whether, in fact, British forces helped at this time or not, however, it is clear that within the next several years, the Wahabis had become a power on the coast, and a menace to British commercial activity. It is reported in Khazal (p. 70) and Dalil al-Kuwayt (p. 57) that in 1805 the British approached Shaikh Abdullah, proposing to protect the shaikhdom from desert attacks; the shaikh refused. And, again in 1807, the British proposed a treaty of friendship with Kuwait, but again, Abdullah refused. Although there is no mention of this in Lorimer, nevertheless the report is consistent with British interests at the time.

Britain's interest in Kuwait at this time was dictated by the tiny shaikhdom's strategic location. First of all, it wanted to keep the Wahabis (or any other power for that matter) from extending their power on the coast to the western reaches of the Gulf. As pointed out earlier, the Wahabis were threatening Kuwait, but never launched a serious attack on the port, no doubt from the fear of large-scale Ottoman and British reprisal and occupation of the port. Neither the Ottomans nor the British would have allowed the establishment of a Wahabi stronghold so close to Basra.

Second, Kuwait's proximity to Basra provided the British with a convenient retreat from Basra, as occurred in 1775 and 1793, and again in 1821–22. In the two latter instances, Britain's withdrawal from Basra was occasioned by problems with the Pasha of Baghdad. Kuwait offered the British a convenient leverage against the authorities of Ottoman Iraq by threatening to withdraw the center of their commercial activities from Basra.

From Kuwait's perspective, on the other hand, the occasional British withdrawals to its port provided brief booms to commerce. But Kuwait could not afford to incur the enmity of either the Ottoman Government of Iraq or the Wahabis by forming an alliance with Britain. While the trade the British occasionally drew to Kuwait was lucrative, its commerce with both Basra and Central Arabia was essential; and throughout the turmoil in both its neighboring regions, Kuwait on the whole followed a judiciously neutral position, attempting to keep lines of communication open on all sides.

Throughout the nineteenth century, in fact, until Mubarak took power in 1896, the policy of alliance with Ottoman Iraq and conciliation towards all factions marked the external relations of Kuwait. During these years, the shaikhdom became a safe refuge for political expatriates from the area deposed in internal power struggles. The chief of the Bani Kaab sought refuge in Kuwait twice (Shaikh Thamir, 1839 and 1841); ex-shaikhs of Bahrein (Abdullah, 1844; Mohammed, 1869); and expatriates from power struggles among the Wahabis (Abdullah bin-Thanaiyin, 1841; and Khalid, de facto Wahabi Amir, in the same year deposed when Abdullah bin-Thanaiyin returned and gained the upper hand).

During this period, however, the British were strengthening their control over the Gulf. Fearing Russian penetration of Ottoman Iraq on the one hand, and Mohammed Ali's ambitions in the Gulf on the other, in 1839 the British considered the suitability of Kuwait as a naval and military station. But their representations in Kuwait were rebuffed by the Shaikh. In 1841, Kuwait temporarily joined the Trucial peace accord with Britain. However, this lapsed after one year and was not renewed. In 1863 and 1865, Colonel Pelly, British Resident in the Gulf, visited Kuwait. Remarking on this visit, Lorimer observed:

> The possible future of Kuwait as a commercial port and as a meeting place of sea-borne and other trade, together with its suitability in certain circumstances for the site of a British telegraph station or coast depot, were clearly realized by Colonel Pelly, who even remarked, with extraordinary prescience, that Khor Abdullah might hereafter become the chief line of

approach by steamer to the commercial capital of Turkish Iraq, and that its head might one day be connected by a railway with the Mediterranean. (vol. 1, pt. 1B, p. 1012)

Throughout these attempts, Kuwait remained very friendly with the British, but firmly resisted British efforts at penetration. Kuwait's commercial and political life throughout the nineteenth century drew increasingly closer to Basra, and the Shaikhs of Kuwait looked to the Ottoman authorities in Iraq as their natural allies if not protectors. The alliance took two principal forms. First was Kuwait's military assistance to Basra. In 1827, Shaikh Jabir put Kuwait's naval fleet under the service of the Mutasalim (Deputy Governor) of Basra when the port was under attack by the Bani Kaab Arabs; in 1836, Kuwait assisted Ottoman forces in quelling an uprising in Zubair; in 1837, it assisted the Ottoman assault against the Persian port of Muhammareh; and in 1845, Kuwait helped defend Basra.[15] The second form was the acquisition by the Sabah family of considerable land holdings in Ottoman territory. During this period, the Sabah family had acquired estates of date palm groves in Fao and Sufiyeh. These groves were acquired primarily as gifts for services rendered by the Sabah family. By the end of the Shaikh Jabir's reign in 1859, these date groves constituted the Sabah family's principal source of income.[16]

If Britain could not bring Kuwait under direct protection, then it was in its interests to preserve the autonomy of the shaikhdom vis-à-vis the Ottoman Empire.[17] British efforts to forestall the development of a real political tie between Kuwait and the Ottoman Empire failed, however. Lorimer reported that Shaikh Abdullah

appears to have maintained very close relations with the Turks, and to have been an obedient and even enthusiastic instrument of Turkish policy. In 1870 or 1871 he became the medium of overtures from Abdullah-bin-Faisal, the displaced Wahhabi Amir, for the assistance of the Turks. In 1870 he supplied sea transport, to the amount of about 300 native vessels, for the Turkish forces sent to conquer Hasa; he accompanied the expedition in person; and it was chiefly through his agency that the Shaikh of Dohah in Qatar was persuaded to accept the Turkish flag. (vol. 1, pt. 1B, p. 1014)

In 1871, Shaikh Abdullah accepted the Turkish title of Qaim-Maqam (sub-governor), and Kuwait became an administrative unit of the Ottoman Empire. There appeared no further contact between

Kuwait and British authorities, and in 1893 the British Ambassador to Istanbul officially acknowledged Ottoman sovereignty along the coast from Basra to Qatif, including Kuwait. However, by 1896 this was rapidly changing in consequence of Mubarak's coup d'etat.

Britain and Mubarak

From the time of Persia's occupation of Basra in 1775, the dominant merchant class in Kuwait was from Basra. These merchants, comprising Indian, Persian, and Ottoman elements, had migrated to Kuwait principally from Basra in the late eighteenth century, and had financed the development of Kuwait's merchant fleet. Representing regional rather than local financial and commercial interests, these merchants had, particularly from the middle of the century, promoted the strong political ties between Kuwait and Ottoman Iraq. A shift in long distance trade routes was an important factor for this.

The long-distance trade between India and Europe was essentially monopolized by Britain by the 1820s. By the 1830s, however, the British changed the route for conveyance of Indian goods to Europe from the Persian Gulf to the Red Sea. The Basra to Aleppo desert post was completely abandoned in 1833, but according to Lorimer (vol. 1, pt. 2, p. 2440), was reestablished in 1843 or 1844 as a camel post between Baghdad and Beirut. This shift of long-distance trade routes diminished both the maritime and caravan traffic activity in the Gulf region. The Ottoman markets of Europe and the Middie East were then the major centers of demand for commerce from the east, and Basra the principal port. Hence, the Ottoman port became the focus of Gulf commerce.

However, by 1862, because of the development of the steam engine, the Persian Gulf route again interested the British. In that year, the British India Steam Navigation Company introduced a six-weekly steam service between Karachi and Basra. By 1874, it was increased to a weekly service and stopped for cargo transfers at the major ports of the Gulf. In the same period, steam service was introduced on the Tigris. The result of the introduction of steam vessels was the dislocation of the regional carrying trade. The native sailing craft of the region were no match in terms of speed or cargo capacity for the British steamers. At the same time, the British steamers carried British goods, displacing the region's nascent industries. Hence, one of the main industries of the Gulf went into decline as British steamers began to monopolize the carrying trade in the Gulf, and further development of the region's productive forces was suppressed by British products.

These changing circumstances weakened the power of Kuwait's merchant class at a time the Ottoman Empire was attempting to strengthen its position in the Gulf. The Utbi merchants of Kuwait— primarily petty merchants and pearl merchants—saw greater opportunity in an alliance with the British than the Ottomans. There is no direct evidence that the British cultivated this proposition, save from inference from succeeding events. Khazal (pp. 119–20), however, reports that as early as 1856, the British had proposed to the Kuwaitis that in exchange for protective rights over Kuwait, Kuwait's trade with Basra could be completely substituted by trade with ports under British hegemony. Although the Shaikh refused the proposition, by the end of the century it must have appeared an inviting alternative to the petty and pearl merchants of Kuwait.

The basis of the inference, however, rests on three facts. First, this transference of trade to ports under British hegemony is what actually occurred in the twentieth century, as will be discussed in the next chapter. Second, the Utbi merchants of Kuwait readily accepted Mubarak's coup d'etat, and Mubarak's first steps were to impose taxation on imports from Basra and other Turkish ports. Finally, and most significantly, was the British connection in Mubarak's coup.

While the British officially denied any complicity in Mubarak's coup, nevertheless, according to an official memorandum by the legal adviser to the British Embassy in Istanbul, prior to the coup Mubarak spent one month in Bushire with the British Resident in the Gulf, F. A. Wilson (a point not denied by Wilson).[18] At the time of the assassination, Yusuf ibn Abdullah al-Ibrahim, a wealthy merchant of Iraqi origin who was Shaikh Mohammed's confidant and adviser, fled Kuwait to seek Turkish assistance in removing the usurper. Shortly afterward, the sons of Mohammed and Jarrah joined al-Ibrahim in Basra. There they petitioned Ottoman authorities in Basra, Baghdad and Istanbul, for support against Mubarak. The government in Istanbul, however, suspicious of British intentions in Kuwait, "unwilling, under the present circumstances, to cause a new complication to arise [in Anglo-Ottoman affairs], decided to ignore the case of the assassination, and intends to grant to Monbarec [sic] the usual investiture, and orders to this effect have been dispatched to the Governor-General of Bussorah, instructing him to avoid all shedding of blood."[19]

From the correspondence that followed between various British officials concerned with the affair—the Prime Minister, Secretary of State, Government of India, Embassy of Istanbul, British Resident in the Gulf, and officials in Basra, Arabia, etc.[20]—there was considerable disagreement between the Foreign Office and the Government of India as to the British role and intent vis-à-vis Kuwait.[21] Two things are clear, however. First the Foreign Office did not want to incur a direct confrontation with the Ottoman Government over Kuwait, if avoidable, so gave at least nominal recognition to Turkish interests (though they denied Ottoman suzerainty) in Kuwait.[22] And second, the government of India was prepared to act if in fact Ottoman authorities took action against Mubarak. A British man-of-war, in fact, visited Kuwait in July 1896, but found no disturbances there as a result of the recent coup. The commander reported:

> Koweit is nominally an independent Arab territory, but in reality the Turks exercise great influence over it, more especially since the new Chief acceded to power, he finds it necessary to play into their hands. I paid him a visit, but he would not come off to the ship; I also noticed that he flew the Turkish flag and taxed him with it, but could not get any satisfactory answer from him.[23]

However, Ottoman, particularly Iraqi, opposition to Mubarak became manifest in the next several months. By early 1897, a concerted action against Mubarak appeared imminent. And in May 1897, the British sent a man-of-war to Basra, no doubt to forestall an overt attack, but under the pretext of piracy.[24] And in November of that year, on rumor that a Turkish gunboat was en route to attack Kuwait, the British dispatched a gunboat there.[25]

In the meantime, there was a concerted effort to find a legitimate reason for Britain to establish a protectorate over Kuwait. Piracy and Russian intervention were proposed during this period as pretexts to establish *de jure* the already *de facto* protectorate without provoking an international accusation of complicity in Mubarak's coup. The case of piracy was already in preparation when Mubarak pulled his coup. And the British continued to cultivate it throughout 1897. However, in November 1897, the Marquis of Salisbury, British Prime Minister, notified the Foreign Office that repression of piracy did not provide sufficient ground for placing Kuwait under British protection.[26] Thereafter, the piracy case was dropped, and Russian "designs" on Kuwait raised.[27] However, this also failed to prove a sufficiently pressing problem to justify establishment of the protectorate. Essentially killing the issue, on February 18, 1898, Admiral Beaumont, Director of Naval Intelligence, wrote to the Foreign Office:

> The anchorage off the town of Koweit is a good one and could well be made into a coaling station, but it is on the way to nowhere, and I cannot

conceive why the Russians should desire to have it. .... It seems to me, therefore, that unless there is a probability of Russia being some day established on the shores of the Persian Gulf, the rumours of her desiring to have Koweit as a coaling station cannot have any military significance or importance.[28]

Throughout this entire period, Mubarak was pressing the British to extend formal protectorate status to Kuwait. The petitions of the sons of the assassinated shaikhs and other protestations from Iraq over Mubarak's coup had been effective, and by September 1898, the Sublime Porte of the Ottoman Empire had sanctioned the appointment of a commission to investigate the complaints against Mubarak. Ottoman intervention in Kuwait appeared imminent, and Mubarak pressed the matter of protection more vigorously. On December 22, 1898, the British Ambassador to Istanbul wrote to the Prime Minister:

> Acts of piracy and of regular Traffic in Slaves would justify the interference of the Indian Government and afford ground for coming to a direct and special arrangement with the Sheikh, which need not necessarily be made public. In course of time this arrangement might be shaped into a more effective form which would serve all practical purposes and give the Indian Government prior lien upon Koweit.

> Though strongly in favour of the maintenance of British supremacy in the Persian Gulf, I am of opinion that it will be advisable to proceed cautiously and as quietly as possible in regard to the establishment of a British Protectorate over Koweit. Any formal declaration to this effect at the present moment would be considered little short of a hostile act by Turkey, and in any case it would be sure to produce very serious diplomatic complications, not only with this Government, but probably also with Russia.[29]

In January 1899, a secret agreement between Shaikh Mubarak and Britain was concluded.[30] By the agreement, Mubarak bound himself, his heirs and his successors

> ... not to receive the Agent or Representative of any Power or Government at Koweit, or at any other place within the limits of his territory, without the previous sanction of the British Government; and further binds himself, his heirs and successors not to cede, sell, lease, mortgage, or give for occupation or for any other purpose any portion of his territory to the Government or subjects of any other Power without the previous consent of Her Majesty's Government for these purposes. This engage-

ment also to extend to any portion of the territory of the said Sheikh
Mubarak, which may now be in the possession of the subjects of any
other Government. [31]

The agreement affixed no obligations upon Britain. Mubarak insisted upon a definite promise of protection. Therefore, in an accom-
panying letter, Colonel Meade, British Political Resident in the Gulf,
assured Mubarak "of the good offices of the British Government towards you, your heirs and successors as long as you...scrupulously and
faithfully observe the conditions of the said bond." [32] The letter also
agreed to pay him Rs. 15,000 (1,000 pounds) and added: "A most
important condition of the execution of this agreement is that it is to be
kept absolutely secret, and not divulged or made public in any way
without the previous consent of the British Government."

Mubarak's two brothers were present to attest the treaty, but
refused to sign the agreement. They wanted British assurances to protect family landholdings in Fao which they feared would be confiscated
by Ottoman authorities. To forestall a split between Mubarak and his
brothers, and guarantee their silence on the secret agreement, in February the Foreign Office approved this stipulation, stating that "Her
Majesty's Government will do what they can to protect the family
estates of the Sheikhs of Koweit at Fao." [33]

Ottoman authorities knew of the British resident's visit to Kuwait [34]
and made some feeble efforts over the next several years to assert
Ottoman suzerainty over Kuwait. These efforts were resisted with the
aid of the British who provided a frequent show of naval power at
Kuwait to ward off potential attacks. By 1902, British control over
Kuwait was a recognized fact in both Istanbul and other European
capitals.

Through the agreement, Mubarak became a tool of British policy
vis-à-vis the Ottoman Empire and in Central Arabia. By denying Germany a terminus in Kuwait for the Berlin to Baghdad railway project,
first proposed in 1899 (a proposal supported by the Ottoman Sultan),
Kuwait helped to forestall the penetration of Germany into the area. [35]

In Central Arabia, Mubarak provided a link for the British with
Abd al-Aziz al-Saud, the Wahabi Amir. With the conquest of Riyadh (the
Wahabi capital) by Ibn Rashid in 1892, Wahabi power in Central Arabia
appeared completely broken. In 1893, Abd al-Rahman ibn Saud, the
defeated Wahabi Amir, took refuge in Kuwait with his family. Abd
al-Aziz al-Saud was then a young boy and grew to maturity in Kuwait
under the personal patronage of Shaikh Mubarak, to whom, notes

Dickson (p. 137) "is due the credit for the political training and pro-British leaning of Abdul Aziz Al Saud, the future ruler of Saudi Arabia."

With his flank protected by Britain from Turkish attack, in December 1900, Mubarak led a large expedition into Central Arabia against the forces of Ibn Rashid. Ibn Rashid, allied to the Ottoman Empire, had been harrying the bedouin adherents of Kuwait, and Kuwait was losing support among the tribesmen. Mubarak wished to re-establish Saudi power in Central Arabia under his patronage, and both diminish Ottoman influence there and re-establish the prestige of Sabah among the tribes. At first, the expedition was a substantial success, but in March 1901, Mubarak's forces lost a major battle and had to hastily retreat from Najd. Britain subsequently had to protect Mubarak not only from more vigorous Ottoman efforts to absorb Kuwait, but also from threats of attack by Ibn Rashid.

However, Mubarak's incursion into Central Arabia had paved the way for the return of Saud. In January 1902, Abd al-Aziz al-Saud recovered Riyadh. With this recovery, Wahabi power in Central Arabia quickly began to grow as tribes deserted the ranks of Ibn Rashid in favor of Saudi allegiance. By 1904, even Ottoman authorities acknowledged Saudi control of Southern Najd and came to terms with Ibn Saud.

There is no direct evidence of a British connection with Mubarak's expedition into Central Arabia and the re-establishment of Saud. Official British correspondence in the period reflects some Foreign Office consternation over Mubarak's aggressive policy in the desert. But this arose from the fear that it would prompt an Ottoman attack on Kuwait and force the open declaration of a Kuwait protectorate.[36] Britain was bogged down in the Boer War in this period and the Foreign Office wished to avoid the international complications that such a declaration would precipitate.

Nevertheless, Britain's international interests were consistent with seeing Ottoman influence in the Gulf and Central Arabia diminished, while maintaining the appearance of empire. The Ottoman Empire was already decaying, and European competition for carving out spheres of influence from the crumbling empire had begun. With the Treaty of San Stefano signed in 1878 ending the Russo-Turkish war, Russia had severed the Balkan provinces from the Ottoman Empire; and Britain, fearing the Empire's complete collapse in the face of European, especially Russian, competition for spheres of influence, sought to shore up the Ottoman Empire in its Asian provinces while establishing its own sphere there. In June 1878, Britain concluded an agreement with Turkey to defend the Asiatic dominions (subject to certain conditions) and in return received possession of the island of Cyprus. In 1882 Britain occupied Egypt.

It is within the context of imperialist competition in the period, then, that British concerns with Central Arabia must be placed. Russia was making advances in Persia, Afghanistan and the Ottoman Empire. Germany, still Britain's logical ally in case of war, was nevertheless rapidly increasing its trade in the Middle East, and had acquired considerable influence in the Istanbul palace, as the Sultan's support for the Berlin to Baghdad railway project indicated. Central Arabia, as the great buffer wasteland between a British occupied Egypt and India, and the sea routes that connected them (as well as a growing empire in East Africa), was a virtual power vacuum. Britain's connection with Mubarak provided the logical avenue of penetration then available.

The availability of arms was one of the single most significant determinants of power in Central Arabian politics at the time. Modern arms held the potential of changing the balance of power in the Peninsula, and it is not merely speculative to suggest that these arms were made available to Saudi forces through Kuwait and similarly denied to Ibn Rashid's forces. Britain had been attempting to control the access of European arms into the Gulf at least since 1881. Through the Gulf, modern arms and ammunitions, mostly of British manufacture, were not only being supplied to the markets of the area but were also reaching Afghanistan and the northwestern frontier of India. According to Lorimer:

> In 1895–96 the estimated number of rifles imported at Masqat was only 4,350, in 1896–97 it was 20,000; and in 1897 no less than 30,000 rifles were believed to have been landed at Bushehr. All the weapons brought to the Gulf were now breech-loaders; and in Southern Persia, in particular, nearly the whole male adult population were armed with weapons of precision and made free use of them. It was ascertained that in 1896 the proportion of arms and ammunition entering the Gulf and absorbed by Persia was about three-fifths of the whole, while about a quarter was taken by countries under Turkish domination and the remainder was disposed of in Arab states and principalities. The great majority of the imports were of British manufacture. (vol. 1, pt. 1A, p. 316)

In attempting to control the arms flow, Britain made formal agreements with Persia, the Sultanate of Oman and Bahrain between 1897 and 1898, giving Britain the right to conduct search and seizure operations on merchant vessels. Kuwait was a principal supply center of arms for Central Arabia, and in 1900, under British advice, Mubarak nominally agreed to its prohibition. Manipulation of arms supply provided an important method of influencing events in Central Arabia, and Britain's interests and ability in this regard cannot be overlooked. Saudi arms came from Kuwait and were a significant factor in the return of Saudi power in Central Arabia.

CONCLUSION

Mubarak's agreement with Britain marks the point of Kuwait's integration into the British colonial system. Unlike many other nations, Kuwait's integration into this system did not emerge from a commercial, but from a distinctly political basis. Nevertheless, as a result, Kuwait became part of an emerging world division of labor, and the impact of this upon Kuwait's internal development for the remainder of the pre-oil period shall be the subject of the next chapter.

3

The Underdevelopment
of Kuwait

$\mathcal{T}$ HE STEADY DEVELOPMENT OF KUWAIT throughout the eighteenth
and nineteenth centuries from a nomadic settlement at the edge of
the desert to a mercantile community at the western edge of the Arab
Gulf was examined in Chapter 2 in terms of the transformation of the
mode of production from nomadic to mercantilist, and the steady
development of productive forces in the mercantile mode. This progress
in the transformation and development of Kuwait's mercantile mode of
production was accompanied throughout the nineteenth century by the
increasing ties of Kuwait with Ottoman Iraq.

The basic autonomy that marked the development of Kuwait as a
mercantile center—the free play of productive and political forces that
contributed to the rapid development of Kuwait—however, was fundamentally curtailed by Britain's penetration of Kuwait at the end of the
nineteenth century. This chapter will examine how Kuwait's peripheral
relationship with Britain as an object of the Empire's Gulf policy affected
the development of Kuwait in the first half of the twentieth century.

KUWAIT UNDER MUBARAK

The subordination of Kuwait to British Gulf policy that was initiated
with Mubarak's coup d'etat in 1896 marked the transformation of political power within Kuwait, and this in turn facilitated the integration of
Kuwait into the emerging world capitalist system of production. It is in
the period of Mubarak's reign that the process of transformation-
integration was essentially completed.

A main feature of this was the transformation of the basis of Sabah authority from a tribally mediated form of community consensus to an externally mediated basis of power. Backed by the British, Mubarak transformed himself from a community leader into an autocratic ruler, in effect transforming the Sabah house into a centralized power structure in the society. One of the first symbols of this power was Mubarak's ability to arbitrarily levy taxes. Prior to Mubarak, customs duties imposed on certain goods were a voluntary contribution of the merchants to the maintenance of the Sabah house. Khazal (vol. 2, pp. 296–97) reports:

> But when Mubarak ruled Kuwait ... he established a regular customs office in 1899 and imposed a five percent tax on all goods coming to Kuwait by land or sea. This increased gradually until it reached ten percent on some goods. He also imposed a real estate tax which required the payment of one-third the total value of a house sold in Kuwait.[1]

Assessing Mubarak's reign, al-Rushaid concluded:

> Mubarak was a tyrant, stubborn and unjust. He was an absolute ruler who loved the accumulation of wealth and was always seeking ways to increase his wealth. He assessed high fines against law-breakers; continuously invented taxes ... and made himself a partner in all building and property [transactions]. As a matter of fact, he was better off than a partner. He received one-third of what was sold or rented, even if this was repeated a number of times a day. (p. 189)

This concentration on the primitive accumulation of wealth was not an end in itself, but was related to the integration of Kuwait into the British division of labor. Mubarak used this wealth to back financially the expansion of the commerce of the Utbi merchants of Kuwait. These were the petty merchants who dealt primarily with the transfer of subsistence products from external sources to the internal and desert markets. Unlike the Basra merchants who migrated to Kuwait in the late eighteenth century and provided the basis for the take-off of Kuwaiti commerce in terms of fostering a dynamic link between productive centers by development of the maritime means of distribution and exchange, the Utbi merchants were middlemen merchants between exchange and subsistence consumption. With increasing British domination throughout the 19th century of the productive centers of India and the Gulf region, as well as the communication lines between productive centers, these merchants increasingly looked to the British for their sources of supply.

The interests of the Utbi merchants, then, were not dynamically linked to the development of productive forces in the region that was emerging in the nineteenth century and ideologically responding to the decay of the Ottoman Empire on the one hand and British imperialism on the other in the form of an emerging Arab nationalism. In fact, Mubarak's usurpation of power severed the dynamic link between Kuwaiti development and regional development, and fostered in its place a link with the British system of production. As a class, the Utbi merchants represented a local bourgeoisie whose interests were narrowly defined in terms of the local market and subsistence consumption. Their linkage with the British system of production rendered Kuwait politically alienated from the development of productive forces in the region, in effect placing them in contradiction with the regionally oriented forces of Arab nationalism emerging in both the Arab centers of the Ottoman Empire and the peninsula hinterland.

Their achievement of dominance in Kuwait over the Ottoman class of merchants through alienation to Britain of Kuwait's autonomy in its foreign affairs in fact marked the alienation to Britain of Kuwait's autonomous development of productive forces. Because of its stark physical environment, such development could only make sense in a regional context. The meagre natural resources of Kuwait provided for only a bare subsistence existence; and its rapid development throughout the seventeenth and eighteenth centuries resulted from the development of its role — productively and politically — in an emerging exchange pattern among productive centers. It was the new structure of colonial relations forged by the linkages with Britain that inhibited the development of productive forces in Kuwait and the region as a whole, initiating the historical process of the underdevelopment of not only Kuwait but the entire region.

The increasing diversity of commodity exchange that typified Gulf commerce in the seventeenth and eighteenth centuries not only indicated the increasing productivity of various centers in the region but also the increasing exchange activity among these centers. In the second half of the nineteenth century, this increased activity was gradually assuming a new political form — articulated in Kuwait by its increasing ties with Ottoman Iraq, and articulated throughout the region by an emerging Arab nationalism. However, this was occurring at the same time Britain was consolidating, in a piecemeal fashion, its hold on the region. The result of British imperialism was that the growing surplus was increasingly being expropriated out of the region by the British. Kuwait's linkage with Britain was part of this overall process.

An important characteristic of Kuwait's integration into the British division of labor was the return of Kuwaiti commerce to a subsistence market basis. This had two interrelated features:

1. The subordination of Kuwait's merchant fleet to British commercial navigation. The role of Kuwait's merchant fleet in a very active Gulf transit trade was already noted in Chapter 2. In 1904, British steamers began to call at Kuwait regularly, and by 1905–06 were, according to Lorimer (vol. 2, pt. 2B, pp. 1055–56), carrying to Kuwait more than 50 percent of the total value of goods imported there. More importantly for Kuwait's role in the transit traffic (since much of what Kuwaiti ships carried during the nineteenth century never touched at Kuwait at all), Busch (p. 307) notes that by 1906, ninety-six percent of the sea traffic to Basra was handled by the British.

2. The types and range of commodities carried on Kuwaiti ships were narrowed to subsistence products for the Kuwaiti and desert hinterland markets. The import-export of surplus products in the region was virtually dominated by the British, leaving Kuwaiti commerce only the marginal subsistence markets and products.[2]

These changes were commensurate with the short-term interests of the Utbi merchants of Kuwait, and their achievement of dominance in Kuwait over the regionally oriented Ottoman class of merchants was an integral part of the process by which Kuwait was integrated into the British division of labor. The immediate effect was to transfer the capital accumulated by the Ottoman merchants to the Utbi merchants. With their transit traffic already marginalized by British competition, Mubarak further weakened them through heavy taxation. This was transferred to the Utbi merchants through liberal loans. The Utbi merchants, in turn, expropriated the shipping fleets as the Ottoman class of merchants fell into their debt and were gradually forced to forfeit ownership of the ships in payment, since they were no longer competitive in the transit trade.

The long-term effect was to transfer out of the region the capital expropriated. The increasing volume of goods coming into Kuwait on British carriers had to be paid for, and this payment was expropriated out of the region. Since the deepening of the commodity market in Kuwait was specifically limited by its subsistence character, the only mechanisms available to the Utbi merchants to compensate for the capital drain were expansion of the size of the subsistence markets served by the Utbi merchants and greater rate of exploitation of labor, represented by the taxation system which diminished the proportion of returns to labor (to be discussed in detail later in the chapter).

Mubarak's attempts to expand his influence in Central Arabia were intimately related to the expansion of the subsistence markets served by Kuwaiti commerce. Kuwait was the principal port serving the markets of Central Arabia. Encouraged by the British in their efforts to weaken Ottoman Iraq's influence in the Peninsula and establish an alliance with Ibn Saud, Mubarak attempted to consolidate Kuwait's relationship with the tribes and expand the limits of Kuwait's territorial sovereignty by fomenting the conflict between Ibn Saud on one side and the forces of Ibn Rashid and Ottoman Iraq on the other. However, Mubarak's aspirations in Central Arabia inevitably brought him into conflict with Ibn Saud whose success in building a territorially delineated nation specifically circumscribed the limits of Kuwait's political and commercial relationship to the area.

Pearling represented the only true form of commodity production in Kuwait. With the dynamic link to productive centers cut off and commerce circumscribed to subsistence markets, pearl production provided the only source of capital for subsistence acquisition, as in early Kuwait. However, unlike early Kuwait, the production cycle was accumulation, not subsistence oriented. Throughout the nineteenth century, the Kuwaiti pearl merchants had realized enormous profits in the exchange-value of pearls, and had enjoyed complete autonomy in shaping the structure of productive relations in the industry. To compensate for the rate of capital drain in commerce with Britain, however, Mubarak attempted to bring this industry under his control to sustain the commercial sector. He established a tax on all pearling boats amounting to one diver's share. In effect, this increased the rate of surplus value realized from pearling by diminishing the diver's share of the profit. But this increase in the rate of surplus value did not benefit the pearl merchants. Rather, it was transferred to Mubarak.

However, Mubarak's efforts to further subordinate the relations of production in the pearling industry to his centralized authority were firmly resisted by the pearl merchants. In 1909, he declared a ban on diving for the season. The major pearl merchants — Hilal Mutayri, Shamlan Ibn Ali and Ibrahim Ibn Mudhif—responded to his interference in their affairs by migrating from Kuwait with their followers (minor merchants, divers, and pearling ship crews) after the diving season. According to al-Rushaid (p. 167), "those migrants and their followers comprised half [of the population] of Kuwait." Mubarak made many concessions to the merchants to return them to Kuwait, and even went to Bahrein himself to convince Hilal Mutayri to return.[3]

With the onset of the First World War, Sheikh Mubarak's relationship to British imperialism in the Middle East was completely revealed. In exchange for Mubarak's assistance to British forces in the pacification of the Shatt al-Arab region and occupation of Basra, Britain guaranteed to Mubarak: (1) Basra, once wrested from Turkish control, would not be returned to Turkish suzerainty; (2) Mubarak's palm tree groves situated near Fao would be permanently exempted from taxation; (3) Britain would guarantee the protection of Kuwait.[4] With the help of Mubarak and other tribal leaders of the region (most notably Ibn Saud and Sheikh Khazal of Muhammerah), on November 21, 1914, Britain occupied Basra.

The British success, however, was not without resistance. Many of the tribes under Sheikh Khazal's suzerainty responded to the Khalife's call for jihad and rebelled against Khazal because of his support to the British. When Sheikh Mubarak attempted to come to Khazal's assistance by mobilizing Kuwaiti forces to help quell the rebellion, Kuwaitis refused to participate. As a result, Mubarak was forced to moderate his demand for Kuwaiti mobilization. Al-Rushaid (p. 175) comments that Mubarak "was disturbed by the degree of enthusiasm for the rebellion common among Kuwaitis, something he had not seen the equivalent of all his life."

Mubarak died suddenly in late 1915, and the amirship of Kuwait passed to his son Jabir. With his death the transformation-integration process was essentially completed. Kuwait had been transformed from an autonomous merchant community to an outpost in what was essentially Britain's Gulf colony. The British Political Agent in Kuwait, first posted there in 1904, was part of the colonial bureaucracy established in the Gulf. He administered the affairs of Kuwait through Mubarak, who became a despot vis-à-vis his people and a bureaucrat vis-à-vis the colonial administration.

KUWAIT BETWEEN TWO WORLD WARS

While the transformation-integration process served the short-term interests of the Utbi merchants, the longer-term effect was the complete drain of resources from Kuwait. By the end of Mubarak's reign, the framework of contradictions of peripheral capitalism—of Kuwait as a regional center of capital accumulation for British expropriation—had been established. These contradictions were: (1) The contradiction of capital accumulation/expropriation; (2) The contradiction of independence/dependence.

Capital Accumulation/Expropriation

The class character of production relations and the capital drain character of peripheral capitalism resulted in the increasing rate of exploitation of labor, not, however, to sustain a rate of investment in the development of productive forces as in classical capitalist development. Rather, the increasing rate of exploitation of labor was required to sustain the level of development against the debilitating force of continuing capital drain.

The form of exploitation depended upon the character of production. Fishing remained an unorganized and unexploited sector participated in freely and at will (or necessity) by all segments of the society. Access to the sea could not be alienated, and the productivity of the sea was neither seasonal nor did it require technical means for exploitation. Production in this sector remained essentially for private consumption.

The autonomous or semi-autonomous character of agricultural and animal husbandry production sustained the inalienability of the means of production of this tribally organized sector of labor. Without the resources for substantial capital investment, these economic sectors could not be brought into commodity production.[5] Nevertheless, the alienation of their meagre surplus through heavy taxation (10 percent) on all supplies they purchased from Kuwait was the mechanism of exploitation.[6] The result of this exploitation of hinterland production was the release of marginal labor to the city. Because of the increasing prices of the necessities they secured from the city markets, it was necessary to sell their labor in the city.

This release of marginal hinterland labor to the city resulted in the rapid growth of population. Estimates of Kuwait's population from 1760 to the turn of the twentieth century indicate that the population remained at about 10,000. A plague that hit the eastern Arabian Peninsula and Iraq about 1831 reduced Kuwait's population to about 4,000, but by 1860 it had reached 10,000 again.[7] By 1910, however, the population jumped to 35,000, and by 1938, to 75,000, primarily as a result of the immigration of the tribes.[8]

The release of labor power to the city markets facilitated the expansion of pearl exploitation and subsistence commerce. Both these sectors relied upon a form of exploitation of wage labor as the mechanism for accumulation. In both, the organization of production was specifically geared to primitive accumulation in the framework of British expropriation.

The Political Economy of Pearling

Because of a favorable world market for pearls and the expansion of labor available to the industry, the Kuwaiti pearl industry rapidly expanded in the first quarter of the twentieth century, reaching a zenith in 1911—called the year of al-Tafha (overflow) in local tradition.[9] In this period of rapid expansion, the pearl merchants gained direct control over the pearling boats and the harvest. New captains entering the industry sought financing for the construction and outfitting of their boats directly from the pearl merchants. In return, they committed their harvest to the merchants, and when the harvest was insufficient to cover the debt, forfeited their independence.

Two general systems of financing existed. In the first, called the System of Fifths (Khamamis), the distribution of proceeds from the harvest was based upon shares.[10] All of the pearls harvested by a boat during the pearling season were kept by the captain who sold them to the itinerant petty merchants making the rounds of the pearling fleets during the season or at the end of the season to the wholesale merchants in the market. From the proceeds of the pearls, the financier and the owner of the boat (whether the captain, the financier, or a third party) each took one-fifth. The financier's portion was a 20 percent rate of interest on the capital he advanced, and the captain was still indebted for the principal. The cost of food and supplies was then deducted, and the captain and crew divided up the remainder on the basis of pre-arranged shares, allocating part to the diving tax instituted by Mubarak. An example of the distribution among the crew is given in Table 1.

This system of financing the pearling ships concentrated the earnings of the industry in the hands of the pearling merchants, and progressively reduced the returns to labor in the industry. The price of the pearl paid by the pearl merchants to the captains in the local market was four to six times below the price realized by these merchants in the main trading centers of Manamah and Bombay.[11] Furthermore, the commitment of the harvest to the merchant financing the voyage reduced competition for the harvest among the pearl merchants. Where the captain and the merchant he was bound to through the financial system disagreed upon the price of the pearls, a third merchant, either agreed upon by the two parties privately or appointed by the Court of Diving (*Salifat al-Ghaus*) mediated the dispute. Finally, the tax levied on the diving ships fell directly upon the crews' shares, further diminishing the returns to labor.[12]

Table 1
Distribution of the Pearling Crew's Income

Description of Crew	Number of Crew	Shares Drawn by Each	Total Shares
Captain	1	3	3
Divers	10	3	30
Haulers	10	2	20
Cook	1	2	2
Haulers' Assistants	2	1	2
*Tax		3	3
Total	24		60

*The tax was not included in the original source, but has been included here to show the complete distribution of income. See al-Qatami, *Guide on Navigation*, p. 222.

SOURCE: Political Agent, Kuwait, *Trade Report for Kuwait, 1937–38*, F.O. File #L/P&S/12/3743, p. 5.

The position of the captain as an independent owner of the means of production was progressively alienated by this system that in effect reduced him to a wage laborer. Where he was able to maintain even nominal ownership of the boat, the costs of construction and the annual costs of outfitting the boat forced him into the hands of the financiers because of the lower return he was receiving in a noncompetitive pearl market. If he was unable to repay the debt at the end of the season, he either forfeited ownership of the boat, or was bound to the same financier for the next season, the more common resolution and indeed one perpetuating the monopoly of the merchants. Divers preferred, of course, to sign on with captains who financed their own voyages, since such captains were then free to sell their pearls in the open market to the highest bidder. In this case of market competition, the system of shares worked to the advantage of labor, and it appears that this was the original system of sharing the returns to pearling before the monopolistic practices of the merchants closed off open competition and independent captains were choked off by the increasing necessity for financing.

The second system of finance, known as the System of Advances, (*al-Salifiyyah*) appears to be an outgrowth of the first, resulting from the increasing inability of captains to perpetuate their independence, the increasing inability of pearling labor to reproduce itself annually from the income realized, and the increasing concentration of capital in the hands of a small class of merchants.[13] In this system, the distribution of income was ideally based upon shares as in the System of Fifths, but this had in fact become a fiction. Because of the inability of divers and their families to subsist on the income earned in a diving season, the captain borrowed from the merchant in order to advance the diver cash prior to the season. If the returns to labor from the season were insufficient to cover the debt (principal plus interest), the diver was bound to the same captain for the next season. If the diver died and was still under debt to a captain, the debt was passed on to his family who continued diving for the captain to pay off the debt, and in the process incurred their own debt. Examining this system, Rumaihi observed, "so the debts of the diver will increase year after year until he finds himself captive of the owner of the ship."[14] Thus, labor lost its market autonomy, and the entire mode of pearl exploitation was held together by a hierarchical debt system that perpetuated accumulation at the top by a system of effective bondage. Villiers observed:

> The whole economic structure of the industry ... was based on debt. Everybody was in debt—the diver to the nakhoda [captain], the nakhoda to the merchant who financed him, the merchant to some other merchant bigger than himself, the bigger merchants to the sheikh. (p. 353)

The whole structure rested upon the shoulders of the divers. Without technical aids, and only the hauler's line to connect them with the surface, they dove to depths of 8 to 16 fathoms, depending upon their skill and daring, to scurry at the bottom for 40 to 75 seconds recovering oysters. Pearl-diving was a particularly hazardous and strenuous occupation, and a pearl-diver's life was generally short-lived. Bowens provides a graphic summary of this labor:

> When the season is over, the diver has weathered the impossible; he has probably completed over 3,000 dives in from 30 to 50 feet of water, and has spent over 50 hours under the surface of the Persian Gulf—that is, over a full forty-hour week without air.... It is not surprising that there are one or two empty stations on each boat; their occupants lie huddled corpse-like under their cloaks in some part of the ship, too sick from scurvy or plain fatigue to dive. After they have been at it for many weeks, the divers are apt to get convulsive shivers when they come out of the water to rest, even though the temperature may be 100°F. ... [15]

The Court of Divers was the tribunal reconstituted yearly by the Amir to resolve disputes in the industry—whether between divers and captains, or captains and merchants. It was composed of the merchants and captains appointed by the Amir to mediate disputes. The decisions were binding on both parties to a dispute. The divers had no representation. In 1940, the Amir codified the practices governing the industry that had evolved out of this tribunal over the years and attempted to introduce a number of minor reforms to ameliorate the worst abuses of the system. The law is reproduced in Appendix 1.

The pearl industry in Kuwait continued to expand until 1929 when the world economic depression weakened the market considerably. Furthermore, the appearance of Japanese cultured pearls in 1930 depreciated the price of pearls generally in the world market. As a result, by the end of the decade many of the merchants and captains were bankrupt, their boats abandoned onshore or taken over by the big merchants in payment of debts.[16] In this period, the divers were reduced to total poverty, but many were bound by the debt system to continue in an industry that could no longer provide even minimum subsistence. Thus, in the diving season, they worked on the pearling fleets to pay off their debts, and the rest of the year eked out a livelihood as best they could. Many returned to the desert, others to petty commerce at sea or fishing, and still others to construction for the nascent oil industry.

The Political Economy of Dhow Commerce

In the period under consideration subsistence commerce expanded rapidly. The increase in Kuwait's population was an important factor stimulating this expansion. The environment of Kuwait could not even provide sufficient drinking water for the town. Brackish water for cooking, gardening and animals was provided by wells outside the town, and drinking water was brought in by donkeys from other villages and sold by peddlers in Kuwait. By 1910, however, because of population expansion, drinking water had to be brought in by dhow from Basra.[17] So it was with other rudimentary subsistence necessities, and local dhow traffic expanded.

In addition, during the First World War, British steamers were brought into the war effort, returning the commerce between India and the Gulf to the dhow trade. Because of the scarcity of goods during the war, huge profits were made by the merchants participating in this trade. Furthermore, the British attempted to blockade commerce via the Gulf to Ottoman territories in the Middle East. Some Kuwaiti merchants accumulated vast fortunes through smuggling. In fact, this activity brought Salim (ruler of Kuwait from 1917–21) into direct confrontation with the British, and precipitated a British blockade of Kuwait in 1918.[18]

However, after the war, the British steamers resumed their commercial activities, and the smuggling traffic died with the end of the blockade. With the British in occupation of Iraq, Kuwaiti merchant capital moved to the purchase of date palm plantations along the Shatt al-Arab, and the transit of wet dates from these groves to India and down the coast of the Arabian Sea as far as Aden became the principal cargo of the Kuwaiti deep-sea fleet.[19] Some ships continued down the East African coast as far south as Zanzibar.

The cargo carried by these ships was Iraqi dates. The voyages to India brought back shipbuilding materials, coir for cordage, and Malabar teak; the return voyages from East Africa brought back mangrove poles from the Rufiji Delta for roofing Kuwaiti houses. In addition, the crews engaged in a variety of lesser trading, both legal and illegal, from trinkets to passenger carrying—anything that could be picked up in one port of call and deposited in another at a profit. The dhow captains were themselves mini-merchants, peddling goods as well as dates to native bazaars along the Indian and East African coasts. "The dhow is a peddlar, as well as a carrier; a storehouse, as well as a ship; a means of livelihood to travelling merchants, as well as to her crew proper," observed Alan Villiers.[20]

These voyages took from four to nine months; the size of the ships ranged from 75 tons to 300 tons, with the size of the crew varying from 20 to 60. In 1939, Kuwait had a registered fleet of 106 ocean-going dhows and from 50 to 60 smaller dhows engaged in inner-Gulf trade.

The system of financing in this industry was based upon the merchant's role in financing the construction of this ship and advancing the date cargo, carried on a freight basis, to finance the voyage. According to Villiers, "finance is always provided by a merchant—usually a merchant with an interest in date plantations on the Basra River . . . who wishes to use the new vessel for carrying his dates."[21] In this way, merchant families would have an interest in a series of dhows. But the loss of a vessel and its freight was carried by the captain, not the merchant. Villiers noted:

> In Kuwait, immediately prior to the outbreak of World War II, there was beginning to be some restiveness about this, and an association of the *nakhodas* had the temerity to issue its demands upon the merchants. These included payment of demurrage when unduly delayed at the loading berths in Basra (a dhow might be kept for weeks waiting for her cargo), a sliding scale of freights for different ports instead of the customary flat rate of 1.5 or 2 rupees a package regardless of destination, liability for the return of advances to cease with the loss of the ship . . . but the merchants' answer was that if the *nakhodas* could make new rules so could they; and they had the real power.[22]

   The merchant who advanced his capital thus took no risk on his investment or cargo, and realized the added dividend of interest which bound the captain permanently to the merchant. The ship, as the productive unit, bore the burden entirely and shared what income the voyage realized. The distribution of income was based upon the system of shares. From the total proceeds of the voyage, the cost of food supplies was deducted. The shipowner took half of the net proceeds, and the remainder was divided among the crew, as shown in Table 2.[23]

   The system of advance to the crew also operated in this industry. But the debt structure was not as debilitating as in the pearling industry, for some subsistence income could still be realized in spite of the structure of exploitation. In fact, during the inter-war period, sailing on merchant vessels superseded pearl diving as the basis of labor's subsistence, and it was only by stringent enforcement of debt obligations that diving was not abandoned altogether.[24] Nevertheless, the ocean-going dhows were being increasingly marginalized by the competition of the European steamships, and it was only the occurrence of the Second World War that gave them a brief boom before air transport and modern shipping in the framework of market monopolies in the world capitalist structure eliminated them completely.

Table 2
Distribution of the Merchant Crew's Income

| | | Number of Shares Drawn by Each | | |
| | | | From | |
Crew	Number of Crew	From Crew's Income	Ship-Owner's Income	Total Shares
Captain	1	1	2	3
1st Steerer	1	1	0½	1½
2nd Steerer	1	1	0½	1½
3rd Steerer	1	1½	0	1½
Foreman	1	1	0	1½
Crew	19	1	0	19
Cook	1	1½	0	1½
Jollyboat	—	1	0	1
Total	25			30½

SOURCE: Political Agent, Kuwait, *Trade Report for Kuwait, 1937–38*, p. 5.

The Polarization of Capital and Labor

The result of the increasing rate of accumulation for British expropriation was the monopolization of capital on the one hand, the proletarianization of labor on the other, and their increasing polarization. The peripheral character of capitalism in Kuwait as established under Mubarak was specified politically and economically by the dependence of this class upon the transfer of British transported commodities to the local and hinterland market. Table 3 reflects the extent to which Kuwait's commerce had passed into the hands of British steamers in the interwar period.

The principal articles coming into Kuwait or being re-exported from Kuwait by steamer were not only the manufactured goods of the industrial world, such as piece goods, hardware and glassware, but also the primary consumption products from other centers in the Gulf, such as coffee, rice, tea, sugar, that had been the mainstay of Kuwait's commerce in the nineteenth century. The greater percentage of goods entering and leaving Kuwait by dhow in 1937–38 was a result of British war preparations.

The merchant class of Kuwait was juxtaposed between the import and re-export of commodities transported primarily by British steamer.[25] As the wholesale merchants in the marketplace, they sold to the small retail traders and merchants at high rates of interest, taking two-thirds of the profits realized through retailing.[26] As the trading

Table 3
Imports and Exports of Kuwait by Mode of Transport, 1935–38

	1935–36	1936–37	1937–38
Imports			
Steamer	73.4%	70.3%	67.7%
Dhow	26.6	29.7	32.3
	100.0%	100.0%	100.0%
Exports			
Steamer	65.8%	44.2%	47.9%
Dhow	34.2	55.8	52.1
	100.0%	100.0%	100.0%

SOURCE: Political Agent, Kuwait, *Trade Report for Kuwait, 1937–38*, pp. 6–24.

center for the tribes of Najd, as well as many of the tribes of Iraq and
north Syria on whose annual migration routes Kuwait lay, their middle-
man commercial role was significant to British commerce, and was,
indeed, the initial basis of their accumulation. When Ibn Saud banned
the tribes of Najd from trading in Kuwait in 1923 (a ban that lasted until
1937), many of the small merchants went bankrupt.

This did not affect the big merchant class, however, for their
interests had become diversified through their financial role in the pearling industry and their investment in date plantations in Iraq. Through the
expansion of labor available to the pearling industry, the rate of accumulation of this class was enhanced by the expansion of production of
exchange value. The merchant class, as the class financing the expansion of pearling, gained control over this means of production. When the
pearl market fell in 1929, it took all of the petty capitalists with it. Only
about eleven families, including the ruling family, remained with capital.

This class of financial merchants, in the meantime, had invested in
the Iraqi wet dates industry and utilized the depressed labor in Kuwait to
exploit labor for the expansion of wet-date commerce. The seafarers not
only made up the crew for the journey but also were responsible for
making the ship's sails, rigging the ship, paying her bottom and floating
her away from the dockyard. All this represented essentially unpaid
labor. The carpenters were only responsible for building the hull and
caulking. In this way, their craft was routinized by reduction to a
minimum set of tasks, and speed of completion, not durability of product, became the criterion of craftsmanship. Similarly in this period the
captains were reduced to wage-earners, and the share system in effect
made much of their work unpaid labor. Thus, the tribal distinctions that
differentiated classes of producers in early Kuwait were obliterated, and
labor in the inter-war period became a homogeneous mass that engaged
in pearling in the summer months and seafaring in the winter. Furthermore, hinterland production, which had been central to the economy of
early Kuwait, was marginal to it by the interwar period.

Independence/Dependence

Throughout the interwar period, Kuwait's character as an independent entity within the Arab Gulf continued to develop within the
framework of British imperial policy in the area. This process had two
essential inter-related facets: economic and political. Kuwait's economic independence from the Gulf, as already discussed, related to the
breaking of its commercial ties with productive centers in the region and

their substitution by commercial ties with the British productive system. Politically, the integration into the British division of labor specifically inhibited the development of labor beyond the bounds of the polity Britain defined as Kuwait. As a result, the development of productive forces was circumscribed to the intensification of pearling for the production of exchange value.

It was in the interwar period that independence as a geographic question of state boundaries and as a legal question of political authority and legitimacy was ultimately alienated from the regional framework of Arab nationalism. It was in this period, in other words, that Kuwait emerged as a national entity—a polity defined in terms of the geographic dimensions of dependent production rather than the social dimensions of culture and history. The solution was a British one imposed to serve imperial interests. It gave geographic form to Kuwait as an independent state without sovereignty and political form to Kuwait as an autocracy without power.

The Question of Boundaries

The question of the geographic area they were willing to defend as Kuwait had plagued the British since the 1899 agreement. In compiling his Gazetteer for British officials in the first decade of the twentieth century, Lorimer (vol. 2, pt. 2B, p. 1059) observed: "The boundaries of the Kuwait principality are for the most part fluctuating and undefined; they are, at any given time, the limits of the tribes which then, either voluntarily or under compulsion, own allegiance to the Shaikh of Kuwait." The Anglo-Turkish Convention of 1913 attempted to resolve the question of the territorial limits of Ottoman sovereignty vis-à-vis Kuwait.[27] However, the First World War changed the power configuration in the region considerably. The dismemberment of the Ottoman Empire, the creation of Iraq as a kingdom under British mandate, and the rise of Ibn Saud and Ikhwan power in Central Arabia all lessened the strategic importance of Kuwait from the British standpoint.

At the Uqair Conference in 1922, Sir Percy Cox, then British High Commissioner in Iraq, attempted to contain the expansion of Ikhwan power under Ibn Saud through a boundary settlement of the frontiers between Iraq, Kuwait, and Saudi Arabia. At the conference, Ibn Saud represented the interests of Najd; Sabih Beg, Iraqi Minister of Communications and Works, represented Iraq; and Major J. C. More, British Political Agent in Kuwait, represented the intersts of Kuwait. After five days of dispute between the Iraqi Minister and Ibn Saud over territorial questions, Dickson (who arranged the conference for Cox and was present throughout) reports:

> Sir Percy took a red pencil and very carefully drew in on the map of Arabia a boundary line. . . . This gave Iraq a large area of the territory claimed by Najd. Obviously to placate Ibn Saud, he ruthlessly deprived Kuwait of nearly two-thirds of her territory and gave it to Najd, his argument being that the power of Ibn Sabah [desert title of the ruler of Kuwait] was much less in the desert than it had been when the Anglo-Turkish Agreement had been drawn up. (p. 274)

The red line was a fait accompli for Iraq and Kuwait, both puppet states of Britain. Ibn Saud was the only independent power negotiating in terms of his nation's interests, but, according to Dickson (pp. 272–73), "he clearly recognized that to defy Great Britain was to court disaster." Sheikh Ahmed (who acceded to the throne of Kuwait in 1921) could only acquiesce to the British settlement. Dickson reports his reaction to the news, however, accordingly:

> Both Major More and myself, I only in a secretarial capacity, were present when Sir Percy broke the news to the ruler of Kuwait that he had been obliged to give away to Ibn Saud nearly two-thirds of the kingdom claimed by Shaikh Ahmad. Shaikh Ahmad pathetically asked why he had done this without even consulting him. Sir Percy replied, that, on this unfortunate occasion, the sword had been mightier than the pen, and that had he not conceded the territory, Ibn Saud would certainly have soon picked a quarrel and taken it, if not more, by force of arms. As it was, he (Sir Percy) had placated Shaikh Ahmad's powerful neighbour and brought about a friendly feeling for Kuwait. Shaikh Ahmad then asked if Great Britain had not entered the war in defence of the rights of small nations. Sir Percy admitted that this was correct. (p. 279)

The settlement did not placate Ibn Saud or the Ikhwan, however. Since Kuwait was economically, geographically, and culturally an integral part of the desert, Saudi pressures on Kuwait continued. In 1923, Ibn Saud banned the Najd tribes from trading in Kuwait, in effect attempting to force Kuwait for economic reasons to forego its ties with Britain and ally itself with the expanding Saudi empire. While the ban had a negligible impact on the merchant class during the twenties, with the fall of the pearl market by the end of that decade the effects were severely felt. By 1933, it appeared to British officials that there was growing sympathy in Kuwait for allying Kuwait with Saudi Arabia, and Sheikh Ahmad and Ibn Saud were secretly negotiating such arrangements.[28]

However, by this period, Kuwait had assumed new strategic importance to Britain since Iraq had gained full independence and was experiencing nationalist unrest. Kuwait's position at the head of the Arab Gulf and on the Arabian Coast air routes to the East gave it a vital strategic position for the British, especially in case of war.[29] To forestall any agreement between Kuwait and Ibn Saud, Britain asserted its right by the 1899 agreement to handle Kuwait's foreign policy. In March 1934, the Political Agent in Kuwait was directed to assert this right to the Sheikh vis-à-vis his correspondence with Ibn Saud.[30] At the same time, the question of tightening Britain's grip on Kuwait was being considered in detail. The assertion of an open protectorate over Kuwait was rejected in favor of more covert methods of tightening control.[31]

The decision not to proclaim the protectorate which in fact existed was based upon the growing force of the pan-Arab, anti-imperialist movement, and the increasing radicalism of the movement resulting from the Palestine issue. Britain's hold on Kuwait was not only threatened by the external pressures on Kuwait emanating from Baghdad and Riyadh; there was growing anti-British, pan-Arab sentiment in Kuwait itself. This had assumed organizational form by the late thirties and was manifesting itself in Kuwait through growing links with the Arab nationalist movement in Iraq and increasing agitation against government oppression and corruption.[32]

The Challenge to Autocracy

The question of the autocratic power of the Sabah family vis-à-vis the merchant community first emerged in 1921 with the sudden death of Salim and the consequent emergence of the issue of succession. At that time, the heads of Kuwait's most influential families organized to form a Consultative Council (al-Majlis al-Istishari) composed of the following twelve members: Hamad Abd Allah al-Saqr, Hilal bin Fajhan al-Mutayri, al-Shaykh Yusif bin Isa al-Qinaie, al-Sayid Abd al-Rahman Sayyid Khalif al-Naqib, Shamlan Ibn Ali bin Sayf, al-Shaykh Abd al-Aziz al-Rushayd, Ahmad Ibn Salih al-Humadi, Marzuq al-Dawud al-Badr, Khalif bin Shahin al-Ghanim, Ahmad al-Fahd al-Khalid, Mishan al-Khudayir al-Khalid, Ibrahim ibn Mudhif.[33]

The immediate objective of the Council was to forestall fac-
tionalism within the ruling family over the issue of succession. To this
end, the members agreed that 1) if the Sabah family agreed upon the
succession of one of the three potential successors — Ahmed al-Jabir,
Hamad Mubarrak, and Abdullah al-Salim—the Council would accept the
nomination; 2) if the Sabah family disagrees, the Council would refer the
matter to the British Political Agent, who would make the selection. It
was the longer-term objective of the organizers to establish their authority in the administration of the country. Ahmed al-Jabir, who succeeded
to the throne unchallenged, pledged himself to work with the Council in
the administration of Kuwait's affairs and sent the following letter to
the Council:

> In the name of God, the beneficent, the munificent: This is what is agreed
> upon between the ruler of Kuwait, Sheikh Ahmed al-Jabir, and his group
> [the Council]:
>
> First: all rulings among the subjects in [governmental] relations and crimi-
> nal acts will be in accordance with the honourable Shari [Islamic] law.
>
> Second: If the convicted claim that the judgement is contrary to the Shari,
> the case of,the plaintiff and defendant and the ruling of the judge will be
> written and will be forwarded to Islamic Ulama [religious leaders], and
> their decision will be the accepted judgement to be implemented.
>
> Third: If the two opposing parties to a dispute agree to find a third person
> who can mediate between them and find accommodation between them,
> accommodation is better because it is one of the accepted means of Shari.
>
> Fourth: Consultation in the internal affairs of the country and the external
> affairs that affect the country and may bring prosperity, inhibit corruption
> and [encourage the development of] a good system.
>
> Fifth: Everyone who has an opinion which may benefit the religious or
> material well-being of the country and its people can bring it to the
> attention of the ruler who will consult with his group [Consultative Coun-
> cil]. If they found it to be beneficial, it will be enacted.[34]

The Council lasted for only two months, however. Fighting among
its members completely crippled it and resulted in the voluntary dissolu-
tion of the body, leaving Sheikh Ahmed with sole authority. Kuwait was
at the height of its prosperity at this time, and the issues of political
power were tangential to this.

Nevertheless, the Amir's pledge became the basis of the demand for parliamentary government as the society edged toward bankruptcy in the thirties as a result of the process of underdevelopment. Bankruptcy, widespread poverty, government maladministration and corruption, and the monopoly of the Sabah family on capital accumulation in a declining economy resulted in anti-government agitation and growing demands for social reform.[35] Encouraged by the British Political Agent,[36] the merchants emerged as the moderate leaders of this movement, seeking reform within the structure of Sabah authority and coalescing the nationalist and pan-nationalist elements behind the movement for parliamentary government. In 1938 they formed a secret society — al-Qutlah al-Wataniyah (The National Bloc) — and sent a petition to the Amir demanding that he fulfill his 1921 pledge and form a legislative council. Under British pressure, the Amir accepted the demands, and an election[37] to the People's Legislative Council (al-Majlis al-Umah al-Tashrii) was organized.[38] There were a total of fourteen representatives elected to the new Council. They were: Shiyan al-Ghanim, Abdullah al-Hamad al-Saqr, Yusif bin Isa al-Qinaie, al-Sayid Ali al-Sayid Sulayman, Yusif Marzuq al-Marzuq, Salih al-Uthman, Mishan al-Khudayir al-Khalid, Abdul Latif Muhammad al-Uthman, Sulayman Khalid al-Adsani, Yusif Salih al-Humayd, Muhammad al-Dawud al-Marzuq, Sultan Ibrahim, Mishari Hasan al-Badr, Khalid al-Abd al-Latif Muhammad.[39]

The first order of business of the new Council was the preparation of the law delineating their powers and responsibilities. The Amir at first refused to sign this law, explaining that while he agreed with its contents, he considered that its implementation should be gradual. In response, the Council sent the Amir the following letter:

Your Highness: The Legislative Council today presented to you a law explaining the basic authority of the People's Council which was unanimously agreed upon by the members of the Council. We learned from Sheikh Abdullah Salim [Chairman of the Council] of your discussion with him when he brought the law to you for your signature. Frankly, we...feel that your response is not satisfactory. Your Highness stated that you are in agreement with the law, but you feel that we should gradually work to implement it. For that reason you saw no reason to sign it at the present time. To answer the queries of Your Highness, we wish to inform you that all the members of the Council ... are dissatisfied with these verbal declarations. Under the circumstances in which you took over the throne you promised to make the rule between you and the nation Shura [consultative]. But as time has passed the nation has not witnessed the achievement of this promise. The deputies of the nation, Your Highness, when they firmly determined to serve the nation and the country were serious, not kidding, and are not reluctant; they swore there will be no obstacles, whatever they may be, between them and their service to the nation. This moment may be one of the most decisive moments in the history of our country. We either [march forward] to prosperity, with you leading your people surrounded by glory, appreciation and love from every side, or the opposite. That is what we are: ready to meet every expected possibility — united on the side of the country, undaunted and unconquerable. At this moment when we submit to you our letter, we all stand together awaiting your decisive written affirmation. We ask God to help us all for whatever is the best.[40]

Faced with this determination, the Amir signed the law on July 2, 1938. In effect constituting a constitution, the law gave the People's Legislative Council far-reaching powers, as indicated by its five articles:

We, the Ruler of Kuwait, in accordance with the decision of the People's Legislative Council, approve this law on the authority of the Council and We have ordered its execution.

Article 1: The people are the source of authority represented in the person of its elected deputies.

Article 2: The Legislative Council must legislate the following laws:

1. The Budget Law, which organizes all the income of the country and its expenditure and directs it in a just manner, with the exception of the private property of al-Sabah which the Council has no right to interfere with.

2. The Law of Justice, the purpose of which is to establish religious and traditional laws in such a manner as to ensure the proper administration of justice among the people.

3. The Law of Public Security, the purpose of which is the maintenance of security inside the country and outside to the furthest borders.

4. The Law of Education, the purpose of which is the enactment of a law for education, following in it the example of the advanced countries.

5. The Law of Health, the purpose of which is the enactment of a health law which protects the country and its people from the dangers of sickness and disease of whatever kind.

6. The Law of Construction; this includes the pavement of roads outside the city and the building of prisons, digging wells, and whatever may help in building the country internally and externally.

7. The Law of Emergency, the purpose of which is the enactment of a law in the country for the occurrence of unexpected events. The authority is authorized to execute all the necessary laws needed to protect the security of the country.

8. The enactment of every other law which the interest of the country requires.

Article 3: The People's Legislative Council is the source of all treaties and internal and external concessions and agreements, and whatever is initiated in this respect will not be considered legal except with the agreement of the Council and its supervision.

Article 4: Since the country has no Court of Appeal, the duties of that court will be given to the People's Legislative Council until the formation of an independent body for this purpose.

Article 5: The Chairman of the People's Legislative Council represents the executive authority in the country.[41]

The formation of the People's Legislative Council represented the ascendance to power of bourgeois interests in Kuwait — that class of capitalist interests that had been most affected by the closure of commerce with Najd and the economic decline of the thirties. The legislation issued by the Council over the several months of its existence concentrated on the reform of customs and taxes to facilitate the expansion of local commerce and the increase of the buying power of the local and hinterland market, the abolishment of monopolies that inhibited free competition, and the organization of public finances to facilitate public services to free enterprise. All of the reforms undertaken by the Council, in fact, reflect the bourgeois ideology of free enterprise in a system of law and order.[42]

The People's Legislative Council, then, represented a progressive expression of autonomous capitalism in Kuwait. Infected with the euphoria of nationalism and seeking the expansion of markets, the bourgeois interests were ultimately in contradiction with the relations of production of dependent capitalism. By constricting the Amir's perogatives and reducing Sabah power to control the economy, the Council significantly reduced the basis of Britain's hold on Kuwait. This had immediate implications in the areas of foreign affairs and oil concessions which, by Article 3 of the law, came under the Council's jurisdiction.

Under this circumstance, confrontation between the Council and the representatives of dependent capitalism in Kuwait—represented by the Amir and the British Political Agent—was inevitable, in spite of the

Council's efforts to minimize tension. For example, although the Council established for the first time in Kuwait's history a distinction between the privy purse and public budget, it allotted 76 percent of total public revenues to salaries for the royal family and its entourage. Furthermore, it attempted to assuage British fears that the Council would abrogate agreements between the Amir of Kuwait and Britain, and on October 29, 1938, sent through the Amir the following letter to the British Resident in the Gulf.

Reference is made to your letter of October 20, 1938, which had enclosed with it the transcript of your speech to the Legislative Council. In reference to my letter to you of October 11, it is important that I clarify the following:

1. After I issued my decree of July 2, 1939, in the form of a law on the authority of the People's Legislative Council, it became evident that by its first article "the nation is the source of authority represented in the form of its elected deputies." It became evident, then, that the country began operating in accordance with a law in a parliamentary fashion. In order for all orders, laws and agreements in the name of the Government of Kuwait to become legitimate and accepted, they must have the approval of the said Council in a formal session.

2. The members of the committee which was delegated from the said Council who met with me, Your Excellency, Sheikh Abdullah Salim and Captain de Gaury [Political Agent] explained to me that the Council, after receiving the summaries of discussions which took place at that meeting, decided the following:

a. The Council depends greatly on Sheikh Ahmed al-Jabir al-Sabah's continuation as the Supreme Head of the State. In order to ease communication between His Majesty's British Government and the Government of Kuwait without infringing upon the authority given to the People's Legislative Council in accordance with His Highness' decree dated July 2, 1938, it elected after previous discussion with Captain de Gaury two of its members to become the communications means between His Highness and the Council.

b. Till now, the Council is convinced that there is no intention of making any new changes of any sort neither from His Majesty's British Government nor from the Government of Kuwait on relations and agreements between the two governments in accordance with the treaties and agreements previously signed between the present Ruler or previous rulers.

c. The Council is convinced of the importance and the advantages of friendship and British support which will always continue to be the aim of the Legislative Council in all political affairs.[43]

From al-Adsani's perspective (p. 44) the letter was a verification of the Council's "care in maintaining English-Kuwait relations" without surrendering "rights previous Kuwaiti rulers did not recognize." The letter, in fact, affirmed the Council's determination to exercise sovereignty, and British support for the Council vis-à-vis the Amir was considerably dampened. As reflected in India Office Records (#L/P&S/12/3894A, especially correspondence between October and November 1938), British authorities in the Gulf considered the Council a permanent addition to Kuwaiti politics and sought to maintain friendly relations with it. Nevertheless, they sought to reinforce the Sheikh's position vis-à-vis the Council and maintain his role as mediator of British authority there.

In December 1938 an open confrontation between the Amir and the Council resulted in the Council barricading itself in the Palace of Nayif, a store for arms. The Amir summoned the tribes to his support, and the palace was surrounded. In return for their peaceful surrender, the Amir guaranteed the safety of the Council members and the integrity of their property. The People's Legislative Council was dissolved only six months after its creation, and the principal nationalist organization, the Shabiba Club, was suppressed.[44]

Nationalist sentiment in Kuwait was still very strong, however. Responding to this, within several days of dissolving the Council, the Amir called a new election. Twelve members of the old Council were re-elected. The ruler introduced to the new Council a new constitution, one which gave him absolute veto powers. The Council rejected it. In this tense situation, a Kuwaiti, just returning from Iraq, gave an inflamed nationalist, antigovernment speech. He was arrested, and when some of his supporters attempted to free him, they were shot. The nationalist was then summarily executed, and many others jailed. As a result, many nationalists fled Kuwait to Iraq, and the movement for reform and representative government ended.[45]

Oil: The New Integration

The re-assertion of autocracy in Kuwait just prior to the initiation of the Second World War brought the inter-war period of Kuwaiti political development full circle. During the war the active nationalist movement in Iraq was suppressed by British occupation of the country. But Kuwait was pacified without the necessity of direct intervention. While the country suffered immense deprivation during the war, following it the autocracy gained a new basis of political and economic power as a result of the initiation of oil wealth.

Around the turn of the century the British Navy began developing oil-fueled ships. By 1907, it had developed the first wholly oil-fueled flotilla of oceangoing destroyers and was pursuing the transition of the entire naval fleet to oil fuel. In addition, oil was increasingly being utilized to fuel the engines of industry. From the turn of the century, then, secure sources of oil became an increasing strategic concern of the British Government. Prior to the First World War, in fact, British oil companies, backed by the power of the British Government, were securing vast oil concessions in the Middle East, and the entire region took on a new strategic importance in the competitive imperialist framework of the time.

It was during this period of competitive capitalism that Britain secured a commitment from Mubarak that "we shall never give a concession in this matter to anyone except a person appointed from the British Government."[46] The entire record of the complex oil concession negotiations which started in 1923 and culminated in the 1934 agreement has been compiled in Chisholm's book, *The First Kuwait Oil Concession*. The important point to be made here is that the entire negotiations were carried on personally by Sheikh Ahmed al-Jabir. Both in these negotiations and the concession finally adopted, the territory of Kuwait and the remunerations from the concession were treated as the private property of the Sheikh. Furthermore, the concession was for the whole of Kuwait, and gave exclusive rights to the Kuwait Oil Company (KOC, an American-British consortium) for oil exploration and exploitation in Kuwait territory.

KOC drilled its first well in 1936, but oil was not discovered until 1938 at the Burgan field (which was to prove one of the largest oil deposits in the world). However, the Second World War interrupted production, and the KOC shut down its operations completely. It was not until 1946 that the first oil was exported from Kuwait.

With the initiation of its role as an oil exporter to the industrial world, the forces of production in Kuwait underwent rapid transformation. How this transformation has affected the framework of the relations of production of dependent capitalism, a framework established in the historic era of the underdevelopment of Kuwait, is examined in Part II.

PART II

Post-Oil Kuwait

4

The New Integration: The Continuity of Dependency

THE PROCESS OF THE UNDERDEVELOPMENT OF KUWAIT throughout
the first half of the twentieth century was examined in Chapter 3
in terms of the transformation of the relations of production from autonomy to dependency and the consequent integration of Kuwait into
the emerging world capitalist division of labor. The framework of contradictions established by the transformation-integration process—capital accumulation/expropriation and independence/dependence — resulted in the limitation on the development of productive forces beyond
the scope of Kuwait's integration into the world division of labor as a
pearling center. The effective result was the concentration of capital and
homogenization of labor in a productive system that by the end of the
inter-war period was no longer able to provide subsistence to the majority of the population.

The new integration of Kuwait as a major oil supplier to the
industrial nations, however, radically transformed the basis of production and the level of surplus realized. Nevertheless, this integration was
established in the framework of the continuity of dependent relations of
production. This chapter will examine the continuity of dependency in
the capital-surplus society.

THE CHANGING STRUCTURE OF AUTOCRACY

The transition to the new basis of integration in the world division of
labor was made within the framework of the continuity of autocracy in
Kuwait, but the structure of autocracy has undergone progressive modification. Sheikh Ahmed al-Jabir died in 1950, and was succeeded by his

cousin, Abdullah al-Salim. Abdullah al-Salim had been an active support-
er of the reform movement in the interwar period; and throughout his
reign (1950–65) he attempted to lessen the more oppressive aspects of
autocracy in Kuwait. Youth associations were allowed to open; a local
press emerged as the active medium for political debate; elections were
organized for important administrative councils; and the foundations of
the welfare state were initiated. However, the expression of nationalism
in the liberalized political atmosphere proved threatening to dependency, and the youth associations and press were banned and the elections to the administrative councils annulled in February 1959.

In this period, Kuwait was still under the British protectorate. And
under British guidance, it moved toward full independence. In June
1961, Kuwait and Britain signed a Treaty of Independence[1] terminating
the 1889 Exclusive Agreement, giving Kuwait formal independence as a
sovereign independent state, and guaranteeing British military assistance if the Amir requested it. Within a month Kuwait joined the Arab
League and in 1963 became a member of the United Nations.

In December 1961, a Constituent Assembly was created to draft a
constitution. The constitution was signed by the Amir on November 11,
1962, and on January 23, 1963, Kuwait held a general election to the
newly created 50-member National Assembly. All male citizens 21 years
and over were eligible to vote. All literate male citizens 30 years and over
were eligible to run for election. Political parties were banned, and
candidates ran on independent platforms, competing for one of five seats
within each of ten electoral districts. About 210 candidates ran in the
election.[2]

The new constitution[3] designated Kuwait as a hereditary Amirate,
and limited succession to the descendants of Mubarak. The Amir was
declared immune and his person inviolable. The Heir Apparent, nomi-
nated by the Amir and approved by a simple majority of the National
Assembly, must be designated within one year of the accession of a
new Amir.

The constitution divided government into executive, legislative,
and judicial functions. Executive powers were vested in the hands of the
Amir, as the Head of State, and a Council of Ministers who were
appointed and dismissed by the Amir. Legislative powers were shared
by the Amir and the National Assembly, which was to be elected every
four years. The size of the Council of Ministers could not exceed
one-third of the number of deputies, but all save one member of the
Council could be selected from outside the National Assembly. Members of the Council of Ministers sat in the National Assembly as ex-
officio members. The Prime Minister (always the Crown Prince by

tradition), a minister without portfolio appointed by the Amir, served as President of the Council of Ministers, and liaison between the Amir and the National Assembly. A vote of no confidence against the Prime Minister was not allowed, but a vote of no confidence was allowed against other ministers. If the National Assembly could not cooperate with the Prime Minister, the Ruler could either appoint a new Prime Minister or dissolve the National Assembly and call a new election.

Although technically all legislation must be approved by a two-thirds vote of the Assembly, in actuality the Assembly's legislative powers were significantly curtailed by the powers of the Amir. The cabinet essentially constituted one third of the votes of the Assembly. Furthermore, in addition to his executive powers, the Amir had the right to initiate, sanction, and promulgate laws, and to rule by decree when the Assembly was not in session. In fact, no law could be promulgated by the Assembly unless sanctioned by the Amir, and the Amir could dissolve the Assembly at will. Also, although disposition of the state's financial resources resided with the Assembly, this was based on recommendations by the Council of Ministers.

The Executive

The functions of the National Assembly, then, were effectively constrained and real power resided with the Amir and his cabinet. These posts circulated among the ruling family, trusted supporters of the ruling family, and members of the pre-oil dominant class.[4] In fact, the Council of Ministers provided the mechanism for bringing into direct government participation and post-oil economic organization members of the pre-oil dominant class. The extent to which the pre-oil elite has actually participated in government and is integrated into the modern economic structure is indicated in Table 4.

Table 4 shows that all but one of the seven families identified by Dickson as the most prominent families (on the basis of his many years of intimate association with Kuwait) served in the 1921 Consultative Council, and five of these served in the 1938 People's Legislative Council. Furthermore, members of all the families on Dickson's list, except the one that participated in neither the 1921 nor 1938 Council, are members of the boards of the major shareholding companies.

Of the five families of the 1921 Council that were not included in Dickson's list, only one served on the 1938 Council, and only one other has ever been a member of a cabinet. From this group, membership on

Table 4

Participation of Pre-Oil Elites in Cabinets and Major Shareholding Corporations

Elites	Basis of Identification			Number of Cabinet Posts Held	Members of Board*	
	Dickson#	1921 Council	1938 Council		Capital*	Industrial
al-Khalid	x	2	1	4	1	3
al-Zayid†	x	1	1	5	4	4
al-Sayf‡	x	1	—	—	1	1
al-Badr	x	1	1	5	—	1
al-Jalil (Nisf)	x	—	—	5	5	7
al-Saleh§	x	1	1	7	5	7
al-Saqr	x	1	1	1	2	4
al-Mutayri	—	1	—	—	2	—
al-Naqib	—	1	—	—	—	1
al-Rushayd	—	1	—	—	—	1
al-Humadhi	—	1	1	1	—	1
Mudhaf	—	1	1	—	—	—
Sulayman	—	—	1	—	—	—
al-Marzuq (al-Daoud)	—	—	2	4	5	3
al-Uthman	—	—	2	—	—	—
al-Adsani	—	—	1	—	2	—
al-Ibrahim	—	—	1	—	—	—
Muhammed	—	—	1	—	—	—

*Includes banks and investment companies.
†Branches of the family include al-Ghanim and al-Qutami.
‡Branches of the family include Ibn al-Rumi and al-Shamlan.
§Branches of the family include Qanaat, al-Issa, al-Mutawa, al-Sultan, Qinaie, Al-Khalid and al-Badr are also related to Qanaat.
#From Dickson, *Kuwait and Her Neighbours*, p. 41.

boards of the major shareholding companies is much less than Dickson's list, and two of them are not members at all.

Finally, of the six families in the 1938 Council that were neither on Dickson's list nor the 1921 Council, only members of one of the families have ever held a cabinet post. And only two families from this group have held board posts.

Dickson's list, then, reflects a high degree of continuity with the 1921 and 1938 Councils, and by itself is the best predictor of subsequent participation in both the cabinets and in the shareholding companies. The shareholding companies form only a small portion of business enterprise in Kuwait, comprising only 95 of the 19,357 operating establishments and representing 14.1 percent of total employment in operating establishments in 1973 (ASA, 1979:120).* Nevertheless, shareholding companies essentially reflect investment and speculative capital, particularly in the seventies with the onset of the international monetary crisis. In 1979, the total market value of the capital of public subscription shareholding companies was KD 4.46 billion. Local capital investments in them amounted to KD 430 million: 42 percent in financial companies (banks, investments and insurance); 22 percent in industrial companies; 12 percent in real estate companies; 24 percent in transport and service companies.[5]

While participation in shareholding companies may not be inclusive of the economic elite, it does provide a strong indicator of the core of that elite. Taken together with Dickson's list, participation in the shareholding companies reflects the high degree of integration of the pre-oil elite in the post-oil elite politico-economic structure.

To what extent does participation in the cabinet correlate with membership on the boards of major shareholding companies? This is indicated in Table 5, which lists the family names that appear on three or more boards of the major shareholding companies.

Table 5 indicates the close correspondence between ministerial participation and membership on boards of major shareholding companies. If participation on three or more boards of governors is somewhat arbitrarily used as an indicator of high participation in the councils of financial power, Table 5 reveals that eleven of the total sixteen names that appear on three or more boards of directors have also participated in cabinets at one time or another between 1962 and 1975. Furthermore, five of the eleven who have participated in the cabinet are names identified in Table 4. However, there are a total of twenty-one names that appeared on cabinet between 1962 and 1975 that were not

*The *Statistical Abstracts* and *Annual Statistical Abstracts* published by the Central Statistical Office, Ministry of Planning will be cited by the abbreviation ASA, year, and page throughout the text, as above.

Table 5
Families That Hold Membership on Three or More Boards of
Major Shareholding Corporations

Family Names	Number of Cabinet Posts Held	Members of Boards	
		Capital*	Industrial
al-Khalid	4	1	3
al-Zayid†	6	4	4
al-Saleh‡	7	5	7
al-Saqr	1	5	4
al-Marzuq	4	5	3
Ghunaym	1	3	2
al-Shai	2	2	1
al-Fulaij	2	5	2
al-Kazimi	2	5	1
al-Nafisi	2	3	1
al-Hamad	1	4	2
al-Bahar	—	7	3
al-Khorafi	—	3	4
al-Rashed	—	1	2
al-Mishari	—	1	3
Behbehani	—	3	3

*Includes banks and investment companies.
†Branches of the family include al-Ghanim and al-Qutami.
‡Branches of the family include Qanaat, al-Issa, al-Mutawa, al-Sultan, and Qinaie.

given in Table 4 (i.e., they were not identified in any of the criteria of pre-oil elite). Of these, six appear in Table 5, while five of the names in Table 5 have never been on cabinet. Thus, the nature of the correspondence between cabinet posts and membership on boards is not straightforward. Nevertheless, it does indicate a close correspondence between the highest posts of political power and the highest councils of finance.

The National Assembly

The National Assembly was envisioned as a rubber stamp for policies set forth by the ruling class as embodied in the executive. However, the National Assembly emerged with a stronger spirit of independence than its architects envisioned. Although political parties were prohibited, a strong opposition bloc developed almost immediately. This bloc reflected the strength of Arab nationalist sentiment in Kuwait. In April 1963, for example, when Syria and Iraq joined President Nasser's United Arab Republic, twelve deputies of the National Assembly demanded abrogation of the Kuwait-British defense treaty and the joining of Kuwait to the Republic.[6]

The opposition bloc continued to emerge in subsequent elections — 1967, 1971 and 1975 — in spite of efforts to gerrymander the electoral districts (geographical not population areas) to increase tribal bloc voting and defeat nationalist candidates.[7] Chief issues of the opposition centered on the nature of the oil concessions and the dominance of the oil companies in Kuwait and the Arab world, Kuwait's close alliance with Britain and the United States, and Kuwait's conservative role in the Arab world.[8] In the 1975 election, the increasing political consciousness of the electorate — a larger, more literate electorate than in any of the previous elections[9] — was reflected in the emergence of election platforms around various groupings and blocs.[10] In spite of the fact that the new Assembly was considered more traditional and conservative than any of the previous ones,[11] it launched a more vigorous attack on government policies which centered more specifically on class issues than before—particularly the growing gap between a small wealthy class and the rest of the population. The opposition had strong support from the press and the public. In August 1976 the government dissolved the Assembly, suspended the Constitution, and introduced restrictions on the press.

Kuwait did not return to the parliamentary system until 1981. Elections were held for the National Assembly on February 18, 1981, and 447 candidates campaigned for 50 seats. The new parliament has an over-representation of 24 members with a bedouin background of loyalty to the ruling family. Furthermore, Shias and Arab nationalists, who formed the recalcitrant opposition in previous assemblies, were substantially diminished. Only three Arab nationalists were elected and only two Shias (who put up a third of the candidates).

THE CHANGING STRUCTURE OF PERIPHERAL INTEGRATION

Kuwait's new integration as an oil producer was made by the linkage with monopoly capital in the form of oil corporations. The Kuwait Oil Company (KOC), which accounts for over 90 percent of oil production in Kuwait, was founded as a joint Gulf Oil and British Petroleum (BP) venture—two of the "majors" or "seven sisters" of oil which include Exxon (Standard Oil of New Jersey), Mobil (Standard Oil of New York),

Chevron (Standard Oil of California), Texaco, and Shell. These "seven sisters" were fully integrated corporations that not only controlled production of Middle East oil but also all downstream operations. Their collusive arrangement, known as the Red Line Agreement, had been instituted to limit the supply of oil on world markets by determining which areas were to be exploited and which areas were to be reserved for future exploitation. [12]

In Kuwait, production began in 1946 under terms fairly typical of the period: BP and Gulf determined the quantities KOC produced, where these would be sold, and the price paid. Kuwait received a fixed royalty of 12.5 percent of the posted price — the value of oil at the well-head which reflected more its cost of production than market value. Over the period 1946 to 1951 this yielded to Kuwait a total revenue of about $42 million. [13]

By 1951, the Kuwait Government had begun to reassess its position, and while not altering the structure of relations with KOC, insisted that KOC be subject to a corporate income tax of an amount equal to 50 percent of the net sales price minus the production costs and royalties. The United States had made provisions that such taxes be deductible as a credit from United States income taxes. A similar arrangement in Britain, plus the fact that Kuwait had just granted a concession in the Kuwait/Saudi Arabia Neutral Zone to the American Independent Oil Company (AMINOIL) under the new terms, all contributed to KOC's willingness to accept the new deal. Revenues to the government were $56 million in 1952 alone. [14]

Despite this gain in receipts, Kuwait remained dissatisfied with the level of production determined solely by KOC in terms of monopolistic market considerations. The government hoped to increase production to some degree and establish some control over production levels by establishing other concessionaires within the country. A step in this direction was taken with the admittance of AMINOIL, and further steps through the fifties involved the Arabian Oil Company (Japan) Ltd. (AOC) and the Kuwait Shell Development Company. Both of these corporations were to include a degree of government participation, with Kuwait acquiring a ten percent share of AOC and an option for 20 percent of the Shell operation. [15] However, a more significant development was an agreement reached in 1955 with KOC calling for it to relinquish 50 percent of its original concession area. This was not a nationalization of oil-producing property, but rather involved undeveloped lands which were to be operated by a nationally-controlled corporation — the Kuwait National Petroleum Company (KNPC). KNPC officially began in 1960 with the government owning 50 percent of the equity. It has not been involved in large-scale production, however, restricting its scope to refining and purchasing its feed-stocks from KOC.

The fifties came to a close with a number of developments changing the nature of the world oil market. A world surplus was emerging, and competition from a number of the smaller independent concessionaires, who had been welcomed into most producing nations under a divide-and-conquer philosophy regarding dealings with foreign corporations, was beginning to force price erosion. In August 1960, the majors announced a reduction in the posted price of Middle East crude, and began enthusiastic development in countries where tax and royalty structures remained strongly in their favor. Reaction from the Middle East was rapid, with Kuwait, Iraq, Iran, and Saudi Arabia joining the formation of OPEC in September. Their sole purpose at that time was to maintain government revenues by either a restoration of the price or a change in the royalty/tax arrangement.

Up to this time Kuwait had been fairly successful in attaining short-term objectives regarding oil. Throughout the post-war period world demand increased rapidly, the industry was extremely profitable, and the majors had a fairly cooperative attitude from the governments of producing countries. The changes that had occurred just prior to 1960 had caused this attitude to change considerably. OPEC found opposition to be quite severe, and the members were relatively unsuccessful throughout the decade. KOC remained very powerful and dominated the industry in Kuwait, granting periodic increases to government revenues of a few cents per barrel. The extent of its power was revealed in 1968, when, amidst a growing feeling of nationalism, the Kuwaiti newspaper, al-Taliah, ran an article accusing KOC of acting as the de facto government. [16] Following this, the newspaper was closed down for a year by Ministerial decree.

However, KOC's position was at a height never again to be enjoyed. The formation of the Organization of Arab Petroleum Exporting Countries (OAPEC) and the events of the 1967 Arab-Israeli War were significant markers of the beginning of a new period of relationships between Gulf countries and oil companies. By 1969 Kuwait and her neighbors were solidly behind an assault on the concessionary terms — terms which had become intolerable to the most conservative governments of the area.

The oil market itself had significantly changed from the surplus situation of the fifties and sixties. By the early seventies, world consumption of oil had increased so dramatically that demand threatened to outpace supply. In this situation, it was a supplier's market, and during the first three years of the seventies the countries acquired the right to significant control in the determination of prices. Most established further claims on control of production through either direct participation or outright nationalization. Because of the threat of oil shortages, a fragmentation of interests had developed among the oil companies themselves, and a much greater diversity of interests existed among consuming nations, who were anxious that future needs be supplied with a high degree of security. The political implications of oil were becoming increasingly important as the world entered 1973, and consuming nations were keenly aware that while the producers were unable to determine among themselves exact levels of production in each country, at least the OAPEC members would cooperate in the ultimate decision as to whether production would take place at all.

Concessions were made therefore to discourage Gulf nations from even voicing the threat implicit in their bargaining position. The world was fairly optimistic in early 1973 that stability in the oil market had been achieved, and the *New York Times* reported on April 16, 1973, that "there [was] little likelihood of even a partial boycott of sales to Western allies of Israel unless there [was] a renewal of Arab-Israel conflict on a large scale."

The Arab-Israeli conflict, however, was already fomenting. In May 1973 Kuwait was among four Arab countries which staged a symbolic protest against Israel by stopping the flow of oil supplies to the West for a 24-hour period. On May 16, 1973, the *New York Times* commented that this action was a demonstration of Kuwait's willingness to close production "the moment the battle against Israel began." Over the summer, a maximum ceiling was placed on oil production. In September, the Kuwaiti Ambassador to the United States, Salem al-Sabah, outlined the reasons for this move as being associated with restricted present development opportunities as well as the international monetary situation, and a concern for the needs of future Kuwaiti generations. He added that "nowadays ... the flag and interest follow trade ... politics may play a role since Kuwait is an Arab country ... it's quite natural that we do not want our oil to participate in oiling the Israeli war machine." [17]

In a speech to the National Assembly in October 1973, the Crown Prince and Prime Minister Jabir al-Ahmed al-Sabah, acting on behalf of the Amir, outlined the government's initiative on oil pricing:

> It was necessary to reconsider Agreements within the framework of future relations between Kuwait and the oil companies operating in Kuwait.... If the companies do not respond, the government will take measures to preserve its oil wealth. In view of the consistent rise in prices of all raw

materials, at an even higher rate than had been anticipated at the time of the signing of the Tehran agreement in 1972, ... we decided without reference to the companies to raise the posted price of Kuwaiti oil by seventy percent as from October 16, 1973, and to adjust these prices in future in accordance with the dictates of national interest and the conditions of the oil markets.[18]

KOC, in which the Kuwaiti government had at this time no participation, regarded the action as a usurpation of its rights, and the decision might well have been rendered ineffective had it been taken in isolation. However, on October 16, the *New York Times* reported that "the Foreign Ministers of Saudi Arabia, Kuwait, Libya and Algeria ... had asked to see President Nixon. ... Arab diplomats reported that Kuwait would seek to stop shipments of her crude, estimated at 65,000 barrels a day, to the United States." Two days later, the paper announced that "the long-awaited formal decision to use oil as a weapon in the Middle East conflict was announced at the end of an eight-hour meeting in Kuwait of Ministers of eleven countries. The monthly export-reduction was set at 5 percent off each previous month's sales, starting with the level of sales in September." This was not a consensus of action, however, as on October 22 the *New York Times* reported that "four Persian Gulf oil producers — Kuwait, Qatar, Bahrain and Dubai — announced a total embargo of oil to the United States." The embargo lingered on in one form or another until March 18, 1975, when at a meeting in Vienna most of the Arab oil countries announced officially they would lift the embargo of oil shipments.

Nevertheless, Kuwait remained aggressive in pursuit of control over KOC. In 1973, the National Assembly had refused to ratify an agreement which called for a government minority share in the company; but in January 1974 a new agreement was reached between KOC and the government which gave Kuwait 60 percent ownership. This was ratified in May and Kuwait acquired its share for a price just equal to the net book value — $112 million.[19]

Throughout 1974 the price of Kuwaiti oil was increased. Before the 29th General Assembly of the United Nations Kuwait explained that this was simply a reaction to the fact that "the companies, the interests they serve and the countries to which they belong, had deliberately frozen the price of oil at a very low level for more than a quarter of a century. Raising the price of oil was in essence the correction of an inequitable situation."[20]

Kuwait continued to restrict output, lowering the ceiling to a maximum of just over two million barrels per day. Such restrictions were hardly necessary, however, for the majors themselves were taking steps to limit the sales of nationally-controlled or wholly state-owned oil companies by working on the gap between the price of crude they bought-back from the producers at a tax-paid cost and the sale price of government participation crude. The latter was agreed to be not lower than 93 percent of the posted price, which at first glance would give the national companies the advantage of being able to sell all they wished. The tax-paid cost on other crude was calculated on the basis of the posted price in such a manner so as to divide the profit (which was virtually all of the posted price) in a ratio of 60:40, with the company receiving the 40 percent. As the posted prices rose, the companies found that they could easily afford to lower their profit margin on buy-back crude, and produce quite profitably at a "cocktail" price which undercut any of the national companies. By summer 1974, with an actual surplus situation again developing in Middle East crude, the national companies found it almost impossible to make any direct sales to third parties at all. [21]

On November 10, 1974, three Arab oil-exporting countries, led by Saudi Arabia, lowered their oil price while sharply increasing the tax and royalties paid by the foreign companies. This was to have the effect of squeezing oil company margins and ensuring a capture by the national companies of the market to third parties. However, Kuwait, Iran, and Iraq argued that a change in the price structure could only be adopted by a full meeting of OPEC ministers, since pricing was the only genuine basis of agreement among OPEC members. Kuwait preferred to move towards complete ownership of oil production, and this became the generally adopted Arab policy.

Kuwait acquired 100 percent of KOC on September 1, 1975. The new arrangement, also used by Saudi Arabia, called for the government to put up all investment capital and be solely responsible for the management of the operation. The ex-concessionaires provide support services and personnel when requested, through the signing of long-term competitive contracts. In Kuwait the companies involved became, quite naturally, Gulf and BP, and these two were allowed to purchase 500,000 and 450,000 barrels per day respectively at a flat fixed discount of fifteen cents per barrel.

Kuwait continued the policy of restrictions on production as a principal means of maintaining price. Further, the government argued that the real returns on oil be kept constant:

> In the last 15 months or so, we estimate that the real price of oil has declined by, say, 25 percent at least. This has been the result of the average

rate of world inflation and the steady decline of the dollar which is still the main...means of payment for oil exports.... The only solution does in fact seem to be in linking the price of oil to some sort of price index.[22]

OIL AND THE CAPITAL SURPLUS ECONOMY

The changes in the structure of autocracy and peripheral integration that Kuwait experienced over the period of its integration into the world division of labor as an oil producer are related to the level of capital surplus realized. From the mid-fifties, at least, Kuwait has been a capital surplus society.[23] Between 1953 and 1961, the government realized KD 897.8 million from oil revenues (ASA, 1968:111). Data for state expenditures in this period are not available. Table 6 shows the surplus realized from 1962 to 1979.

The deficit reflected in the period 1965/66 was the result of decreases in the rate of increase in oil revenues in the sixties. Between 1953 and 1958, production increased by 67 percent and revenues by 112 percent (ASA, 1972:180). The more rapid rate in the increase of revenues was due to adjustments in terms of trade with KOC, as discussed earlier. By 1960, however, these had reached their limit within the framework of the concessions. Between 1960 and 1964, oil production increased by 61 percent, while revenues from 1960/61 through 1964/65 increased by only 30 percent (ASA, 1972:156, 180). Thus, the relation-

Table 6

Actual State Revenues and Expenditures (KD million), 1962/63–1978/79

	Revenues	Expenditures	Surplus Millions KD	Percent
1962/63–1964/65	619.4	523.7	95.7	15.4
1965/66–1967/68	808.8	852.0	−43.2	−5.3
1968/69–1970/71	918.1	853.9	64.2	7.0
1971/72–1973/74	1,519.8	1,355.0	164.8	10.8
1974/75–1976/77	8,462.1	3,984.1	4,478.0	52.9
1977/78–1978/79	5,014.0	4,697.7	316.3	6.3

SOURCE: Data for 1962/63 through 1970/71 from *Statistical Abstract, 1972*, p. 187; government expenditures in 1971/72 from *Statistical Yearbook of Kuwait*, 1974, p. 144; remaining data from *Annual Statistical Abstract, 1979*, pp. 297–301.

ship between increasing production and increasing revenues was essentially reversed in this period and remained the same throughout the decade. Government expenditures, on the other hand, increased from KD 165.2 in 1962/63 to KD 285.5 in 1969/70 (ASA, 1972:187), a 73 percent increase over the period.

The phenomenal surplus realized in the period 1974/75–1976/77 was a result of the inability of the government departments and agencies to absorb the sudden increases in revenue generated by the changes in the oil industry. By 1977/78, the situation was ameliorated, as reflected in Table 6, by substantial increases in public expenditure. These increases are reflected in Table 7.

Public expenditure is made up of three budgets: the general budget includes the Head of State, ministries, and departments; the attached budget (attached to the general budget) includes the National Assembly, municipality and acquisition department; the independent budget includes financial and non-financial public enterprises. Table 7 reflects the substantial increases in these budgets in the period.

The struggle with the oil companies that culminated in state sovereignty over oil production by 1975 may be understood in terms of the class structure that resulted from the new integration of Kuwait as an oil producer. In the new integration, the basis of class power had been transformed from ownership of the means of production to control of the means of allocation — namely the oil revenues. Since all oil revenue accrued directly to the ruler under the terms of the concession, the executive in fact became the appropriator of the new wealth. Revenue allocation through ministries transformed the articulation of economic and political power, and transformed the basis of power from control over the means of production to control over the means of allocation.

Table 7
Increases in Public Expenditures by Budget Allocation, 1974/75–1978/79

| | Budget (KD 000) | | |
	General	Attached	Independent
1974/75	1,087,045	14,629	35,049
1975/76	1,034,874	24,479	65,587
1976/77	1,377,885	23,433	321,118
1977/78	1,753,370	25,820	381,299
1978/79	1,941,000	31,265	564,917

SOURCE: *Annual Statistical Abstract, 1979,* pp. 300–301.

Oil revenues are the major source of funds for financing of consumption and investment in the post-oil economy. The capture of public expenditure is the basis of private enterprise in Kuwait in the post-oil era. In this situation, the capture of public revenue became the focus of intra-class competition, in effect consolidating rather than fragmenting class cohesion behind the ruling family. Under the new integration the executive, represented by the ruler and his Council of Ministers, became the political superstructure of an economic infrastructure based upon expropriation of the nation's oil resources.

As a capitalist class, the executive first struggled with the problem of increasing the rates of accumulation by increasing returns to the state from oil production. The next logical step (in terms of capitalist interests) was to gain control over the means of production themselves. Between 1971 and 1978, in fact, production decreased by 33 percent, but revenues between 1971/72 and 1978/79 increased by 500 percent (ASA, 1979:163, 297).

Throughout the struggle with the oil companies, the National Assembly spearheaded the attack on the oil companies, and because of inflamed Arab nationalist sentiment due to the Arab-Israeli conflict, accelerated the process of gaining control over the means of production. However, once this was achieved and the oil companies could no longer provide a scapegoat for nationalist unrest, the National Assembly posed a threat to the class itself. For although the state had gained control over oil production, this had been achieved within the framework of dependency.

Under the impact of capital surplus, the mechanisms of expropriation have included both increasing rates of commodity imports from the Western capitalist nations and increasing rates of capital export. Between 1954 and 1960, the value of Kuwait's annual imports increased from KD 29.9 million to KD 86.4 million, an increase of 189 percent; and between 1961 and 1971, the value of annual imports increased by 161 percent (ASA, 1972:247). Between 1970 and 1977, the importation of goods and services increased from KD 223.3 million, to KD 1,387.0 million, a 521 percent increase over a seven-year period (ASA, 1979:231). Kuwait's imports from Japan, the European Common Market and the United States in 1977 accounted for about 65 percent of the total value of imports (ASA, 1979:236–38). Between 1970 and 1975, the importation of consumption and intermediate goods accounted for over 70 percent of total imports, while capital goods other than transport equipment accounted for 15 percent or less (ASA, 1976:267).

Table 8 reflects the relative importance of different sectors in the expropriation of capital from Kuwait for the years 1966/67, 1970/71, and 1974/75.

Table 8
Balance of Payments, 1966/67, 1970/71, and 1974/75 (in KD million)

Transactions	1966/67	1970/71	1974/75
Oil Sector			
Government Receipts	292.1	321.1	2,203.5
Expenditure of Oil Companies	23.3	27.8	25.0
Transactions of KNPC	—	2.4	140.8
Total	315.4	351.3	2,369.3
Other Current Transactions			
Exports	14.5	26.4	130.5
Imports	−176.1	−240.6	−552.6
Freight, Insurance, Travel	−26.8	−21.0	−21.8
Investment Income	75.2	102.8	202.6
Total	−113.2	−132.4	−241.3
Balance of Current Transactions	202.2	218.9	2,128.0
Capital Transfer			
Government Transfers	−15.3	−40.9	−286.7
Current Private Transfers	−2.8	—	−75.0
Private Capital (Other)	−114.7	−59.3	−532.6
Total	−132.8	−100.2	−894.3
Loans			
Government Loans (net)	−5.5	4.5	16.7
KFAED loans	−6.0	1.8	−145.0
Total	−11.5	6.3	−128.3
Balance of Capital Transactions	−144.3	−93.9	−1,022.6
Monetary Sector			
Net Commercial Banks Assets	−62.0	−24.5	23.3
Government Assets	4.1	−100.5	−1,138.1
Total	−57.9	−125.0	−1,114.8

SOURCE: *Statistical Yearbook of Kuwait, 1976*, p. 183.

Table 8 reflects both the increases in imports and capital transfers over the period 1966/67–1974/75. There was a 573 percent increase in the rate of capital transfers between 1966/67 and 1974/75. In 1966/67, private capital made up 88 percent of these transfers, but by 1974/75, government transfers had increased to 32 percent. The most spectacular increase, however, was in government assets. Table 9 shows the substantial increase in Kuwait's foreign investments between 1970 and 1977, and the distribution of these investments by allocation of funds.

From the mid-sixties, the intermediate position of Kuwait's dominant class between importation and local consumption was protected by law which required all businesses in Kuwait to be 51 percent Kuwaiti. This provided the limits of nationalism of the peripheral capitalist class in the sixties when 75 percent of Kuwait's surplus was absorbed in internal development, and the 25 percent surplus went into reserves and foreign investments.[24] But the phenomenal increases in oil revenues in

Table 9

Kuwait Foreign Investments 1970, 1975, and 1977 (in KD million)

Allocations	1970	1975	1977
Reserve Fund			
Government Organizations	113.9	395.6	612.7
International Organizations	9.4	169.2	295.4
Kuwait Investment Office (reserve)	41.8	290.0	1,253.2
American Shares and Bonds	52.4	536.7	1,080.3
Other Foreign Shares and Bonds	34.6	486.2	1,555.3
Local Shares	41.0	108.7	281.8
Local Loans and Deposits	78.1	249.4	701.6
Foreign Loans	119.9	98.1	120.9
Deposits in Foreign Banks*	42.1	80.1	93.8
Real Estate	6.1	52.7	102.1
Other Accounts	0.8	−120.9	80.8
Total	540.7	2,345.8	6,177.9
Current Fund			
Kuwait Investment Office Current	7.3	63.0	839.6
Current Bank Accounts	2.4	0.1	9.9
Total	9.7	63.1	849.5
General Total	550.4	2,408.9	7,027.4

*Listed as "Loans for Foreign Governments" in ASA, 1978.

SOURCE: *Annual Statistical Abstract, 1977,* p. 224, and *Annual Statistical Abstract, 1980, p. 318.*

the seventies reversed the relationship between allocations to internal development and surplus. In 1970, Kuwait's surplus in foreign transactions amounted to KD339.7 million and comprised 29 percent of the disposal of current receipts; by 1975, the surplus amounted to KD 1,939.2 million, and comprised 64 percent of the disposal of current receipts (ASA, 1977:211). After 1972, the export of financial capital emerged as a major industry in Kuwait.

The Financial Industry

The financial industry of Kuwait is comparatively young. Before the seventies, funds channelled outside Kuwait were mainly in the form of time deposits and loans, as reflected in Table 9. However, by the end of 1973, foreign investments had become the major outlet of the country's huge capital surplus. In December 1973, the Crown Prince and Prime Minister, Jabir al-Ahmad al-Sabah, outlined the foundations of a foreign investment policy as a means to increase gradually reserves by secure and rewarding investments of capital. He stressed that Kuwait should "distribute investments among various world markets and in various kinds of investments so as to achieve the highest yield with the minimum of risk."[25] Over the period 1973 to 1975, many new banks and investment corporations were established and began to engage actively in participation internationally and to underwrite private issues on a world-wide scale. By 1976 the banking and financial system of Kuwait comprised:

1. The Central Bank of Kuwait, which executes all local and foreign business transactions for the government ministries and agencies.

2. Six commercial banks: four fully owned by the private sector; two jointly owned by the government and the private sector.

3. Three specialized banks: one privately owned; one jointly owned by the government and the private sector; and one fully owned by the government. The Credit and Savings Bank (government-owned) and the Real Estate Bank (private) provide financing mainly for real estate activities, and the Industrial Bank (joint sector) provides financing and technical assistance to the industrial sector.

4. Fifteen investment companies (most of which were established since 1972): two jointly owned by the government and private sector; the others fully owned by the private sector or by the private sector with foreign participation (not exceeding 49 percent). Twelve of the companies are closed corporations and the remainder are shareholding companies. The

three shareholding companies — Kuwait Investment Company (joint sector), Kuwait International Investment Company (private) and Kuwait Foreign Trading, Contracting and Investment Company (joint sector) — held 92.5 percent of the assets of all investment companies and 97.3 percent of their total capital and reserves in 1976.

5. Several insurance companies, including three national companies, one re-insurance company, and a number of foreign companies operating through local agencies. [26]

In the seventies, this financial structure emerged as the major intermediary between accumulation in Kuwait and the central financial markets of the world by channelling a major part of local savings and surpluses outside the country. By 1976, the commercial banks had 38.6 percent of total assets in foreign assets, the specialized banks had 35.0 percent of total assets in foreign assets, [27] and the investment companies had 62 percent of total assets in foreign assets. [28] It is especially through the investment companies, then, that the country's vast financial resources are funnelled into the world market.

The scope of operations of the investment industry in Kuwait was indicated by their activities. In 1975, for example, twenty-two bond issues totalling over half a billion dollars were managed by Kuwaiti investment companies, and there was participation in another thirty-nine issues, the total amount of which was not disclosed. [29] In 1976, the investment companies managed, co-managed, and participated in issues totalling KD 2,411.8 million, a 41 percent increase over 1975. Of this, KD 127 million were locally marketed. Furthermore, of the KD 2,411.8 million, about KD 81 million were marketed in Kuwaiti dinars, and KD 27 million were marketed for the benefit of Arab countries. The balance of the total issues was in foreign currencies: 60 percent in U.S. dollars; 24.4 percent in Deutsche mark; 9.7 percent in Canadian dollars; and the remainder in other foreign currencies. [30]

The major investment corporations are under the direction of the Ministry of Finance, which administers the bulk of the State's revenues in foreign exchange and which is the main provider and manager of funds. Over the past several years, the Ministry has established its own "efficient global network similar to the best of the old professional institutions." [31] The criteria of profitability is obviously met; Kuwait is earning as much as 15 percent return on money in Europe. [32] In 1976, the government owned $14 billion in foreign assets, and private interests owned another $4 billion; [33] by 1978, the government's foreign assets had increased to $25 billion, divided about equally between equities and money market instruments, with two percent of it in real estate. [34]

DEPENDENCY AND CLASS IN THE CAPITAL SURPLUS SOCIETY

Kuwait is a particular case of dependent capitalism—a case where the producing nations have achieved a monopoly over a resource that is vital to the economies of the industrialized nations. In this case, capital surplus rather than capital shortage is the effective result. Nevertheless, like other dependent nations, dependency in Kuwait is specified by its narrow specialized role in the world division of labor as an oil producer and the expropriation of capital from Kuwait is specified by its narrow specialized role in the world division of labor as an oil producer and the expropriation of capital from Kuwait to the centers of world capitalism. The narrow specialization is revealed by the role of crude oil in Kuwait's balance of payments, and expropriation is also revealed by the balance of payments which reflects the extent of flow out of capital. Because of the volume of capital involved, the flow out of the nation has taken the forms of foreign investments and surplus reserves in addition to ever-increasing imports.

Kuwait's integration into the world division of labor is a function of the relations of production in a world system—of the functional division of labor between central capitalism and peripheral capitalism. This functional division of labor was established in the historical era of underdevelopment when the ruling family was politically dependent upon Britain for its power, and economically dependent upon a class of financial and commercial interests initially related to pearling (the production of exchange value for external markets) and commerce (the transfer of British-transported commodities to local and hinterland markets). The relations of production in Kuwait were determined by these relationships, and adjusted over time within the general framework of these relationships.

The new integration of Kuwait into the world division of labor as an oil producer rendered the ruling family economically independent of financial and commercial interests in Kuwait and consolidated the relationship between central capitalism (in the form of monopoly capital—the oil companies) and primitive accumulation in Kuwait. In transforming the basis of power from ownership of the means of production to control over the means of allocation, the new integration also consolidated the articulation of political and economic power behind the ruling family. In this situation, the dominant class interests remained essentially the same. That is, the basis of power remained externally mediated through Britain (and now the oil companies), the basis of production remained the creation of exchange value for expropriation, and the basis of accumulation remained the transfer of commodities from the industrial nations to the local markets.

The achievement of state sovereignty and sovereignty over the oil industry did not alter the structure of these relations. Rather, both occurred within the framework of this structure. The essential structure of dependency — specialized primary production in the periphery, accumulation by a peripheral capitalist class for expropriation to the center —remains fundamentally unaltered. It does, however, reveal the nature of peripheral capitalism in Kuwait. The class is peripheral in the sense of its relationship to the level of development of productive forces in Kuwait. It is integrated into the level of development of productive forces in the world centers of capitalism. Both the achievement of independence and the achievement of sovereignty over resources occurred in congruence with the level of integration of this class, and both have strengthened Kuwait's integration into the world division of labor as an oil producer.

As a class, in fact, peripheral capitalists in Kuwait are dependent upon the maintenance of the structure of dependency and fundamentally antagonistic to any development of productive forces in Kuwait that alters this structure. This is examined in Chapter 5 in terms of the transformation of productive forces in Kuwait resulting from Kuwait's new integration into the world division of labor as an oil producer.

5
The Transformation
of Kuwait

*T*HE EMERGENCE OF KUWAIT AS A MAJOR OIL SUPPLIER to the industrial nations radically transformed the economic infrastructure of Kuwait. The traditional seafaring industries, already depressed in the interwar period, were essentially obliterated by the early fifties by the dynamic expansion of the oil sector. In 1948, for example, only 82 ships went pearling; and by 1955 only eleven. Similarly, the last Kuwaiti deepsea dhow was purchased by the Office of Education in 1954 for preservation as an historical memorial. Dhow construction, maritime commerce, and pearling, then, already marginalized in the interwar period by the forces of production of the industrial world, were essentially extinguished as productive sectors by the new integration.

THE ECONOMIC TRANSFORMATION

In the post-oil era, the character of Kuwait's economic infrastructure was transformed from production of surplus value to consumption of surplus products. Government expenditure on development was the principal mechanism facilitating this transformation. At its core was the transfer of public revenue to the private sector. Within the structure of peripheral capitalism, development took the form of the expansion of the consumer market for the commodities of the industrial world. In the fifties and early sixties, both the physical infrastructure of the affluent society and the bureaucratic infrastructure of the welfare state were created from the huge oil revenues flowing into the nation. Both facilitated private accumulation from public revenue and expropriation to the world centers of capitalism.

The physical transformation of Kuwait City from a sun-baked adobe town, four miles long on its desert side, to a modern metropolis of the most contemporary design and ostentatious architecture, 25 miles long on its desert side by 1963, was one of the initial mechanisms of private accumulation-expropriation of public funds. As early as 1950, foreign consultants were brought in to draw up a Master Development Plan for Kuwait City, and its suburbs, identifying the sites for public institutions, industrial areas, ports, and residential areas.[1] In 1952, a Development Board was established to co-ordinate construction activity, especially the development of a public utilities infrastructure. The Board devised a program of development projects for the period 1952/53–1956/57 at the cost of KD 91.5 million. Expenditure on development projects between 1956 and 1965/66 amounted to KD 345 million.[2]

The relationship between public expenditure and private accumulation-expropriation was evident in the land acquisition and construction program. Within the city, the government bought up huge tracts of land for public projects and resold the improved surplus at about four percent of its cost to the treasury, setting off lucrative land speculation. In addition, the government-owned banking institutions made substantial advances to merchants investing in land. Outside the city, in the once public domain of the desert, those who had insight into expansion plans fenced in and claimed ownership of huge tracts of the barren sand. The government then purchased these lands at handsome prices to accommodate expansion. According to the report of the mission of the International Bank for Reconstruction and Development (IBRD) sent to Kuwait in 1961 and 1963:

> The Government buys land at highly inflated prices for development projects and for resale to private buyers. Land purchases amounted to between KD 40 million and KD 60 million in most recent years. Whatever the political or developmental justifications for this practice, the prices fixed by the Government for these transactions and the small amount thus far collected on the resale of the land make the public land transactions a rather indiscriminate and inequitable way of distributing the oil revenues. In addition, probably the largest share of these funds are invested abroad, so that the land purchase program fails to accomplish its main objective of invigorating the Kuwait economy.[3]

Fakhry Shehab further observed:

> Enormous private fortunes were amassed by both selling to, and buying from, the state. It has been estimated that between 1957 and 1962 close to $840,000,000 of public money was spent on land.

This huge expenditure would have been justified on the grounds that it engendered economic activity and diffused a large portion of the new wealth, were it not that in fact only a limited amount was piped into the local economy. By far the larger part was remitted abroad either directly, or indirectly through the banking system.[4]

In spite of IBRD recommendations in its report, *The Economic Development of Kuwait* (p. 89) that "the purchasing of land at high prices in excess of development needs" as a mechanism for disbursing public funds to the private sector be replaced by more economically productive mechanisms, this continued to be an important component of development expenditure, as reflected in Table 10.

Another example that demonstrates the government's essentially paternal relationship to private accumulation occurred in 1977. Following a considerable expansion of stock market speculation throughout 1975 and 1976, there appeared a slump in the market in 1977, indicated both by a 30.6 percent decrease in the volume of traded shares compared to 1976 and an overall average decline of 38 percent in the price of shares. In an effort to offset the considerable losses experienced by speculators as a result of the slump, in December 1977 the Government undertook to purchase any quantity of shares that might be offered for

Table 10

State Expenditure on Property Acquisition
and Revenue from Sales of State Owned Property,
1964/65–1971/72 (in KD millions)

	Expenditure on Property Acquisition	Percent of Development Expenditures	Property Sales Revenue
1964/65	KD 45.0	50.0%	KD 2.5
1965/66	29.2	38.2%	1.5
1966/67	10.0	12.3%	2.0
1967/68	30.0	33.7%	1.5
1968/69	17.0	29.5%	1.5
1969/70	10.0	14.8%	1.8
1970/71	25.0	33.0%	1.7
1971/72	29.7	33.0%	1.6

SOURCE: Data for 1964/65–1967/68 from *Statistical Abstract*, 1968, pp. 113–15; data from 1968/69–1971/72 from *Statistical Abstract*, 1972, pp. 182–85.

sale at prices it prescribed.[5] By February 1978, it was reported that the gesture cost the State KD 125 million.[6]

The government's efforts to modernize the City of Kuwait resulted in a construction boom, particularly in the period 1952 to 1965. Foreign planning consultants, architects, engineers, construction firms, and labor planned and created a city with the best material and technologies the industrial world could supply.[7] In contrast to the land acquisition program, however, government outlays in this period to create social overhead capital did generate considerable economic activity. In addition to a great many public buildings, commercial centers, apartment blocks, and suburban community projects built in the period, the following were also constructed:

1. 176 government schools and 32 private schools.

2. 8 hospitals, 2 sanatoria, 37 dispensaries and health centers, 148 school dispensaries and 9 centers for preventive medicine.

3. 1,100 meters of paved roads.

4. A number of electric power stations and an expansive network for distribution and street lighting laid; between 1956 and 1965, installed capacity increased from 30,000 kwh to 370,000 kwh.

5. Water desalinization plants with a capacity of producing 15 million gallons per day; in addition, development of underground brackish and sweet water resources producing a total of 23 million gallons per day.

6. The creation of Kuwait Airways and the development of support and maintenance facilities.

7. The expansion of port facilities.

8. The creation by the Ministry of Public Works of several industries supplying construction materials.[8]

The development of the bureaucratic infrastructure of the welfare state was also related to the expansion of the consumer market for the commodities of the industrial world. In this case the target was to increase the consumer capacity of the population by raising its standard of living. Two mechanisms have been utilized to achieve this: through the expansion of social services, and in the form of wages to public sector employees. This program was facilitated through the transformation of Kuwait into the welfare state — the total service society with almost every human need from the cradle to the grave serviced by institutional arrangements. Health, education, welfare, housing were transformed from the private family sector to the public service sector. Between 1962/63 and 1978/79 expenditure on public services increased from KD 27.4 million (ASA, 1976:182) to KD 291.5 million (ASA, 1979:302).

Corresponding to the growth of public services was the increasingly bureaucratic organization of society. From the simple structure of a ruling family that served as the government administration in the pre-oil era, by 1979 the government was composed of seventeen ministries. As early as 1955, 55.6 percent of the labor force was employed by the government. In 1978, the civil service comprised 133,248 employees, about 44 percent of the labor force and representing approximately one civil servant for every ten persons in the population.

The civil service is actually overstaffed, however, by the policy of guaranteeing to all Kuwaiti citizens a job in the public sector. This has been a major mechanism for increasing the standard of living of the population. Commenting on the administrative effects of overstaffing, the IBRD mission to Kuwait observed:

> Even a cursory passage through administrative offices reveals great segmentation, showing little groups of two to five persons performing a few moves in an administrative process. This fragmentation seems unnecessary in what is after all a small State and administration. ... There is a profusion of forms and ledgers, often individually well designed and always beautifully printed, which have to be filled out laboriously, in many cases with data that already are easily accessible in other forms and ledgers. At the same time, important data are seldom available. The amount of work done by each person or section is often small because there sometimes simply is not enough work to fill the day. ... There are, of course many exceptions to this general image, but a classified civil service of about 36,000 members serving a population of about 350,000 speaks for itself.[9]

The increasing standard of living of the Kuwaiti population as a result of liberal government welfare and employment policies is reflected in the increasing level of consumer demand for goods and services. In 1975, average per capita income in Kuwait was $11,365, one of the highest in the world. The corresponding growth in the level of consumption is indicated by the shift in living space. While in 1957, there were 2.1 persons per room in Kuwaiti dwellings, by 1965 this had decreased to 1.9; and by 1970 to 1.5. Correspondingly, the rooms per dwelling reflected a steady increase from 3.3 in 1957, 3.5 in 1965, to 4.2 in 1970 (ASA, 1975:335–36). The increasing standard of consumption is also indicated by private car ownership. In 1965, there were 0.18 cars for every person in Kuwait 15 years or over, or 0.70 cars per household; by 1970, this had increased to 0.25 cars for every person 15 years or older, or 0.92 cars per household; and by 1975, to 0.35 cars for every person 15 years or older, or 1.3 cars per household (ASA, 1976:277). In fact, on every indicator of standard of living, the population of Kuwait improves yearly its consumption capacity for luxury commodities.

Table 11 reflects that the economic infrastructure of Kuwait is increasingly dependent upon oil. The calculation of gross domestic product is based on the value of all goods and services produced in Kuwait for final use. Nevertheless the calculation of GDP at market prices introduces some error. Had the impact of inflation been taken into account, the real growth between 1970 and 1979 would have been considerably less than the figures indicate. For example, price indices rose from 117.5 in 1973 to 175.6 in 1979 (1972 = base year).

Table 11 does not by itself reflect the role of oil revenue in the generation of GDP. Data on GDP uses provide an indication of the pattern of consumption and development expenditure, and the roles of the private and public sectors in social and economic development. However, such data is only available for 1977 but may be used as an approximate indicator, as reflected in Table 12.

As Table 12 indicates, expenditure on exports represented 75.1 percent of total expenditure on GDP, while total private and government consumption and capital formation represented 41 percent and 26 percent respectively. The ratio of private consumption expenditure to total consumption expenditure amounted to 62 percent in 1977. The high ratio of expenditure on imports to GDP (45.3 percent), and the ratio of import expenditure to consumption and capital formation expenditures (67.7 percent), reflect how greatly the Kuwaiti economy depends on the outside world to satisfy its needs for goods and services. It also provides an indicator of the role of public expenditure in generating private sector economic activity. Private enterprise in Kuwait, in fact, is fundamentally based on public revenue transfer to the private sector.

Government transfers to the private sector occur through three main mechanisms — current expenditures, which provide the basis of purchasing power of the population and sustain the increasing level of imports, land purchases (discussed earlier) and capital expenditure which together provide the basis for the direct transformation of public revenue to private capital. Table 13 provides a summary of these for the period 1973/74 to 1979/80.

Table 13 shows that wages and salaries represent the largest single item of current expenditure. General expenses, which represent outlays on goods and services, constituted the second major item in current expenditure. The relative importance of these expenditures decreased from 59.1 percent of the total in 1973/74 to 49.1 percent in the 1979/80 budget. However, this was a result of substantial increase in capital

Table 11

Gross Domestic Product (at Current Prices), by Industrial Origin, 1970, 1975, and 1979 (KD million)

	1970 KD	Percent	1975 KD	Percent	1979* KD	Percent
Oil Sector	579.5	57.2	2,363.3	70.0	4,650.3	72.3
Non-Oil Sector						
Agriculture and Fisheries	3.0	0.3	8.8	0.3	14.4	0.2
Manufacturing	45.1	4.5	196.7	5.8	349.6	5.4
Electricity, Gas, and Water	7.2	0.7	13.3	0.4	26.3	0.4
Construction	28.7	2.8	70.0	2.1	160.0	2.5
Wholesale and Retail Trade	81.0	8.0	211.3	6.2	331.6	5.2
Transport, Storage, and Communication	26.8	2.6	55.0	1.6	84.7	1.3
Financial Institutions	32.6	3.2	59.2	1.7	173.9	2.7
Insurance	0.6	0.1	6.0	0.2	13.3	0.2
Others	208.9	20.6	393.9	11.7	626.4	9.8
Total	1,013.4	100.0	3,377.5	100.0	6,430.5	100.0

*Central Bank of Kuwait estimates.

SOURCE: Central Bank of Kuwait, *Economic Report for 1979*, pp. 28–29.

Table 12
Gross Domestic Product Uses, 1977

	Amount (000)	Percent
Private Final Consumption	986,205	25.4
Governmental Final Consumption	604,289	15.6
Total Capital Formation	1,006,671	25.9
Change in Stock	130,000	3.3
Exports	2,918,000	75.1
Imports	−1,760,000	−45.3
Expenditure on GDP	3,885,165	100.0

SOURCE: Central Bank of Kuwait, *Economic Report for 1979,* p. 30.

expenditures rather than cutbacks. The absolute increases in wages and salaries and general expenses reflect inflation as well as substantial real expansion in expenditure on goods and services.

Domestic transfers consist of a number of items, the most important of which are the exceptional allowances for retirees, social allowances, price subsidies for some basic commodities, assistance to the General Housing Authority and some other outlays to social affairs. The relative importance of these outlays remained consistent, reflecting the pressures of inflation on dependent groups.

Capital expenditure consists of direct development expenditure, loans to, and participation in domestic institutions. Direct development expenditure represented a major portion of total domestic expenditure over the period 1973/74 to 1979/80. The relative importance of this item increased from 15.7 percent to 29.1 percent over the period. However, a high portion of this increase was accounted for by the rise in world prices of construction materials, equipment, and labor. The development expenditure primarily represents allocations to the development of electricity, water, transport, communications, trade, and housing. In addition to the development expenditure, the Government provides financial assistance to domestic companies and institutions. This assistance is given either in the form of loans at low rates of interest, or through direct participation when the private sector is short of funds.

Over the post-oil period, development in Kuwait has been purchased at the cost of increasing dependence upon specialization in the world division of labor as an oil producer. In this period, dependence has been transformed from a specific to a universal characteristic of

Table 13

Summary of Domestic Expenditures, 1973/74, 1976/77, and 1979/80 (KD million)

	1973/74 KD	1973/74 Percent	1976/77 KD	1976/77 Percent	Budget 1979/80 KD	Budget 1979/80 Percent
Current Domestic Expenditure						
Wages and Salaries	197.5	44.2	368.2	26.0	645.4	28.8
General Expenses	66.4	14.9	314.3	22.2	453.1	20.3
Domestic Transfers and						
Unclassified Payments	17.0	3.8	63.5	4.5	97.9	4.4
Land Purchases	19.4	4.3	108.4	7.6	330.0	14.7
Development	70.2	15.7	353.1	24.9	650.9	29.1
Local Loans	13.7	3.1	35.2	2.5	–	–
Contributions to:						
Shares in Local Companies	45.8	10.3	51.6	3.6	–	–
Government Financial						
Institutions	16.6	3.7	123.5	8.7	60.0	2.7
Total	446.6	100.0	1,417.8	100.0	2,237.3	100.0

SOURCE: Central Bank of Kuwait, *Economic Report for 1980*, p. 50.

Kuwait's structure by policies that tie private and public consumption levels directly to oil revenues. Even the development of productive forces that has occurred in manufacturing, energy, and water production and transport and communications infrastructures has served to increase dependence rather than decrease it by increasing dependence upon externally produced technologies, raising consumer absorption capacities for imported luxury commodities and reducing the capacity of labor, to develop autonomously interdependent rather than dependent productive forces. This is examined in the next section in terms of the transformation of labor.

THE TRANSFORMATION OF LABOR

The development of Kuwait as a consumer society and welfare state is directly related to the capital surplus economy and the dominance of a peripheral capitalist class integrating itself into the dominant centers of world capitalism through expropriation. The distribution of labor in Kuwait over the post-oil period among divisions of economic activity, as indicated in Table 14 reflects this.

Table 14

Percentage Distribution of Active Labor Force by
Division of Economic Activity in Census Years

	1957	1965	1970	1975
Agriculture, Hunting, and Fishing	1.2%	1.2%	1.7%	2.5%
Mining and Quarrying	6.3	3.9	3.1	1.6
Manufacturing Industries	7.7	10.0	13.7	8.2
Construction	10.0	16.1	14.4	10.8
Electricity, Gas, and Water	—	3.9	3.1	2.4
Wholesale and Retail Trade	9.6	12.8	14.1	13.3
Transportation and Communication	4.1	5.6	5.2	5.3
Services	51.3	46.0	44.4	55.9
Activities not adequately defined	9.8	0.5	0.3	—
Total	100.0%	100.0%	100.0%	100.0%

SOURCE: *Annual Statistical Abstract*, 1977, p. 86.

Table 14 reflects the changing distribution of labor in Kuwait between 1957 and 1975 according to division of economic activity. It demonstrates that throughout the period, the major portion of the labor force has been concentrated in the service sector (which includes both government and private sector services). Mining and quarrying, which makes the greatest contribution to GDP is a capital intensive industry and a minor component as a proportion of labor force participation. The steady growth in the proportion of the labor force occupied in wholesale and retail trade, on the other hand, reflects the expansion of this sector with the progress of consumerism in Kuwait.

The table does not reflect the fact that Kuwait's labor force over the period expanded from 80,299 in 1957 to 304,582 in 1975[10]; a 279 percent increase in the size of the labor force in an eighteen year period. What is striking about Table 14 in the light of this fact is the relative stability in the proportions of labor distributed by economic activity. What this indicates in terms of the transformation of productive forces in Kuwait in the post-oil era is the stability of the relation between peripheral capital and labor in a period of unprecedented expansion both in the volume of capital and the size of the labor force.

The relation between peripheral capital and labor in Kuwait is specified by the concept of underdevelopment of productive forces. In dependency theory, development of productive forces refers to the relationship between living labor as the subject of development and natural and man-made resources as the objects of development. The common indices of development standard in the literature are generally aggregated indices of consumption levels or productivity levels that treat resources as the subject and labor as the object of development. While poverty and low productivity have been the characteristic correlates of underdevelopment, nevertheless, level of development of productive forces is an analytically distinct concept from these measures. Its indicators are more appropriately specified by the distribution of labor in terms of the production of value. An increasing level of development of productive forces, then, is indicated not only by increasing productivity levels in value production (quantity of labor), but also by the diversification of labor in terms of value production (quality of labor). In the capitalist system where production is concentrated in the creation of exchange value (commodity production), and labor itself is a commodity, shifts in the distribution of labor across productive sectors, mediated through the labor market, may be utilized as an indicator of the level of development of productive forces.

In these terms, narrow specialization of productivity and unequal development of productive forces are indicators of underdevelopment.

Although the level of productivity may be high in the productive sector, specialization in a world division of labor specifically limits increasing productivity across economic sectors and diversification of productive labor. This limitation on the level of development of productive forces is a function of the relations of production in a world system — of the functional division of labor between central capitalism and peripheral capitalism.

The relation between peripheral capital and labor in Kuwait is specified by the process of marginalization — that is, by the increasing unproductivity of labor in terms of value production in an economy specified by intense specialization of productive forces and consumption of capital surplus. This is indicated in Table 15, which shows the percentage distribution of the labor force by occupational division and economic sector in 1975.

As Table 15 demonstrates, production and related workers and laborers, the largest group in the occupational category, are, however, occupied in social services, the economic sector that in fact occupies over 53 percent of the labor force. Clerical and related workers, sales workers and service workers together account for about 47 percent of the occupational distribution and are primarily concentrated in social services and wholesale and retail trade. Professional, technical, and related workers, the third largest single category, are predominantly concentrated in social services. What Table 15 demonstrates is the dominance of employment related to consumption and services (the transformation of social relations into commodities). Social services are the major commodity occupying the Kuwaiti labor force. Productive labor—that is, labor that works upon material and man-made resources to produce goods—constitutes no more than 26 percent of the labor force in Kuwait. Here productive labor includes professional, technical, and related workers; production and related workers and laborers; and agriculture, animal husbandry, fishing and hunting. Only these occupational groups that are occupied in the following economic sectors have been included: transportation and communications; electricity, gas, and water; construction; manufacturing industries; mining and quarrying; agriculture, hunting, and fishing.

The limited development of primary sector occupations is accounted for historically by Kuwait's lack of an agricultural basis and the nomadic nature of its hinterland population. Oil and gas exploitation, the major primary sector industry, is highly capital intensive, with total employment in 1975 of 4,476.[11] Fishing, a traditional activity in pre-oil Kuwait, and one with potential for development of productive forces, was one of the early industries to develop in the post-oil period. The

Table 15
Percentage Distribution of Labor Force by Occupational Divisions and Economic Sectors, 1975

Occupational Divisions	Economic Sectors									
	Social Services	Financial Services	Transportation and Communications	Wholesale and Retail Trade	Electricity, Gas, and Water	Construction	Manufacturing Industries	Mining and Quarrying	Agriculture, Hunting, and Fishing	TOTAL
Professional, Technical, and Related Workers	10.9%	0.5%	0.4%	0.5%	0.6%	0.3%	0.5%	0.3%	0.1%	14.1%
Administrative and Managerial Workers	0.3	0.2	0.1	0.2	0.1	0.0	0.1	0.0	0.0	1.0
Clerical and Related Workers	7.3	1.0	1.4	1.4	0.4	0.2	0.6	0.3	0.0	12.6
Sales Workers	0.0	0.2	0.0	7.7	0.0	0.0	0.1	0.0	0.0	8.0
Service Workers	23.1	0.2	0.3	1.7	0.3	0.1	0.3	0.1	0.1	26.2
Agricultural, Animal Husbandry, Fishermen, and Hunters	0.4	0.0	0.0	0.0	0.0	0.0	0.1	0.0	2.2	2.7
Production and Related Workers and Laborers	11.7	0.1	3.0	1.8	9.4	1.8	6.5	0.9	0.2	35.4
Total	53.7%	2.2%	5.2%	13.3%	10.8%	2.4%	8.2%	1.6%	2.6%	99.9%

SOURCE: *Annual Statistical Abstract, 1977*, p. 94.

limitation on development of productive forces imposed by specialization in the world division of labor and integration into the world market is highlighted in this sector, however. While in 1966 the contribution of fishing to gross domestic production prices was KD 3.3 million, by 1971 this had decreased to KD 0.3 million. In 1974, the contribution had increased to KD 0.7 million (an increase that is at least partially accounted for by the substantial rise in the price index over the period), and the number of persons engaged in fishing was 2,181 (ASA, 1977:176–77). In that year Kuwait exported fish and fish preparations (primarily shrimp to the U. S.) of KD 1.6 million and imported KD 0.8 million from this commodity group (ASA, 1977:286). Specialization and integration, then, have actually produced the decline of fishing, and the potential for development of productive forces in terms of stimulating the growth of associated industries has not been utilized.

The limitation on the level of development of productive forces is more evident in the oil sector, where Kuwait's resources and potentials are apparent. Noting the availability of cheap capital in Kuwait and the abundance of hydrocarbon raw materials, the IBRD mission to Kuwait in 1963 reported on the favorable prospects for the development of capital intensive oil refining and petrochemical industries.[12] Some development in this direction has taken place. Between 1967 and 1974, for example, production of fertilizers and chemical products — urea, ammonium sulphate, ammonium hydroxide, sulphuric acid — increased from 228,876 metric tons to 1,248,876 metric tons, a 446 percent increase (ASA, 1975:130). Between 1968 and 1974, oil refinery products increased from 99.4 million barrels to 121.2 million barrels, a 22 percent increase over the period (ASA, 1975:112). Industrial activities other than crude petroleum and natural gas production contributed KD 171 million to gross domestic production prices in 1974, representing a 119 percent increase over 1966. The manufacture of industrial chemicals, other chemical products and petroleum refineries constituted 74 percent of this contribution (ASA, 1977:176–7). Nevertheless, manufacturing industries contributed only five percent to GDP in 1975/76 and constituted only 8.2 percent of the labor force in 1975.

What this indicates is that while refining and petrochemical industries have experienced development over the period, these remain specific, limited aspects of economic infrastructure that the availability of capital and resources makes feasible. In terms of capitalist development, such development would only be feasible in terms of international markets. And this would place Kuwait capital in direct competition with the petrochemical and refining industries of the world centers of capitalism, particularly the United States which has the most advanced petrochemicals industry. In terms of the interests of peripheral capitalism, however, such development is non-economic. Investment capital flows out of Kuwait, and labor in Kuwait is occupied in either the public sector which services private accumulation from public revenue or in the private sector which services expropriation.

The greatest concentration of employment in the private sector is in wholesale and retail trade—a total of 45,402 employees accounting for 33 percent of employment in the private sector in 1975 (ASA, 1979:122). There were 11,710 wholesale and retail establishments in Kuwait in 1975 with less than five employees, accounting for 51 percent of the employment in this area (ASA, 1979:122). In Kuwait, in other words, there is a preponderance of petty shopkeepers.

Private sector manufacturing was the second largest category in terms of employment, accounting for 28,103 or 21 percent of the private sector labor force in 1975. About 74 percent of the manufacturing establishments had less than five employees; another 20 percent had from five to nineteen employees (ASA, 1979:122). The distribution of employment among manufacturing industries indicates that the majority of them are small craft-like or specialty operations that cater to luxury or specialized markets (furniture and fixtures, metal products, printing and printing products), or intermediate assembly and maintenance operations that assemble or service imported items (transport assembly and repair, assembly and repair of electrical equipment).

Private sector services were the third largest category in terms of employment, accounting for 19,525 or 14 percent of private sector labor force. Establishments of less than five employees accounted for 86 percent of these establishments and 41 percent of employment in this sector (ASA, 1979:122).

The distribution of labor in Kuwait reflects the transformation of the economic infrastructure from production of surplus value to consumption of surplus products. Productive labor has been subordinated to and marginalized by the importation of capital intensive technologies, and marginal labor has been absorbed by the transformation of social relations into commodities. The high standard of living made possible by the capital surplus economy masks the contradictions inherent in an economy where consumption, not production, is the basis of socioeconomic activity. Nevertheless, the contradictions in Kuwait are apparent in the demographic transformation that has occurred in the post-oil era.

THE DEMOGRAPHIC TRANSFORMATION

In 1949, Kuwait's population was estimated to be approximately 100,000. Table 16 reflects the dramatic demographic transformation of Kuwait in the post-oil era.

Table 16 demonstrates that Kuwait's population increased 557 percent between 1957 and 1975, an annual average increase of 24 percent over the twenty-three year period. Foreign immigration constituted the largest component of increase, and by 1965 Kuwaiti nationals constituted a minority in the nation.

The large-scale immigration into Kuwait resulted from the demands for labor emanating from the ambitious development programs undertaken by the government. In 1957, 53.9 percent of the non-Kuwaiti population were males in the labor force age range of 15 to 39 (ASA, 1977:40–1). By 1975, when 29.1 percent of the immigrant population had been in Kuwait ten or more years, the considerable skewing of the non-Kuwaiti population pyramid caused by the predominance of labor force age males had been reduced to 28.1 percent, although males still constituted a larger proportion—58.8 percent (ASA, 1977:140–41). Over the period, the pattern of migration had shifted from males in the labor force age range to family units with the male head in the labor force age range. Reflecting this, by 1975 16.6 percent of the non-Kuwaiti population was in the dependent age range of 0 to 5, compared with 7.0 percent in 1957 (ASA, 1977:40–41).

In contrast to the non-Kuwaiti population pyramid, the Kuwaiti population pyramid in the five censuses from 1957 to 1975 reflected the typical population pyramid, with the male/female ratio approximately

Table 16
Population of Kuwait in Census Years

| | Kuwaiti | | Non-Kuwaiti | | Total | |
	Number	Percent	Number	Percent	Number	Percent
1957	113,622	55.0	92,851	45.0	206,473	100.0
1961	161,909	50.4	159,712	49.6	321,621	100.0
1965	220,059	47.1	247,280	52.9	467,339	100.0
1970	347,396	47.0	391,266	53.0	738,662	100.0
1975	472,088	47.5	522,749	52.5	994,837	100.0
1980*	562,065	41.5	793,762	58.5	1,355,827	100.0

*Preliminary Results

SOURCE: *Annual Statistical Abstract*, 1980, p. 27.

equal and the age distribution wide at the base years—reflecting the high birth rate of about 53 per thousand over the period and the greatly lowered infant death rate due to improved sanitation and medical care— and gradually tapering off to a peak at the upper limits of life expectancy. Correspondingly, males in the labor force age range of 15 to 39 made up 18.1 percent of the Kuwaiti population in 1957 and 17.8 percent in 1975 (ASA, 1977:40–41).

What is significant about the demographic transformation of Kuwait in the present context is the fact that the distinction between Kuwaiti nationals and non-Kuwaiti nationals is the fundamental classification of the population in every category of each of the censuses. According to Article 1 of the citizenship law of 1959 (Amiri Decree #157), amended 1960, 1965, and 1966, Kuwaiti nationality is recognized for those and their descendants who resided in Kuwait before 1920 and maintained residence there to 1959.[13] All others are classified as non-Kuwaitis. By 1975, 16.4 percent of the non-Kuwaiti population had been in Kuwait 10 to 14 years, and another 12.7 percent had been in Kuwait 15 or more years (ASA, 1977:63). By 1975, in fact, 29.9 percent of the non-Kuwaiti population had been born in Kuwait (ASA, 1980:32). In spite of this, they remain classified as non-Kuwaitis and have little option to change this status because of the restrictive naturalization requirements.

The requirements of naturalization—Articles 4 to 8—provide that naturalization for non-Kuwaitis of Arab origin requires a ten-year residency before application for citizenship decree; for immigrants from other than Arab origins, the residency requirement is fifteen years. Time spent in Kuwait prior to the publication of the citizenship law does not count toward the residency requirement. Furthermore, Article 4 of the law restricts the number of naturalizations allowable in any given year to 50. Even after application, the decree is by no means routine. In fact, it takes considerable political influence to attain a decree. Total discretion rests with the Minister of the Interior. However, naturalized citizens are second class citizens; they may not vote in elections until they have been citizens for twenty years (Article 6); they may not run for elected office at the sub-cabinet level or above in the executive branch (Article 6). Also, they are subject to deportation and their citizenship status subject to revocation at the discretion of the Minister of the Interior. Most sweeping are subsections iv and v of Article 13 which provide that citizenship can be revoked from naturalized citizens "if the supreme interest of the State or its external security requires," or "if the specific authorities have proof that the person is propagating principles which may destroy the social and economic system in the country, or belongs to a foreign political organization." Furthermore, according to the Kuwaiti newspaper *Al-Rai al-Amm,* February 2, 1975, the law does not allow for naturalization of the children when the parent is naturalized; and naturalized citizenship cannot be transmitted to offspring.

Non-Kuwaiti is a status distinction that permeates the entire social structure of Kuwaiti society and places manifold disabilities upon the population so classified. Non-Kuwaitis have no legal rights in Kuwait. A non-Kuwaiti cannot secure a working permit or residency without the guarantee of a Kuwaiti national who is responsible for the non-Kuwaiti in all legal and financial dealings (called the System of Guarantees). A non-Kuwaiti must leave the country once unemployed. Furthermore, non-Kuwaitis do not have access to the welfare system that Kuwaitis have. While free medical care is provided to all residents of Kuwait, only Kuwaitis are eligible for the low-interest housing loans and income security programs. Regular public education is available to non-Kuwaitis only in certain occupational categories — doctors, engineers, pharmacists, and teachers; many evening schools are available for the children of non-Kuwaitis who cannot afford the expensive private schools. In the labor market, non-Kuwaitis may not unionize. Within the civil service, which was made up of 59.8 percent non-Kuwaitis in 1976 (ASA, 1977:112) only Kuwaitis obtain permanent appointments and are entitled to a pension. Non-Kuwaitis work on a contract basis and are only entitled to a gratuity calculated on a lower actuarial basis. Contracts are subject to termination with two months' notice. Furthermore, Kuwaitis are preferentially recruited, require lower qualifications for the same grade as non-Kuwaitis, and are preferentially promoted over non-Kuwaitis irrespective of qualifications.

Politics of the Demographic Transformation

The heavy influx of immigrant labor in the early fifties resulted from the heavy labor demands of the booming construction industry, the new opportunities of an expanding consumer market, and the rapid growth of the government bureaucracy. Until 1954, immigration was unrestricted and unsupervised. However, in that year, an uproar by unskilled Kuwaiti labor over high unemployment in their ranks due to competition with foreign labor drew the government's attention to the issue of immigration.[14] As a result, the Office of Social Affairs conducted a survey of the labor force in April 1955 and discovered that only 13 percent of the labor force was made up of Kuwaiti nationals.[15] This brought to the forefront the question of not only the economic but also the political role of a large immigrant population and the nature of the social structure that would result from heavy dependence upon immigrant labor—particularly in the elite decision-making occupations.

The problem that large-scale immigration and structural change posed for the ruling class is one of boundary maintenance: namely, having made the commitment to modernization, the problem of maintaining class legitimation based essentially upon tribal ideology within a modernizing institutional infrastructure is compounded by the pervasive influence of cultural diversity, an influence that is most prominent — indeed, essentially unchallenged in the fifties—in the elite occupations that were in fact creating and administering the institutional transformation to the consumer society. This is indicated in Table 17.

The progressive expansion of the Kuwaiti component of professional and technical workers[16] between 1957 and 1975 resulted from social engineering policies inherent in the planning process, initiated about 1960, that specifically aimed at the containment and gradual replacement of non-Kuwaiti occupational elite with Kuwaitis. The role of social engineering in Kuwait will be discussed in the next chapter. The point to be made here is that these policies were specifically aimed at decision makers in the public sector and were reinforced by employment and naturalization policies, discussed earlier, that aimed at the isolation of non-Kuwaitis from participation in the social structure. The attitude adopted toward the immigrant population was that their role in Kuwait was based purely upon a transient economic exchange of labor for wages, and as such had no past nor future in the society. As one government publication explained, "Kuwait is not open for immigration, although she welcomes all who wish to stay and work or operate a business, provided their stay is temporary."[17]

Table 17
Professional and Technical Labor Force
by Nationality in Census Years

| | Professional and Technical Workers | | | | | |
| | Kuwaiti | | Non-Kuwaiti | | Total | |
	Number	Percent	Number	Percent	Number	Percent
1957	484	12.8	3,299	87.2	3,783	100.0
1965	1,528	11.2	12,093	88.8	13,621	100.0
1970	3,734	14.6	21,888	85.4	25,622	100.0
1975	9,739	23.3	32,097	76.7	41,836	100.0

SOURCE: *Annual Statistical Abstract*, 1977, p. 95.

The reason for the heavy reliance upon immigrant labor in professional, technical, and other skilled occupational categories was related to the irrelevance of the post-oil economic infrastructure to the indigenous labor of the society. The post-oil infrastructure depended upon the importation of foreign technologies and required a division of labor based upon knowledge of techniques and skills alien to the Kuwaiti population. Educational level is the standard measure of knowledge of modern techniques and acquisition of modern skills—that is, techniques and skills related to the market economy and capital intensive technologies. In 1957, 62.6 percent of the Kuwaiti population was illiterate; 27.9 percent had knowledge of reading and writing but had not completed primary school; 1.5 percent had completed primary school; and only 0.4 percent had completed a level of education above the primary level (intermediate, secondary and university). In contrast, 6.8 percent of the non-Kuwaiti population had a secondary certificate or more (ASA, 1977:36).

By 1975 the intensive efforts to raise the educational distribution of the Kuwaiti population, to be discussed in the next chapter, had reduced illiteracy to 44.6 percent; correspondingly, 6.8 percent had completed secondary school or more. However, the continuing demands of an increasingly tertiary-oriented economy had proportionately increased the demand for highly skilled labor, a demand that was filled by importation. Consequently, by 1975, 18.3 percent of the non-Kuwaiti population had completed secondary school or more (ASA, 1977:36).

As noted earlier, it is the government's policy to employ all Kuwaitis not absorbed in the private sector. Hence, Kuwaitis are highly concentrated in the public sector. In 1975, 72 percent of the Kuwaiti labor force was in the public sector.[18] The transfer of oil revenue in the form of wages to a population whose skills are non-marketable in the labor force has been a principal mechanism for the expansion of consumerism. The policy, in effect, disguises unemployment and confounds bureaucratic inefficiency. It has, however, also served to reinforce status distinctions between Kuwaitis and non-Kuwaitis by guaranteeing to Kuwaitis a form of economic security not available to the non-Kuwaitis, fostering a sense of privilege among the Kuwaiti population and a sense of insecurity in the non-Kuwaiti population, and supporting higher consumption levels of the Kuwaiti population.

In spite of the high concentration of Kuwaitis in the public sector, however, they made up only 40.2 percent of the civil service labor force in 1976 (ASA, 1977:112). The reason for the civil service's dependence upon immigrants is indicated in Table 18.

Kuwaitis do not have the kinds of skills related to the functioning of the modern welfare state bureaucracy or the capital export economy.

Table 18
Government Civil Servants
by Educational Attainment, February 1976

Educational Attainment	Percentage Distribution	
	Kuwaitis	Non-Kuwaitis
Illiterate	24.1%	26.9%
Read and Write	31.3	28.4
Primary	8.1	3.9
Intermediate	13.3	4.7
Secondary	13.0	15.0
Below University Level	3.8	2.4
1st University Degree	6.1	17.4
Post Graduates	0.3	1.3
	100.0%	100.0%

SOURCE: *Annual Statistical Abstract*, 1977, p. 95.

Table 18 reflects that while only 6.4 percent of the indigenous Kuwaiti civil servants have a university degree or more, 18.7 percent of the immigrant civil servants have achieved this educational level. Considering the educational attainment distribution, higher bureaucratic posts are disproportionately distributed among indigenous Kuwaitis, as indicated in Table 19.

Table 19 reflects the practice of preferentially placing Kuwaitis in positions within the civil service hierarchy, and the attempt, particularly at the higher levels of decision making, to maintain a balance between Kuwaiti and non-Kuwaiti incumbents to office. Even though incumbency assignment is ascriptively biased, however, there remains heavy dependence upon immigrants even at the highest levels. Furthermore, unskilled or semi-skilled non-Kuwaitis (those with minimal or no educational qualifications) are concentrated in the labor categories, while only 9.8 percent of Kuwaitis are in these categories even though 24.1 percent are illiterate.

Dialectics of the Demographic Transformation

While highly skilled non-Kuwaitis are lured to Kuwait by high salaries and a high standard of living, a system of job insecurity and political disenfranchisement functions to control their political involve-

Table 19
Government Civil Servants by Range, February 1976

	Kuwaiti	Non-Kuwaiti
Range I	0.4%	0.4%
Range II	11.0	4.9
Range III	45.5	31.3
Range IV	33.2	18.0
Contracts	0.0	2.4
Fixed Salaries	0.1	10.5
Permanent Laborers	9.8	30.9
Casual Laborers	0.0	1.6
	100.0%	100.0%

Note: Range denotes the broadest level of classification of civil service posts in the hierarchical authority structure of Kuwait's civil service bureaucracy, Range I being the highest posts.

SOURCE: *Annual Statistical Abstract*, 1977, pp. 116–17.

ment. By 1965, non-Kuwaitis constituted 52.9 percent of the population, 76.7 percent of the labor force, and 88.8 percent of the professional and technical elite. Kuwaitis, in essence, represented not only a numerical minority in the nation, but also a leisured minority dependent upon government subsidy for a high standard of living, and dependent upon immigrants to administer their health, welfare, and security. Furthermore, the dynamics of dependency in Kuwait continued to generate greater demands for imported labor, and by 1970, non-Kuwaitis represented 53 percent of the population.

There are profound political implications of a large expatriate population disenfranchised from the political sphere but dominating the occupational, educational, and cultural spheres. In practical terms, the problem posed for the ruling class is to maintain legitimation when a major portion of the population has no commitment to the political system but forms the occupational elite in both public administration and the private sector. While Kuwaitis share the sentimental heritage of living under the same ruling family since 1756 — a heritage that gives legitimacy to Kuwait's class structure—they also share with the major portion of the non-Kuwaiti population a common cultural and historical heritage that is the basis of Arab nationalism—the ideology of Arab unity, anti-imperialism, and social transformation that challenges the class nature of underdevelopment and dependency in the Arab world.

In 1975, 80.2 percent of the 522,749 non-Kuwaitis were nationals of other Arab countries. Furthermore, 50.7 percent came from two Arab countries: Jordan and Palestine (39.1 percent), and Egypt (11.6 percent) (ASA, 1977:61). These nationalities, in fact, accounted for 72 percent of the non-Kuwaiti professional, technical, and related workers in 1975 (ASA, 1977:91). Nationals from Lebanon, Syria, and Iraq (which together accounted for 20.7 percent of the non-Kuwaiti population), comprised another 10.7 percent of the non-Kuwaiti professional, technical, and related workers (ASA, 1977:91).

A major portion of the non-Kuwaiti professional and technical elite, then, are expatriates of other Arab countries, the most politicized countries of the Arab world. Kuwait has encouraged the immigration of the educated malcontents of the region to facilitate its modernization program by constitutionally prohibiting the extradition of political refugees (Article 46). The price of a politicized educated elite, however, is a heavy burden for a highly conservative, Western-oriented ruling class. Due in no small part to the pressures of this group, Kuwait has adopted the polemics of regional integration and Arab development supported by an economic assistance policy to Arab nations that consumes about ten percent of its national income annually — more than any other foreign aid donor.

The Kuwait Fund for Arab Economic Development, established in 1961, is the principal agency for funneling funds to the Arab world.[19] The role of economic assistance and regional integration in the present class structure of Kuwait has served not only to further Kuwait's integration into the world capitalist structure but the region's integration as well. The projects funded generally serve to (1) increase the capacity of receiving nations to supply raw materials to Western markets by funding the importation of technologies of scale, and (2) increase the capacity of recipient regimes to stay in power against popular opposition.[20] The funds invested in regional aid, in other words, have essentially replaced the functions of Western aid and are funneled back to the centers of capitalism, as pointed out by El Mallakh, Kadhim and Poulson:

> It must be emphasized that a greater commitment to regionalism and assistance to other developing countries, though reducing the direct flow of capital channeled into various investment outlets in the West, does not necessarily affect adversely the total flow of petro-dollars — direct and indirect — into Western economies. Whether or not, and to what extent, funds provided for regional development and assistance to the developing countries are re-cycled to OECD countries in the form of higher import levels depends principally on the patterns of trade of recipient countries. However, since the OECD countries are by far the leading exporters to the majority of recipient countries, the leakage effect must indeed be small.[21]

The contradiction inherent in the goals of Arab nationalism and peripheral capitalism are played out on a small scale in Kuwait in the relation between the immigrant population and the political structure. Dependent upon external forces of production, labor in Kuwait, and the entire Arab East, is specifically inhibited from developing beyond the bounds of the political divisions established by imperialist powers. The effective result is that the entire Middle East, including Kuwait, remains underdeveloped and dependent, in spite of the unprecedented levels of capital accumulation in the area.[22] Progressive movements seeking a new integration of the region's labor are increasingly radicalized by the apparent contradictions.

In Kuwait, the problem for the ruling class is one of exploiting the expertise of immigrant labor to serve the functions of dependency while isolating their political involvement and maintaining the legitimacy of class power when the tribal base of legitimacy is diminishing. Policy responses to this problem have been, on the one hand, to control the immigrant population by a system of insecurity in terms of their tenure in Kuwait; on the other hand, through paternalistic policies toward the Kuwaiti population, to engender dependence on the ruling class and status distinctions between the Kuwaiti and non-Kuwaiti groups.

The contradiction is that the dynamics of dependency in Kuwait's capital surplus economy generate continued demands for the increment of the skilled labor force. Removal of status rewards to the Kuwaiti population to force greater participation in the labor force would weaken a principal mechanism of legitimation and separation from non-Kuwaitis. However, immigration to fulfill these demands further increases the non-Kuwaiti population. A concerted population policy to hold down the rate of increase of the immigrant population and increase the rate of growth of the Kuwaiti population reduced the proportion of non-Kuwaitis from 53.0 percent in 1970 to 52.5 percent by 1975.[23] A major mechanism of this policy was to increase the rate of settlement of bedouin tribes from the desert areas adjacent to Kuwait. Unlike the immigrant population classified as non-Kuwaitis, these tribes are automatically and immediately given first class citizenship in Kuwait and are provided major social assistance, especially housing allowances, upon citizenship acquisition. Between 1965 and 1970, there was a net increase to the Kuwaiti population from immigration of 62,278 (ASA, 1976:87); and between 1970 and 1975, 38,120 (ASA, 1977:64).

Immigration of the tribes is relevant to the stability of relations of production in Kuwait. It reinforces the tribal basis of legitimacy. However, these tribes are irrelevant, in the short term, to the forces of production in Kuwait since they are primarily illiterate bedouins skilled in nomadic desert production and alien to urban modes. Their settlement

requires the expansion of government services to aid them in the transformation from nomadic life and socialize them to the patterns of urban
life. The expansion of these services, in turn, increases demands for
skilled labor.

The principal contradiction of peripheral capital and labor in
Kuwait relates to the marginal role played by the indigenous population
and the dependence upon immigrant labor. This results from several
interrelated factors: the predominantly tertiary sector orientation of the
economy, the role of a financial and commercial class in facilitating the
external flow of capital, the role of the government in promoting a high
consumption society. The effective result is that the economy of Kuwait
has developed independent of the labor of the society's population. The
population functions as consumers, not producers, in an economy that is
organized around externally developed and oriented forces of production. Like most everything else in Kuwait, then, an exploitable labor
force had to be imported too.

The Exploitation of Immigrant Labor

The exploitation of immigrant labor is apparent in establishments
operating in the private sector. These establishments accounted for 45.5
percent of the total labor force in 1975. However, only 2.6 percent of
employment in these establishments was Kuwaiti (ASA, 1977:103).
Immigrant labor not only from the surplus labor pools of the Arab world
but also from Pakistan, India, and Iran serve to keep the returns to labor
in the private sector minimal. This is reflected in Table 20, which pin-
points the concentration of immigrant labor in the private sector and the
wage differential between Kuwaiti and non-Kuwaiti.

As Table 20 demonstrates, Kuwaiti workers classified as laborers
earned three times as much as their non-Kuwaiti counterparts. A disparity is also reflected in these establishments among workers classified as
administrative and technical workers. Of the total 25,222 workers in this
classification, 93 percent were non-Kuwaitis. They earned an average
monthly wage of KD 120, while the 1,662 Kuwaitis in this classification
earned an average monthly wage of KD 265 (ASA, 1977:106–107).

The public sector also reflects a wage disparity between Kuwaiti
and non-Kuwaiti civil servants. This is indicated in Table 21, which
shows the average monthly wage of Kuwaiti and non-Kuwaiti civil
servants by occupational classification.

Table 20

Operating Establishments by Section of Economic Activity,
Number of Laborers and Average Monthly Wages (in KD), 1974

	Kuwaiti		Non-Kuwaiti	
	Number	Wages	Number	Wages
Agriculture, Hunting, and Fishing	—	—	1,550	29
Mining and Quarrying	721	207	674	133
Manufacturing	142	195	17,908	49
Electricity, Gas, and Water	—	—	5	52
Construction	—	—	12,705	46
Wholesale and Retail Trade	22	147	22,082	48
Transport, Storage, and Communications	29	95	4,049	91
Finance, Insurance, and Business Services	3	106	1,286	38
Other	7	205	11,827	48

SOURCE: *Annual Statistical Abstract*, 1977, p. 107.

Table 21

Government Civil Servants by Occupational Division and
Average Monthly Wages (in KD), February 1976

	Kuwaiti		Non-Kuwaiti	
	Number	Wages	Number	Wages
Professional, Technical, and Related Workers	10,089	245	22,260	198
Administrative and Managerial Workers	460	556	33	503
Clerical and Related Workers	14,181	198	7,075	158
Sales Workers	93	253	14	200
Service Workers	11,085	162	16,672	80
Agricultural, Animal Husbandry, and Fishermen	318	191	1,816	69
Production and Related Workers and Laborers	10,543	204	21,812	79

SOURCE: *Annual Statistical Abstract*, 1977, pp. 123–25.

As Table 21 reflects, Kuwaiti wages in the civil service are an average of 35 percent more than the wages of their non-Kuwaiti counterparts. The largest disparities occurred in unskilled and skilled manual occupations. Kuwaiti workers classified in the division of production and related workers and laborers, for example, earned an average of 158 percent more than non-Kuwaitis in this division. In the 1975 census, of the 105,608 members of the labor force classified under production and related workers and laborers, 84.5 percent was immigrant labor (ASA, 1977:92–93). Of the 15,348 Kuwaitis in this classification, about 68 percent worked in the public sector, where the average monthly wages were 86.5 percent higher than in the private sector.[24] In contrast, of the 90,260 non-Kuwaitis in this classification, only about 24 percent worked in the public sector (ASA, 1977:123–28).

Thus, non-Kuwaitis are exploited in the Kuwait labor market, and Kuwaiti labor is buffered against exploitation. Immigrants, in effect, constitute a cheap source of labor that can be expelled from the nation when the growth rate begins to subside. At current rates of oil exploitation, it is estimated that Kuwait's oil resources will be depleted in from 80 to 100 years.[25] The building of alternative sources of income is based upon income from external investment and the creation of capital intensive industries. A large percentage of the current labor force will be superfluous, and the ability to expel surplus labor will be politically expeditious.

CONCLUSION

This chapter identified three aspects of Kuwait's new integration into the world capitalist division of labor: the transformation of the economic infrastructure, the transformation of labor, and the demographic transformation. The relationships among these three categories of transformation were examined in terms of the relationship between peripheral capital and labor. In this context, the contradiction between the relations of production of peripheral capitalism and the forces of production of marginalized labor were identified in terms of government policies. Chapter VI expands this argument in terms of the politics of stratification in the welfare state.

6

The Politics of Stratification: Social Change and Social Control in the Welfare State

*I*N THE PREVIOUS CHAPTER, the welfare state in Kuwait was identified as a fundamental function of the relations of production of
dependency. The emergence of the welfare state was identified in terms
of its role in promoting consumerism and sustaining the accumulation-
expropriation structure of dependency. Embodied in the policies of the
welfare state are also the social control functions of peripheral
capitalism—specifically, the control of marginalized labor. This chapter
examines the social control functions in terms of the politics of stratification and planning in the capital surplus society.

THE POLITICS OF STRATIFICATION IN THE WELFARE STATE

In the post-oil era in Kuwait, the ruling family effectively controls a
tremendous surplus that has made its lifestyle one of the most oppulent
in the world and far out of reach of the average Kuwaiti. The shaikh's
personal income from oil revenue in 1973, for example, was KD 8
million. [1] With the introduction in 1961 of a distinction between the privy
purse and public revenue, members of the ruling family began receiving
a substantial share of oil revenue in the form of permanent salaries —
amounting to 8 percent of oil revenue in 1975. [2]

The power of the ruling family is based upon dependence of the
community on oil revenue and the ability of the ruling family to manipu-
late these revenues. The wealth of the nation has filtered down to the

population from the ruling family, friends of the family, servants, and so on to the periphery of the population. What has emerged within the indigenous population is a stratification system essentially based on distance from the ruling family. The range of stratification is reflected in Table 22.

Table 22 demonstrates that within the indigenous population, 5.5 percent of the households capture 31.6 percent of the total income. For households in the KD 1,000 or more income bracket, 17.4 percent of the income is derived from wages, 42.2 percent from private business, and 40.4 percent from other sources—i.e., rents, income from investments (ASA, 1977:225). Only in this highest income bracket and in the lowest bracket (income less than KD 100) did wages contribute to less than 50 percent of income. The 12.5 percent of the households whose income was less than KD 100 per month captured only two percent of total Kuwaiti household income. Wages contributed an average of 48.5 percent, private business 17.0 percent, and other sources (i.e., welfare assistance) contributed 34.5 percent (ASA, 1977:225). This is in contrast to the middle income brackets—KD 100 to KD 399—which comprised 64.8 percent of Kuwaiti households and 39.2 percent of total household

Table 22
Distribution of Kuwaiti Income Levels by
Proportion of Income Captured, Persons,
Households, 1972/73

Income Per Month (KD)	Income	Percentage Persons	Households
Less than 50	0.5	3.5	5.4
50–99	1.5	4.7	7.0
100–149	4.9	9.9	13.6
150–199	9.2	17.3	18.7
200–249	7.9	12.9	12.8
250–299	7.2	9.7	9.4
300–399	10.0	11.7	10.3
400–599	15.4	13.8	11.5
600–999	11.8	8.3	5.8
1000+	31.6	8.2	5.5
	100.0	100.0	100.0

SOURCE: *Annual Statistical Abstract*, 1977, p. 224.

income, where wages constituted an average of 80.2 percent of total monthly income (ASA, 1977:225). In the 17.3 percent of households whose monthly income was between KD 400 and KD 999, wages constituted an average of 62.3 percent of total monthly income, private business 16.7 percent, and other sources 21.0 percent (ASA, 1977:225). This group captured 27.2 percent of total Kuwaiti household income.

Income in Kuwait, then, is highly concentrated in the hands of the ruling family and wealthy merchant families who have direct and indirect interests in virtually all of the private and quasi-private establishments in the country. Commenting on the concentration of wealth within a few families, one observer noted:

> It is as if such a merchant is repeating what Caliph Maawiyah said one day: "Go, O dinar, wherever you wish because wherever you drop it will be in one of my pockets."[3]

As might be expected, the non-Kuwaiti stratification structure is in sharp contrast to this, as indicated in Table 23.

Table 23
Distribution of Non-Kuwaiti Income Levels
by Proportion of Income Captured, Persons, Households,
1972/73

Income Per Month (KD)	Income	Percentage Persons	Households
Less than 50	1.1	4.9	5.5
50–69	2.2	7.3	7.5
70–99	6.0	14.7	14.6
100–149	12.6	22.2	20.9
150–199	13.8	16.3	16.1
200–249	11.2	10.2	10.3
250–299	10.2	7.3	7.6
300–399	13.8	7.8	8.1
400–599	15.1	6.5	6.5
600–999	7.8	2.2	2.2
1000+	6.2	0.6	0.7
	100.0	100.0	100.0

SOURCE: *Annual Statistical Abstract*, 1977, p. 224.

Table 23 demonstrates that the distribution of households by income level is not as polarized at the upper income level as in the Kuwaiti case. The middle income brackets—KD 100 to KD 399—represented 63.0 percent of non-Kuwaiti households and captured 61.6 percent of total non-Kuwaiti income; wages constituted an average of 75.5 percent of their income. Furthermore, non-Kuwaiti households earning less than KD 100 per month represented 27.6 percent of total non-Kuwaiti households and captured 9.3 percent of total non-Kuwaiti household income; 80.5 percent of this income was derived from wages. Only in the 0.7 percent of non-Kuwaiti households earning KD 1000 or more per month did wages as a source of income constitute a minor portion of income— 12.6 percent. For this group, income from private business provided the main source of income, 58.4 percent, and other sources (i.e., investment income) 29.0 percent (ASA, 1977:225).

A comparison of the income stratification structures of Kuwaitis and non-Kuwaitis reveals that non-Kuwaitis are primarily wage earners concentrated in the lower half of the income distribution hierarchy, with income from wages constituting 70.0 percent of total non-Kuwaiti household income. Kuwaiti wage-earners, on the other hand, are concentrated in the upper half of the income distribution hierarchy. Income from wages constituted only 53.8 percent of total Kuwaiti household income; but only for the uppermost income brackets did income from sources other than wages constitute a major portion of income. Kuwaitis in the uppermost brackets form a small capitalist class in Kuwait whose income derives from private business or investments.

For Kuwaitis, the degree of inequality within Kuwait is mediated by the welfare system which buffers them against all the economic vicissitudes of dependency and misfortune. What this paternalistic welfare system has done is to transform the indigenous population into a leisure class with a capacity for consumption of luxury foreign goods and a dependence upon the ruling class to sustain the consumption level. In effect, it has served to mitigate the creation of class consciousness within the Kuwaiti population. Although economic and social stratification have increased substantially as a result of the distribution of oil wealth, Kuwaiti nationals are a privileged ethnic minority—the largest ethnic minority group—within Kuwait. The humblest Kuwaiti has more rights, greater economic and social security, and better opportunities for social mobility than a highly skilled non-Kuwaiti.

For non-Kuwaitis, the ethnic stratification system also serves to mitigate class consciousness by reinforcing ethnic cohesion and fragmenting class cohesion. Non-Arab immigrants are essentially at the very periphery of Kuwait's social, economic, and political spheres. The bulk of the non-Arab immigrant labor force is from India, Pakistan, and Iran

—in 1975, 95 percent (ASA, 1977:91–93). They are concentrated in menial service and manual occupations in the private sector where wages are low and working conditions degrading. Ineligible for housing subsidies or limited income housing, they live in shack towns that fringe the city or in some of the barrack-type projects designed as temporary accommodations. Fragmented among themselves by language, cultural, and religious differences, however, and in a very insecure position in terms of their tenure in Kuwait, they appear to have been largely ineffective in organizing to improve their lot.

Indeed, when a labor strike broke out among these groups in 1969 to protest the discriminatory labor laws and resulted in violence, the government deported hundreds of Arabs rather than the demonstrators. The government's rationale behind the deportations was that:

> ... the workers' strike was provoked by certain "destructive elements," because most of the demonstrators were Pakistanis, Indians, and Iranians who were not familiar with the Arabic language. How then could they write statements in a complicated, doctrinal style? The government circles then went on to say that the strike was intended to paralyze oil production and to spread to other sectors for the purpose of creating economic confusion as well as chaotic conditions. The government accuses "Arab partisan elements" of instigating strikes and destructive activities.[4]

This points up the government's fears of the political and social role of its Arab immigrant population. Sharing the same language and the same cultural and religious heritage, Arab immigrants can cooperate with each other and operate within the Kuwaiti social milieux. Denied access to legitimate political participation, they nevertheless have considerable input into the decision-making process by virtue of their professional and technical occupations. Also, they are a highly politicized group who have the skills, the time, and the financial resources to afford dabbling in politics. They are the middle-class agents of social and political change as much as the instruments of economic change. Controlling their role in the society while promoting their role in the economy has taken considerable rationalization of the social control process.

THE RATIONALIZATION OF SOCIAL CONTROL: PLANNING

The Development Board, created in 1952, was the first manifestation of planning in Kuwait. Although its terms of reference were to guide national development, at this time the concept of planning in Kuwait focused on physical development and not the "financial, economic and social aspects of a comprehensive development policy." [5] Thus, the sudden inflow of wealth in the early fifties resulted in large-scale construction and expansion projects — schools, hospitals, roads, port facilities, office buildings — and in grandiose schemes of physical modernization of old Kuwait City. Essentially the entire core of the city was bought up by the government at enormous expense and developed for public use or resold at considerable loss for private development. This policy had a two-fold purpose — to pump public money into the private sector and to facilitate the reconstruction of the city.

The rapid development of Kuwait City was not only transforming the city physically, however. By the mid-fifties, it was apparent that the entire social structure of the society — the role and distribution of both capital and labor, the demographic and social composition of the population — had undergone rapid transformation. These transformations had contributed to the increasing isolation of the ruling family within the polity since its power and wealth were rendered independent of the social structure by the new integration. This isolation was manifested in growing opposition from all sectors of the society to the status quo of autocracy. It was in this context of increasing isolation that the concept of planning as an institutionalized social control function was initiated.

The concept of comprehensive planning in terms of short-term and long-term interrelated economic and social goals became manifest in 1961 when the government invited the International Bank for Reconstruction and Development to send an economic mission to Kuwait. The mission in 1961 was followed up by another in 1963. These missions made a comprehensive survey of the potentials of and limitations to economic development in Kuwait and recommendations regarding investment policies and rationalization of public administration. [6] Most of the recommendations never became incorporated into government policy. Most significant here, however, is the fact that as a result of the mission's recommendations, the planning process itself became institutionalized to ensure social stability through rationalization of the allocation of oil revenues.

In 1962, a centralized Planning Board (superceded by the Ministry of Planning in 1974) was established as an independent body directly attached to the Council of Ministers. The Prime Minister was to function as Chairman and the Minister of Finance and Industry as Deputy Chairman. Its other members included the Ministers of Public Works, Education, Social Affairs, and Commerce, the Minister of State for Cabinet Affairs and four prominent Kuwaitis from the private sector. [7] The Board was given comprehensive powers for the "formulation of the general economic, social and population policy, and the establishment of development programs and the supervision of their implementation."[8] This broad mandate was to be manifested in a series of five-year plans. The first one was completed and adopted in 1967 to span the period to 1971/72.

The first five-year plan explicated the long-term objectives of planning in terms of several unassailable, abstract goals. These included: (1) the creation of a diversified economy with a self-sustaining rate of growth; (2) insuring an equitable distribution of income; (3) insuring the training of human resources for the development of specialized skills; (4) the achievement of Arab economic integration.[9] The operationalization of these goals in terms of priorities and policies to be pursued over the planning period, however, more clearly specified the social control nature of the plan's objectives. These included: (1) increasing the scope of the public services infrastructures — a principal mechanism of rendering the interests of the Kuwaiti population dependent upon the ruling class; (2) replacing non-Kuwaiti occupational elite with Kuwaitis by increasing the level of education of the Kuwaiti population; (3) stemming the growth in the proportion of the non-Kuwaiti population by increasing Kuwaiti participation in the labor force and upgrading their skills through training; (4) promoting the integration of private capital and public expenditure.[10]

The social control of marginalized labor was explicated in the plan in terms of the priority of human resource development. The plan explained this accordingly:

> In spite of the integration and interrelation of the Plan's objectives, the greatest emphasis during the Plan period will relate to manpower in the Kuwaiti society. The objectives here are to raise productivity, increase the participation of the Kuwaitis in the total labour force, diversify skills and produce specializations among the Kuwaiti labour force. Briefly this means *an attempt to make the members of the Kuwaiti labour force more efficient, more productive and more capable of realizing the projections and expectations of the Plan.*[11]

In post-oil Kuwait, institutionalized education had been rapidly developing as the major socialization agency of the state. The emphasis placed upon it in the Plan rationalized the expanding role of education to include not only socialization to consumerism in the capital surplus economy but also socialization to competitive labor market principles in the consumer society. This rationalization took on the neutral title of human resource development.

Human Resource Development

Kuwait's public educational system began rapid expansion in 1954 when there were only 41 schools in the nation. The foundations of the present educational system were laid in 1955 under the guidance of two prominent Egyptian educationists. In addition to an educational hierarchy that funnels students through an academic stream there also are programs of vocational education.

The Educational Hierarchy

In addition to a kindergarten program, three stages of education were established — primary, intermediate, secondary — that last four years each. The goals of this educational program were two-fold: at the lower levels to eliminate illiteracy in the young population and at the upper levels of secondary and post-secondary education to prepare them for careers in the modern work force. Between 1958 and 1965, total enrollment (Kuwaiti and non-Kuwaiti) at the primary level in government schools increased from 22,118 to 44,131; at the intermediate level from 6,530 to 19,006; at the secondary level from 1,270 to 4,823 (ASA, 1973:78). In 1965, Kuwaiti enrollment represented 71.2 percent of total enrollment at the primary level, 68.3 percent at the intermediate level, and 49.6 percent at the secondary level. To encourage enrollment of Kuwaiti children in the school system, all clothing, books, transportation, and meals were provided free of charge.

By 1965, 76.5 percent of Kuwait's labor force was non-Kuwaiti (ASA, 1977:81) and educational expansion assumed a new urgency. In that year, education between the ages of six to fourteen was made compulsory for all Kuwaitis. However, popular resistance to compulsory education in general, and female education in particular (even though education at all levels is segregated), made this difficult to achieve quickly. Rather than attempting to enforce this law against popular resistance, the government undertook a vigorous program through the mass media and instituted a reward system for educational achievement to overcome resistance to education. By the 1975/76 academic year there were 92,240 students enrolled at the primary level (49.8 percent Kuwaiti) 59,767 at the intermediate level (66.4 percent Kuwaiti) and 29,962 at the secondary level (56.9 percent Kuwaiti) (ASA, 1976:300). Although the percentage of the school age population actually enrolled cannot be ascertained, nevertheless, by the 1975 census, illiteracy in the 10–19 age bracket of Kuwaiti nationals had been reduced to

22.1 percent — and 74.0 percent of this illiterate group were females (ASA, 1979:39) — compared with 40.0 percent illiteracy in this age bracket in 1957.[12]

Aside from overcoming resistance to compulsory education, Kuwait has faced three related problems in the rapid expansion of its public education system: (1) the rapid expansion of the school age population as a result of the high birth rate and rapid settlement of desert hinterland tribes; correlatively, (2) the increasing need for adequate physical facilities; (3) the increasing need for qualified teachers. Between 1957 and 1975 Kuwait's indigenous population increased from 107,246 to 472,088. Furthermore, in this period the 5–14 year age group increased as a proportion of the population from 24.0 percent to 29.9 percent (ASA, 1977:40–41). In addition, by the late sixties sectors of the immigrant population were successfully pressing their demands for access to public education. Between 1967 and 1977, non-Kuwaiti enrollment in government schools increased from 26.3 percent to 45.5 percent of total enrollment (ASA, 1977:348).

The pressure on facilities and teaching staff has been met by huge budget allocations to education. Expenditures on education have steadily increased from about KD 6.5 million in 1955/56 (ASA, 1973:94) to KD 62 million in 1974/75 (about 14 percent of total government expenditures) (ASA, 1975:285). Because of its capital surplus situation, then, Kuwait can afford to import both the materials and labor to facilitate rapid educational expansion. Reflecting this ability to meet the material and staff requirements of continuously expanding enrollment, between 1967/68 and 1978/79, the average number of students per classroom at the primary level actually decreased from 34.8 to 30.8, and the number of students per teacher similarly decreased from 22.3 to 16.9; at the intermediate level in this period, the students per teacher from 16.7 to 13.2; finally, at the secondary level, the students per classroom decreased from 31.1 to 28.2, and the students per teacher from 11.7 to 8.8 (ASA, 1979:332–33).

By offering high salaries and a high standard of living, Kuwait has siphoned off the available talent from neighboring Arab countries to staff its expanding educational system. In 1957, virtually the entire staff of teachers (89.6 percent) at all levels of education was non-Kuwaiti (Population Census, 1957:282–82). However, in addition to sending students abroad for teacher training, in the early sixties Kuwait developed its own system of teacher training institutes, the first graduates of which entered the profession in 1965. Since then, the number of Kuwaiti teachers has increased rapidly. Between 1971/72 and 1976/77, for example, the number of Kuwaiti teachers at the primary, intermediate, and secondary levels increased from 2,767 (ASA, 1972:93) to 4,402 (ASA, 1977:349). Nevertheless, the educational system was expanding more rapidly than the production of teachers, and the proportion of Kuwaiti teachers at these levels actually decreased from 32.3 percent in 1971/72 to 27.7 percent in 1978/79 (ASA, 1979:338).

The task set for the educational hierarchy in terms of career preparation is on the one hand to remove the young from family and environmental influences that foster traditional collective attitudes towards work and status, and on the other to socialize the young to the individualistic achievement-oriented norms of occupational mobility — to instill a set of skills, attitudes, motivations, and career preferences that are compatible with national political, economic, and social development programs. The first task has been undertaken by developing a system of kindergarten education for four to six year olds. The first kindergarten was founded in 1954; and by 1963 there were twenty kindergartens with an enrollment of 6,000 children. From 1963 to 1979, the number of kindergartens increased to 57, with a total enrollment by 1979 of 16,199 (ASA, 1979:331). During this period, the student-teacher ratio was progressively lowered from 22.3 in 1964/65 to 12.6 by 1974/75 (ASA, 1975:296) climbing to 13.9 by 1978/79, however (ASA, 1979:331). Within the kindergarten setting, young children learn to work with their hands through handicraft lessons, learn to care for small animals (rabbits, pigeons, ducks, chickens) and learn individual responsibility in interpersonal and task-oriented exercises that are isolated from the ascriptive, particularistic, and protective family environment.

The development of competitive, achievement-oriented norms and attitudes of individualistic career alternatives, preferences, and choices is systematized at the primary and intermediate stages of education. While the four years of primary school are aimed at instilling basic language and math skills, at the intermediate level emphasis is placed upon the discovery and development of individual aptitudes and talents and their relationship to occupational alternatives. At the secondary stage, then, students are streamed into either arts or science studies.

Completing the structure of the educational hierarchy, in 1966 the University of Kuwait opened its doors. With an initial enrollment of 500 students, by the 1978/79 academic year the university accommodated 17,123 students (ASA, 1979:358). Between 1972/73 and 1975/76, the university graduated 2,347 students (60.5 percent Kuwaitis by nationality). The distribution of these graduates by field of study was 18.8 percent in the sciences, 41.4 percent in literature, 7.4 percent in law, 20.1 percent in commerce, and 12.3 percent in economics and political science (ASA, 1977:366). In 1975/76, the university opened a Department of Petroleum Engineering, and in 1976/77 a medical school.

Other post secondary institutions are also available that are more job-specific than university education. These include the Teachers' Training College, the Agricultural Institute, Arab Planning Institute, Banking Studies Center, and the Civil Aviation Training Center. All of these institutes suffer from under-capacity enrollment, high costs of operation, and low productivity in terms of number of completers.[13]

The performance of Kuwait's educational hierarchy in terms of upgrading the educational status of Kuwaiti nationals may be assessed from Table 24.

Considered in terms of the distribution of the population by educational qualification, there was a 20.6 percent increase between 1957 and 1975 in the proportion of the Kuwaiti population 10 years and over that had primary certificates; an 11.8 percent increase in intermediate certificate holders, a 5.2 percent increase in secondary certificate holders, and a 1.2 percent increase in university degree holders. Thus, over the period, the educational status of Kuwaitis has increased not only in terms of absolute number, but also as proportions of a rapidly expanding population.

Nevertheless, the educational status distribution is less than expected given the enrollment figures over the seventeen-year period from 1958 to 1975. The enrollment figures are somewhat misleading as they mask the high drop out and repeater rates. Over the period, drop outs between the primary and intermediate levels have ranged between 30 to 40 percent, while drop outs between the intermediate and secondary level have ranged between 40 to 50 percent. Reflecting the high repeater rate, it was estimated that the twelve years of education from primary through secondary school cost the state a total of KD 4,508 per student, assuming continual progress of the student through the curriculum; in actuality, it was found that the student required an average of eighteen years instead of twelve years to complete the curriculum, increasing the cost per student 37 percent.[14]

Table 24
Kuwaitis 10 Years and Over by
Educational Status, 1957 and 1975

Educational Status	1957	1975
Primary Certificate	1,077	66,188
Intermediate Certificate	—	35,415
Secondary Certificate and below University level	197	16,603
First University and Post-graduate Degrees	51	3,979

SOURCE: *Annual Statistical Abstract,* 1977, p. 35.

The performance of Kuwait's educational hierarchy in terms of preparing Kuwaitis for participation in the labor force may be considered in terms of labor force participation in 1975. Considered in terms of the distribution of Kuwaiti males 15 years and over by age groups, 47.2 percent of the 15 to 24 age group was in the labor force, 93.9 percent of the 25 to 49 age group and 59.0 percent of the 50+ age group (ASA, 1977:33, 83). Because of extension of the educational process, Kuwaitis enter the labor force at a later age than previously. Furthermore, early retirement policies and liberal pension benefits greatly reduce participation in the 50+ population. In the active labor force group 25 to 49, there is 6.1 percent non-participation—a high figure for males in this age group.

However, if females are included, the percentages for labor force participation are cut almost in half in every age category. In 1975 there were only 7,477 Kuwaiti females in the labor force, even though they comprise approximately 50 percent of the total Kuwaiti population and approximately 43 percent of Kuwaiti enrollment in the public school system. Cultural constraints have been major barriers to female participation, and the state's comprehensive welfare system has obviated economic factors as a cause of female participation.

Nevertheless, the heavy dependence upon immigrant labor has led to government efforts to overcome cultural barriers that keep half the population inactive. *The First Five Year Plan* (p. 133) outlined as an objective of population policy "encouraging the participation of Kuwaiti females in occupations which are better suited to the nature of women, by offering them priority in employment." Between 1965 and 1975, in fact, Kuwaiti female participation in the Kuwaiti labor force increased from 2.5 percent to 8.1 percent (ASA, 1977:82). This increase, however, was virtually confined to social services (which accounted for 80.8 percent of female employment in 1975) (ASA, 1977:85). In fact, the increase in female employment within the Kuwaiti population reflects the labor market demands emerging from sexually segregated social service structures. Hence female professionals and service workers — teachers, social workers, etc.—are needed to service the female population in a segregated welfare system. Outside these structures, there has been virtually no growth of Kuwaiti female participation.

In contrast, the participation of non-Kuwaiti females in the non-Kuwaiti labor force increased from 5.4 percent in 1962 to 13.0 percent in 1975 (ASA, 1977:82). While 45.2 percent of this labor force component was concentrated in the social service sector, 43.8 percent was in personal and household services—reflecting the personal service demands of an affluent population (ASA, 1977:95).

Vocational Education

The programs of vocational education in Kuwait are specifically employment oriented, in contrast to the educational hierarchy which is academically or professionally oriented. In addition, there are special training programs offered by various ministries. These programs are designed to pick up the high number of drop outs from the academic system for semi-skilled and skilled occupational preparation. In 1979/80, there were a total of 5,901 students enrolled in these programs (ASA, 1979:334).

The vocational institutes and programs are restricted to Kuwaiti nationals and except for the secondary institutes, generally offer a monthly stipend to trainees. According to Socknat (pp. 14–17), in addition to the general proliferation of programs, these programs suffer from a number of problems: overlapping and duplication of curricula, the expense of operation (in part due to the high drop out rates, low program output and under-capacity operation), and competition among the programs to attract students. To provide coordination for training programs, in 1973 Kuwait established a Central Training Department which assumed admission and budget functions for most vocational institutes and programs in 1975.

The contribution of the vocational education institutes and programs may be assessed in terms of Kuwaiti participation in semi-skilled and skilled labor in both white collar and manual occupations. Most of these occupations fall within two occupational classifications: clerical and related workers, and production and related workers and laborers. Between 1957 and 1975, there was a five-fold increase—from 7,657 to 38,018—in the size of the labor force classified under clerical and related workers. Kuwaiti participation in this occupational category increased from 42.2 percent in 1957 to 47.0 percent in 1975 (ASA, 1977:95). In the same period, the amount of labor classified under production and related workers more than doubled—from 49,623 to 105,608. However, Kuwaiti participation in this category decreased from 22.5 percent in 1957 to 14.5 percent in 1975 (ASA, 1977:95).

These figures reflect the preference of Kuwaitis for white collar jobs, and their ability to secure white collar jobs in the public sector due to government employment policies that preferentially hire and promote Kuwaitis over non-Kuwaitis in the civil service. The effective result is that the Kuwaiti labor force is highly concentrated in the civil service—accounting for approximately 72 percent of total Kuwaiti employment in 1975.

It appears, then, that training in manual occupations has been somewhat irrelevant to the occupations actually undertaken. While no follow-up studies of institute graduates and program trainees are available, one survey reported that 60 percent of the graduates of training institutes preferred supervisory jobs over the manual occupations they were trained for, and 49.2 percent would not accept manual labor.[15]

Commercial education, then, appears more relevant to the kinds of jobs Kuwaitis actually enter. It may also be more relevant to the occupational structure emerging from Kuwait's social and economic development policies. This is reflected in Table 25.

Table 25 demonstrates that while production and related workers are still the largest single occupational division, this category has significantly decreased as a proportion of the division of labor. Clerical and related workers and sales workers, on the other hand, have both increased. The greatest change occurred in service workers—a category of generally menial personal service occupations that are occupied by non-Kuwaiti labor—except for fire fighters, policemen, and detectives which had been completely Kuwaitized by 1975 (ASA, 1977:91–93). This category, then, reflects more the demand for personal services resulting from the affluence of the Kuwaiti population than substantive changes in the mode of production.

Table 25
Percentage Distribution of the Labor Force,
by Occupational Division, 1957 and 1975

	1957	1975	% Change
Professional and Technical Workers	4.4%	14.0%	+ 9.6
Administrative and Managerial Workers	1.5	1.0	− 0.5
Clerical and Related Workers	9.0	12.7	+ 3.7
Sales Workers	7.1	8.1	+ 1.0
Service Workers	11.0	26.2	+15.2
Agricultural, Animal Husbandry, Fishermen and Hunters	1.5	2.6	+ 1.1
Production and Related Workers	58.0	35.4	−22.6
Not Adequately Defined	7.5	—	− 7.5
Total	100.0%	100.0%	

SOURCE: *Annual Statistical Abstract*, 1977, p. 95.

Professional vs. Vocational Education

The substantial increase in the proportion of professional and technical workers, on the other hand, does reflect the increasingly technocratic organization of Kuwait resulting from capital surplus investment policies and welfare state organization. The proliferation of post-secondary educational facilities, in spite of the relatively limited production of secondary certificate holders, may indeed be related to the importance of this category.

This importance stems not only from the increasing proportion of professional and technical workers in the division of labor, but also from the role this group plays in terms of policy formulation and implementation. The carrying out of government goals of economic and social development depends to a large extent on program formulation and implementation at the level of highly skilled professional and technical elite, and these levels are dominated by immigrants. As noted earlier, the question of the social and political impact of a non-Kuwaiti elite dominating the occupational structure is a central one in Kuwait. Thus, a primary concern of the educational system is to replace skilled immigrant professionals and technicians with Kuwaitis.

One of the problems with vocational education is that the educational process itself builds in a bias towards higher status occupations, in effect reinforcing negative status-conscious attitudes towards manual labor. This may be a secondary concern in Kuwait, however, as economic development plans recognize that the nation's economy will be substantially dependent upon immigrant labor into the long-term future. The more immediate problem, and one identified by *The First Five Year Plan* (p. 5), seems to be the dependence at highly skilled technical and professional levels; a dependence that is certainly not amenable to rapid solution, but one that may be served by biases built into the educational process and supported by welfare policies.

The Second Five Year Plan

The second five year plan — Proposal of the Five Year Plan, 1976/77–1980/81 — covered the period 1976/77–1980/81. Unlike its predecessor, this plan was never officially adopted as national policy because the National Assembly was suspended in 1976. Nevertheless, its projections served as the basis of policy guidelines, and it was in effect implemented.

In the period since the development of the first plan, Kuwait had achieved total sovereignty over oil exploitation and had experienced a tremendous growth in revenue. Furthermore, two Arab-Israeli wars had been fought (June 1967 and October 1973), heightening popular consciousness of the contradiction between the level of wealth in the Arab world and the inability of the area's governments to defend the Arab people against aggression. In addition, American intervention on behalf of Israel during the 1973 war heated the friction between conservative regimes in the area and the Arab nationalists. In this situation, social control of the large Arab expatriate population in Kuwait assumed added urgency. This is reflected in the second five year plan's emphasis upon forecasting labor force requirements over the planning period and the extent to which educational production could meet these demands.

In the area of the development of human resources, the plan (p. 10) identified the "strategic" components accordingly:

1. Raising the productivity of available human resources and developing them through education, training, and retraining to satisfy labor force demands.

2. Following a selective policy of immigration based upon labor force needs, providing them with social stability and security.

3. Organizing the labor market to ensure a balance between supply and demand in all specializations.

4. Increasing the level of female participation in the labor force in all social and economic sectors.

5. Relating the level of salaries and wages to worker productivity levels, guaranteeing a minimum wage adjusted to the standard of living.

Figure 1 shows the plan's projections of population growth and labor force growth in the planning period. It was estimated that of the 91,844 Kuwaitis in the labor force in 1975, 89,200 would remain in the labor force to the end of the plan period; and 30,400 Kuwaitis would enter the labor force for the first time during the period. The total Kuwaiti labor force by the end of the plan period, then, would be 119,600. Assuming that the size of the non-Kuwaiti population remained constant over the plan period, and the non-Kuwaiti labor force at the end of the period was 155,000 the plan estimated the size of the total labor force in 1980 to be 274,600. However, based upon economic expansion plans during the period, it was estimated that total demand for labor would be 412,200 by 1980. Hence, immigration would be required to fill the gap of 137,600 workers. These estimates were the basis of the population projection shown in Figure 1, which reflects the anticipated higher growth rate of the non-Kuwaiti population due to immigration. Based upon these projections, by the end of the plan period, then, it was

Figure 1
Population and the Labor Force
1976/77–1980/81

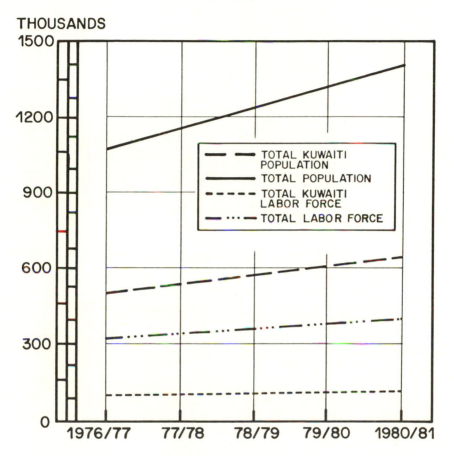

THOUSANDS

TOTAL KUWAITI
POPULATION

TOTAL POPULATION

TOTAL KUWAITI
LABOR FORCE

TOTAL LABOR FORCE

SOURCE: *Proposal of the Five Year Plan, 1976/77–1980/81*, p. 29.

estimated that non-Kuwaitis would comprise 54.4 percent of total population and 71 percent of the total labor force.

Table 26 shows the origin of demand for labor during the plan period by sectors of economic activity, based upon the expected growth arising from public expenditure on development projects. This table demonstrates that public administration and defense were anticipated to generate the largest increase in demand for labor, 19.8 percent, in effect

Table 26

Estimates of Labor Force Demand, by Kind of Economic Activity, 1980–81

	Supply 1975	Demand 1980–81	Increase in Period Number	Increase in Period Percent
Agriculture	6,671	10,250	3,580	3.1%
Hunting	843	1,500	660	0.6
Crude Oil and Natural Gas	4,476	5,100	620	0.6
Quarrying	383	660	280	0.3
Manufacturing Industries	24,467	34,400	9,930	8.6
Electricity and Water	7,271	12,000	4,730	4.1
Construction	32,256	42,000	9,740	8.5
Wholesale and Retail Trade	39,559	57,000	17,440	15.2
Transport and Storage	11,822	15,400	3,580	3.1
Communications	3,863	5,400	1,540	1.3
Financial Institutions, Insurance, and Real Estate	6,523	8,400	1,880	1.6
Public Administration and Defense	68,887	91,600	22,710	19.8
Sanitary Public Services	4,430	6,640	2,210	1.9
Educational Services	29,879	41,950	12,070	10.5
Health Services	12,548	23,300	10,750	9.4
Social Services	1,634	2,100	470	0.4
Recreational and Cultural Services	2,478	3,500	1,020	0.9
Personal and Household Services	39,370	51,000	11,630	10.1
Total	297,360	412,200	114,840	100.0%

SOURCE: *Proposal of the Five Year Plan, 1976/77–1980/81*, p. 25.

reflecting the continued high rate of expansion of government bureaucracy over the period. Wholesale and retail trade was expected to
generate the next largest increase in demand, 15.2 percent, reflecting the
anticipated expansion of consumerism in the period. The expected
increase in demand for labor from educational services, 10.5 percent,
reflects the emphasis put upon expansion of the educational institution
in the plan. Finally, the 10.1 percent increase in demand for labor from
personal household services suggests the anticipated increase in the
level of affluence of the Kuwaiti population.

Table 27 shows the distribution of demand by occupational groups.
It demonstrates that the largest growth in demand is expected to occur in
production and related workers and laborers, 30.2 percent. Since manufacturing industries are only expected to account for 8.3 percent of the
labor force in 1980/81 (Table 26), it may be assumed that most of the
demand for this occupational category will come from the social service
and public utilities sectors, and this is congruent with plan policies for
expansion in these sectors (pp. 102–14). Professional, technical, and
related workers and service workers are the next two occupational
groups in terms of projected labor force demands. This is also congruent
with the expansion of services outlined in the plan.

The anticipated distribution of sectoral and occupational demands
for labor indicates the continuation of the pattern of growth of Kuwait's
economic infrastructure discussed in Chapter V. The real concern em-
phasized in the plan was not in terms of the pattern of growth but rather
in terms of the source of supply for increasing demand in the "strategic
professions," those occupations defined by the plan (p. 69) as requiring
"organized training" and whose "practice by citizens is considered
essential." These professions were defined as technical, skilled, and
semi-skilled occupations. The plan called for a substantial increase in
enrollment in existing and new training programs for these occupations.
Quantitatively, the aims of the "strategic professions" policy are delineated by Figure 2. Qualitatively, the aims of a policy (pp. 73–74) for
the "strategic professions" was delineated accordingly: (1)to meet the
needs of a technical labor force through training and retraining programs; (2) to achieve through the programs both horizontal and vertical
mobility in the strategic professions; (3) to achieve administrative effi-
ciency at the supervisory levels in the strategic professions, concentrat-
ing on the level of foremen and heads of departments; (4) to integrate the
Kuwaiti labor force in the industrial sector and to create specialized
groups indoctrinated with the values of the industrial sector.

Furthermore, the plan outlined (pp. 79–80) the following policies
to attract the Kuwaiti labor force away from the soft civil service jobs

Table 27

Distribution of Total Demand by Major Occupational Groups, 1980–81

	Supply 1975	Demand 1980–81	Increase in Period Number	Increase in Period Percent
Professional, Technical, and Related Workers	41,737	69,100	27,360	23.8%
Administrators	2,511	3,450	940	0.9
Clerical and Related Workers	37,602	50,000	12,400	10.8
Sales Workers	24,090	34,530	10,440	9.1
Service Workers	78,191	103,150	24,960	21.7
Agricultural, Animal Husbandry, Fishermen, and Hunters	7,697	11,750	4,050	3.5
Production and Related Workers and Laborers	105,532	140,220	34,690	30.2
Total	297,360	412,200	114,840	100.0%

SOURCE: *Proposal of the Five Year Plan, 1976/77–1980/81*, p. 27.

Figure 2
The Goals of Training in Strategic
Professions During Plan Period, 1976–1980

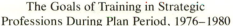

SEMI-SKILLED   SKILLED WORKERS   TECHNICAL WORKERS

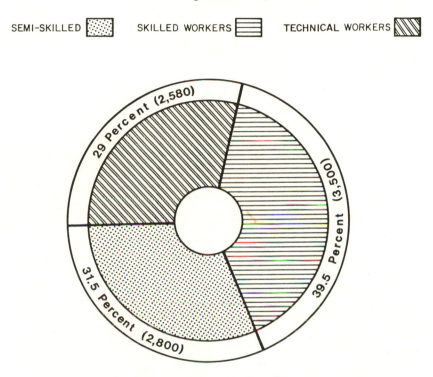

SOURCE: *Proposal of the Five Year Plan, 1976/77–1980/81*, p. 77.

into the "strategic professions:" (1) the expansion of training opportunities — on-the-job training programs, institutes, training scholarships
abroad—that will offer rapid upward mobility; (2) the opening of chan-
nels between technical training and professional education; (3) the expansion of training efforts to include the private sector as well as the
public sector; (4) the reassessment of wage and incentive policies that
encourage the concentration of the Kuwaiti labor force in white collar
civil service jobs; (5) the achievement of integration with Arab exporters
of labor to secure an additional source of a trained labor force; (6) the
enactment of a system of incentives to encourage the private sector to
employ the graduates of training centers and make available to them
opportunities for advancement.

Preliminary results of the 1980 census reveal that the non-Kuwaiti population increased to 58.5 percent of the total population — a much larger increase than anticipated in the plan. While the Ministry of Planning's 1979 population projections predicted the 1985 non-Kuwaiti population at 51.8 percent (ASA, 1979:67), the Ministry's 1980 population estimates for 1985 put the non-Kuwaiti proportion at 64.7 percent (ASA, 1980:28).

CONCLUSION

Stratification in Kuwait serves to fragment the emergence of class consciousness in the marginalized labor force. Through the planning process, the mechanisms of social control through differential stratification have been expanded in response to the proportional increase of a disenfranchised labor force. The main concern of human resource development in the plans is not the Kuwaitization of the labor force, or the return of the Kuwaiti population to majority status. Under the impact of continuing economic expansion—an imperative of peripheral capitalism in a capital surplus society—dependence upon immigrant labor and the consequent increase in non-Kuwaitis as a proportion of the population was recognized as a structural imperative of growth. The concern of the plans centered on the superordinate-subordinate relationship between Kuwaitis and non-Kuwaitis in the labor force. While the first plan concentrated on the development of a professional cadre of Kuwaitis to function in supervisory capacities vis-à-vis non-Kuwaiti professionals in public administration, the second plan expanded its scope to include supervisory cadres throughout the occupational structure. The social control function is exercised through Kuwaitis (a privileged minority in the labor force as well as the population) over non-Kuwaitis (a disenfranchised majority).

7
Conclusion

*D*EPENDENCY, AS OUTLINED IN THE INTRODUCTION, has been identified above all as a historical process of the development of underdevelopment. This process, fostered by the imperialist penetration of pre-capitalist societies, induced the integration of these societies into an emerging world division of labor. This integration took the specific form of external domination and narrow specialization of productive forces, resulting, in effect, in expropriation of surplus product. It is this historical process that must be addressed first in the characterization of Kuwait as a dependent mode.

The underdevelopment of Kuwait through its integration into an emerging British colonial system was initiated in the nineteenth century in the context of British imperial policy in the Arab Gulf. By a coup d'etat in 1896, encouraged (if not engineered) by Britain, the dominance of a regionally oriented merchant class was broken. This class had been dynamically linked through their interests in regional commerce to emerging productive centers in the Gulf and along the coast of the Arabian Sea. Throughout the second half of the nineteenth century, this growing mercantilism was gradually assuming the political form of integration with Ottoman Iraq. By the middle of the century, it was ideologically responding to the decay of the Ottoman empire on the one hand and imperialist penetration of the Gulf on the other in the form of an emerging Arab nationalism.

The interests of the petty commercial class who achieved dominance in their place through the coup d'etat were not dynamically linked to the development of productive forces in the region that was emerging in the nineteenth century. This class was composed of middlemen merchants between exchange and local subsistence consumption. With increasing British domination throughout the nineteenth century of the productive centers of India and the Gulf region, these merchants achieved dominance in Kuwait by severing the dynamic link between Kuwaiti development and regional development, and fostering in its place a link with the British system of production.

Through the secret agreement with the usurping Amir in 1899, Kuwait became a British protectorate, a relationship that lasted until 1961 when Kuwait achieved formal independence and provided the basis for the perpetuation of this class against internal and external threats. Within the framework of this agreement, the relations of production within Kuwait were transformed from a tribally mediated form of community consensus to an externally mediated form of autocracy. This transformation of the nature and basis of class power in Kuwait facilitated the integration of Kuwait into the British division of labor. This integration was a specific part of the integration of the entire Gulf region into the British colonial empire in the Gulf—a process based upon breaking the emerging dynamic link between productive centers and markets in the region and subverting the development of an autonomous capitalist class.

Through the dependence of the local commercial class upon British protection for its perpetuation and upon the importation of British transported commodities for the local and desert hinterland subsistence markets, the surplus realized from the pearl industries was expropriated out of the region. This surplus had provided the basis for the development of Kuwait's merchant fleet in the eighteenth century. With the merchant role marginalized by British domination of Gulf commerce, the dynamic link to productive centers in the region cut off by the commercial and political link with Britain, and the surplus realized from pearling (Kuwait's only form of large-scale commodity production) drained by commerce with Britain, the development of productive forces in Kuwait became specifically limited to intensification of pearl exploitation.

The examination of the political economy of the pearling industry revealed this enterprise to be essentially capitalist in character—that is, commodity production, with the rate of accumulation based upon the rate of exploitation of labor power. Accumulation, however, did not foster expanded capitalist production—the deepening of the capitalist infrastructure. Rather, it fostered an expanded rate of expropriation through British commerce. Kuwait's strategic location vis-à-vis Gulf commerce in general and Basra commerce in particular had been at the very basis of British sponsorship of the ascendance to power and perpetuation of the local commercial class. The attempt by the local commercial class during the First World War to expand commerce autonomously—that is, outside the framework of British expropriation—was suppressed by the British blockade of Kuwait. And during the inter-war period, the attempt of the dominant local commercial class to open commerce with Saudi Arabia was responded to by the tightening of British political control over Kuwait.

The major stimuli to the attempt at autonomous development was the resurgence of Kuwaiti mercantilism during the First World War when Britain's commercial fleet was occupied in the war effort and the decline of the pearling industry in the inter-war period. The first contributed to the revitalization of the dynamic link between Kuwait and regional development and facilitated accumulation without expropriation. The availability of investment capital and the regional opportunities for investment and market expansion promoted the impetus toward autonomous development within the wider regional framework. Furthermore, the second revealed the economic fragility of narrow specialization, contributing to the outward orientation and the identification with Arab nationalism. By the end of the inter-war period, the drive toward autonomous development took the form of a political movement that directly challenged Sabah autocracy and indirectly challenged British domination. This movement was suppressed with force, like similar movements throughout the Arab world during the period, closing the historical possibility of autonomous capitalist development in the Arab world in general and Kuwait in particular.

It is the argument here, then, that it was the forces of autonomous capitalist development that British imperialism confronted and ultimately vanquished during the inter-war period in the Arab world in general and Kuwait in particular. In Kuwait, autonomous capitalist class interests found their ideological expression in Arab nationalism. The confrontation between the interests of autonomous capitalism and British imperialism in Kuwait ended the historical role of an autonomous capitalist class in Kuwait. Thereafter, the emergence of oil wealth resulting from the integration of Kuwait into the world capitalist division of labor as a major oil-producer transformed the basis of power and the relationship between central capitalism and peripheral capitalism in Kuwait. Accumulation as a motive force for autonomous capitalist development was dissipated in the unprecedented levels achieved through oil exploitation.

DEPENDENCY IN THE POST-OIL ERA

In the post-oil era, the capitalist class was coopted into the ruling class through an expanding government apparatus and participation in oil revenue allocation. The nationalist effort became absorbed in maximizing rates of return to the government from oil exploitation, not in changing the productive substructure or political superstructure — that is, not in changing the structure of dependency. This struggle was spearheaded by the opposition in the National Assembly who found their ideological expression in the anti-imperialist struggle of Arab nationalism. The focus on the oil company as a nationalist rallying point served the interests of the dominant class in terms of maximizing rates of return to the government from oil exploitation and diverting attention from issues of class structure. Once the struggle with the oil company was over, ending in full sovereignty of the government over oil exploitation, however, the usefulness of the opposition had ended. Furthermore, by this time Arab nationalist ideology had articulated the linkage between imperialist exploitation and class domination. With the oil company no longer as a scapegoat, the opposition in the National Assembly began focusing on class issues. The government responded by suspending the democratic façade and oppressing opposition elements where it could not coopt them.

The point to be made here is that although the level of accumulation in Kuwait increased rapidly in the post-oil era, the essential structure of dependency — specialized primary production for the world capitalist market, accumulation by a class who controls the means of production for expropriation to the centers of world capitalism—remains fundamentally unaltered in terms of the functional division of labor between central capitalism and peripheral capitalism established in the historical era of imperialism. Dependency, in other words, is specified by narrow specialization in the world division of labor and expropriation of capital to the world centers of capitalism. Under the impact of capital surplus, the mechanisms of expropriation in Kuwait have taken new forms: expansion of the consumer market through welfare state programs, foreign investment and surplus reserves.

In these terms, narrow specialization of productivity and unequal development of productive forces are indicators of underdevelopment. Although the level of productivity may be high in the productive sector, specialization in the world capitalist division of labor specifically limits increasing productivity across economic sectors and diversification of productive labor. The effective result is the marginalization of productive labor rather than its continuing development in a deepening capitalist infrastructure.

In Kuwait, this limitation on the level of development of productive forces was examined in terms of economic transformation. While substantial development in the building of utilities, transportation, and communications infrastructures has been achieved, these have served to increase integration into the world capitalist division of labor as a crude oil exporter and to increase dependence upon oil exportation as the motive force of the economic infrastructure. Furthermore, the physical modernization of Kuwait, the dependence of utilities, transportation, and communications infrastructures upon technologies produced in the central capitalist nations and the increase in the standard of living of the population have all served to increase the level of expropriation under the impact of increasing capital surplus. The result of development policies, in other words, has been to increase dependence of the economy on the oil sector in correspondence with the growth in the level of surplus. Hence, by 1975/76, the perpetuation of Kuwait's economic infrastructure was more dependent upon its continuing integration into the world capitalist division of labor as a major crude oil exporter than it was in 1967/68.

This limitation on the level of development of productive forces is a function of the relations of production in the world capitalist system. These relations are specified by the level of integration of the peripheral capitalist class into the central capitalist productive substructure. The level of integration, correlatively, is determined by the level of expropriation. Primitive accumulation in Kuwait has taken the form of increasing the rates of return to the government from oil exploitation. Integration has taken the form of increasing the rates of expropriation to the centers of world capitalism to invest in the level of productivity of that system.

Because of its stark physical environment and small population base, development of productive forces in Kuwait could only make sense in a regional context. Its rapid development throughout the eighteenth and early nineteenth centuries resulted from the development of its role—productively and politically—in an emerging exchange pattern among productive centers in the region. It was the new structure of the relations of production forged by British penetration of the region that inhibited the development of productive forces, specifically limiting development beyond the bounds of the political divisions established by imperialist powers, and initiating the historical process of the underdevelopment of not only Kuwait but the entire region. In the post-oil era, the role of capital surplus has served to further the integration of the dominant class into the world capitalist structure and has served to strengthen the structure of political divisions that inhibit a new integration of labor. The entire economic infrastructure of Kuwait has developed around activities that produce no value but consume the surplus in such a way as to sustain and enhance expropriation. The effective result is that productive labor in Kuwait is progressively marginalized by imported technologies that service high productivity in the specialized sector and imported consumer commodities that obviate the economy of development outside this sector.

This process of marginalization was examined in terms of the transformation of labor in the post-oil era. The concentration of labor in tertiary sector activities was related to the class dynamics of peripheral capitalism in terms of its relations to expropriation. The distribution of labor in Kuwait reflects the transformation of the economic infrastructure from production of surplus value to consumption of surplus products.

However, the objective link between peripheral capitalism and central capitalism is the rate of expropriation of surplus. In Kuwait, the increasing level of surplus generation from oil exploitation has resulted in the continuous expansion of the mechanisms of expropriation. The institutionalization of these mechanisms has generated increasing demands for immigrant labor to provide the skills required by modern capitalist technologies and their associated forms of bureaucratic organization.

To control the impact of an expatriate population that constitutes an ever-increasing proportion of the population and over three-quarters of the labor force, the government has specifically denied the immigrant population citizenship rights and employment security and has institutionalized status distinctions between Kuwaitis and non-Kuwaitis. These status distinctions were examined in terms of income stratification and the policies of human resource development. These policies were identified in terms of their social control functions. Under the impact of tremendous increases in capital surplus resulting from acquisition of sovereignty over oil exploitation, the imperatives of increasing rates of expropriation generate policies that require a continuous increase in the rate of expansion of the non-Kuwaiti population. To preserve class power in a situation where class legitimacy is based upon an ever diminishing proportion of the population, the social control function has assumed an increasingly prominent role in government policies. These policies, however, serve to alienate further the non-Kuwaiti population from the relations of production of contemporary Kuwait.

In Kuwait, then, there is a fully developed contradiction between the relations of production and the forces of production. Only the contemporary capital surplus situation keeps the contradiction from exploding, but only by fostering political and economic policies that are an incipient negation of Kuwait's dependent capitalist system. In other words, the social composition of the Kuwaiti labor force—representative of the entire Gulf region—is indicative of an emerging productive substructure that transcends and is constrained by the existing political divisions and relationships in the region. The relations of dependency are the most manifest limitation on the development of these productive forces. Political policies that foster regional cooperation and development and economic policies that foster a new social integration of labor are both necessitated by and in contradiction with the dynamics of dependency in the capital surplus situation. Social policies that serve to fragment the interests of labor vis-à-vis peripheral capitalism also serve to heighten the contradictions.

DEPENDENCY THEORY IN RETROSPECT

Among the principal contributions of dependency theory to the study of development in the Third World are (1) identification of the historical process of the development of underdevelopment; and (2) identification of the external mechanisms that induced and perpetuate a situation of capital expropriation from these nations—asymmetrical exchange; integration into a world division of labor, unequal development of productive forces. However, the concentration in dependency research on these external mechanisms has raised the central theoretical question of whether autonomous capitalist development is possible through international adjustments that stem the flow of capital out of these nations. In other words, is dependency a result of capital shortage, or is it a result of class dialectics that obviate autonomous capitalist development, capital shortage being only one symptom of this?

What has to be demonstrated in dependency theory if it is to address this question is that the flow of capital out of the nation and other structural features identified with dependency—progressive subordination of all sectors of the socioeconomic infrastructure to the demands of a limited primary commodity export economy; dependence of the productive sector upon the importation of the products of Western technologies; dependence of the internal market on the importation of essential consumer goods; proletarianization of labor; low levels of employment in the productive economic sector (marginalization of labor); rapid growth of the tertiary sector; increasing concentration of wealth and power—are the result of objective class relations fostered by the linkage of imperialist nations with pre-capitalist societies. In addressing the issue of autonomous development, then, we must address the class dialectics that constitute the dynamics of dependency.

It is this central question of the relationship between capital and labor that structured this examination of Kuwait. Contemporary Kuwait is one of the super-affluent, oil-rich sheikhdoms of the so-called Fourth World. Kuwait, like other nations in this category, occupies an anomalous position in terms of theories of development, underdevelopment and dependency. It is a single-resource dependent, capital-surplus nation, with one of the highest per capita standards of living in the world.

By applying dependency theory to Kuwait, this study attempted to address the following questions: (1) the nature of class dynamics in pre-oil Kuwait from the historical perspective, beginning with the foundation and development of the community in the eighteenth century; (2) whether the process of the development of underdevelopment is an historical experience of Kuwait; (3) whether dependency theory is relevant to the study of the capital surplus society; that is, does it provide the analytic categories for examining the historical development of contemporary Kuwait, and for interrelating the multifaceted features of continuity and change; (4) the nature of class dynamics in contemporary Kuwait. The central focus of the study, then, was not upon the international dynamics of dependency, but upon its internal dynamics as a class phenomenon.

In the introductory chapter several conceptual issues regarding dependency theory were raised. These included:

1. Whether dependent societies constitute a homogeneous category in terms of the concept of mode of production.

2. Does peripheral capitalism operate by a different dynamic than capitalism in the developed industrial nations.

3. Is there an objective link between peripheral capitalism and central capitalism that defines the structural dynamics of dependency.

This case study of Kuwait suggests that contemporary Kuwait forms an integral unit of world capitalism. Contemporary world capitalism constitutes an historically developed international mode of production, not a national mode, and the capitalist class has evolved through historical development into a world class, not a national class. In examining the historical development of class in Kuwait, dependency theory provided the essential categories for analyzing how Kuwait was integrated into the emerging supra-national capitalist mode of production. The processes of imperialism and the development of underdevelopment provided the framework for this analysis. Within this framework, the transformation of the basis of class power from dependence upon world capitalist relations of production (mediated through British imperial power in the Gulf) to dependence upon external forces of production (mediated through the oil companies) can be identified as the point of integration of the dominant class in Kuwait into the world capitalist class.

This identification of a transformation in the basis of class power suggests that a distinction between dependent capitalism as a class dependent upon external force for its perpetuation and peripheral capitalism as a class dependent upon external economic factors for its perpetuation may be useful in dependency theory in attempting to differentiate between class dynamics operating in Third World nations. The case study of Kuwait suggests that in dependent capitalism, the integration of the dominant class into the world capitalist structure is incomplete, and the articulation of social forces within the nation in terms of the capitalist dialectic is fragmentary. In peripheral capitalism, on the other hand, the integration into the world capitalist class is complete, the dominant class is a capitalist class, and the articulation of social forces within the nation is in the framework of the capitalist dialectic.

In Kuwait, the objective link between peripheral capitalism and central capitalism was identified in terms of the rate of expropriation of surplus from capitalist exploitation. In terms of a supra-national capitalist class, peripheral capitalism in Kuwait is peripheral to the level of development of productive forces there, but central to the level of development of productive forces in the world capitalist system. The integrating mechanism of peripheral capitalists into the superstructure of world capitalism is the level of expropriation of surplus. In terms of this, the question of autonomous capitalist development is obviated. The economics of capitalist development simply render integration into the most developed sectors of the capitalist structure more profitable in the short run and in the long run in terms of checking the tendency for the rate of profit to fall. However, this does not obviate capitalist development of productive forces, but only insofar as such development facilitates expanded expropriation.

The contemporary structure of Kuwait is a particular case of dependency — a case where the producing nations have achieved a monopoly over a resource that is vital to the forces of production of central capitalism. In this case, capital surplus rather than capital shortage is the effective result. Dependency in Kuwait is specified by its narrow specialized role in the world division of labor as an oil exporter, and its reciprocal role as an expropriator of capital to the industrial world. The relations of production in this dependent mode are specified by the integration of financial and commercial capital into the world capitalist system.

The nature of the dependency relationship is evident in the subordination of development to the forces of production of central capitalism. The structure of development in Kuwait insures the recirculation of capital accumulated through oil exploitation back into the central capitalist system. Thus, in spite of the benefits of capital surplus, Kuwait reflects the same syndromes of underdevelopment present in other dependent nations that are generally attributed to capital shortage: the destruction of the traditional economic infrastructure to accommodate a single resource export economy, dependence of the productive sector upon the importation of capitalist technologies; destruction of internal markets (in Kuwait's case, regional exchange patterns) by the importation of consumer goods from the world centers of capitalism; high levels of technological development and low levels of employment in the productive economic sector; and the rapid growth of the tertiary sector. The forms of development that have occurred in terms of productive forces are determined by the imperative of peripheral capitalism to expand expropriation.

Hence, in Kuwait's capital surplus situation, the expansion of expropriation and not the production of value is the imperative of development. This has resulted in the generation of development policies that conceive of human development in terms of consumerism, and social development in terms of gross consumption indices. The comprehensive welfare program is the principal mechanism of this policy. It disguises unemployment and exploitation resulting from the narrow specialization of the forces of production for the benefit of a class integrating itself via expropriation into the central capitalist system.

In the limitations placed upon the level of development of productive forces that Kuwait's dependency relationship generates, the dialectic of social class in Kuwait is apparent. As in developed capitalist nations, the relationship between capital and labor is still specified by the objective link between the level of development of productive forces and the rate of exploitation of labor. However, in the case of peripheral capitalism, exploitation takes the form of the expansion and deepening of the structure of expropriation rather than the expansion and deepening of capitalist production. The development of productive forces is specifically limited by the dynamic of this imperative. The result is the marginalization of productive labor rather than its continuing development in a deepening capitalist productive infrastructure. This is the dialectic of social class in the capital surplus dependent society. It remains an empirical question whether it is the dialectic of social class in other nations of the Third World.

Appendix 1

The Law of Divers*

In the name of God, the merciful
The Law of Divers in Kuwait
Issued in the Year 1359h.–1940 A.D.

We the ruler of Kuwait!
Ahmad Al-Jabqr Al-Sabah

In accordance with the suggestion of the chairman of the consultative committee and because of our wish to reform the country and our subjects, we order the following: This is called the Law of the Divers and is composed of 51 articles.

Article One

It is obligatory for every sea diver to appear before his captain at least half a month prior to the official diving trip to service the ship. This order is effective inside and outside the country except in cases of a legitimate excuse [for absence]. If the diver fails to appear without an excuse, he shall be punished.

Article Two

The seamen are obliged to obey the orders of the captain during the season of diving whether they are on sea or on land. They have no right to disobey or object to his orders whatever they may be. However, if anything occurs which may disturb the system of diving, the captain then should have the crew or others witness it and take the issue to the ruler.

*Translation based on a comparison of the law in Adil Muhammad al-Abd al-Mughni, *al-Iqtisad al-Kuwayti al-Qadim* (The Traditional Kuwaiti Economy) (Kuwait, 1977), pp. 225–34, and Badr al-Din Abbas al-Khususi, *Dirasat fi Tarikh al-Kuwayt al-Ijtimai wa al-Iqtisadi: 1913–1961* (Studies in the Social and Economic History of Kuwait: 1913–1961) (Kuwait: Sharikat al-Matbuat Lil Tawzi wa al-Nashr, 1972), pp. 429–39.

Article Three

When a seaman receives *salaf* [an advance] from his captain and is absent without a legitimate excuse, then he is obligated to return the advance. In addition, he will have to pay the penalty decided upon by the Government at the end of the diving season.

Article Four

A seaman signs with a captain for diving and receives the advance. If the ship stops in one of the ports and the seaman stays behind, then his case will be taken to the ruler.

Article Five

When a seaman is a month or more late in appearing for the official trip of the diving season without a legitimate excuse, then the captain has the choice of either levying the official fine *(fasal)* or reducing the advance by half and allowing the seaman to join the ship. This is only if half of the season has not passed. But if more than half of the season has passed, then the seaman has to pay the approved penalty.

Article Six

If the season is over and the seaman did not appear and did not have a legitimate excuse for his absence, then he has to pay the penalty levied.

Article Seven

If a seaman escapes from diving two times or more and is apprehended, he will not be released without the bond of a guarantor.

Article Eight

For any seaman who does not fulfill the service expected from him on the land or the sea the captain has a choice of either paying him only half of the advance or taking from him half of the advance and releasing him, or accepting from him a note promising one-third of his share.

Article Nine

If a seaman gets sick, it is the duty of the captain to take care of him as well as circumstances allow. If the seaman could not stay on the ship due to illness, it is the captain's duty to send him home. When the seaman reaches home, he is expected to see a doctor. If God grants him recovery, then he must return to his captain.

Article Ten

If a seaman claims to be sick and is sent home by his captain for treatment and the doctor discovers he is not sick, then he will be punished and must return immediately to his captain.

Article Eleven

The penalty [levied on the seaman] for the diving captain is the same amount decided by the government, for the advance.

Article Twelve

If a captain signs a seaman to duty and the seaman has a penalty levied against him [by a former captain] in an explanatory note and was not able to pay the penalty ... the former captain can write a note for the penalty and the latter captain has no right to the levied penalty.

Article Thirteen

If a captain was unable to dive and [because of being] late and could not pay the penalty [to the crew], then he must write a note [guaranteeing to the crew] one-third of the share for one full year and the captain [who the crew signs on with] does not get any part of it.

Article Fourteen

If a seaman diver borrowed money [from the captain] after the return, then he is required to take the advance and travel with [the captain] for the dive [the following season] and he has no right to ask his captain for a note that year.

Article Fifteen

All seamen who are diving together: the living pay the debts of the dead, the present of the absent, on the condition that those who participate have reached the age of maturity. The agreement should be written in the presence of all those who are participating and witnesses. No participants should break up until all debts on all of them are paid.

Article Sixteen

The captain has no right to pay money to any of the participants except in the presence of all [members of the crew] or a legal authorization from those absent. If the captain paid one of them and the rest did not approve it, then it becomes a special [arrangement] with the receiver.

Article Seventeen

If one of those participating in the dive dies and leaves anything besides his house, his [belongings] will be distributed among his debtors in accordance with the amount of debt. As for the house, it will be under the jurisdiction of Articles 18 and 19.

Article Eighteen

If a seaman dies and leaves a house and has no inheritors, this house if it came from the money of the diving captain, and he can prove it, is for the captain. But if it was owned as a result of inheritance or purchased from money not derived from diving, then it will go to all the debtors, each in accordance with his debt.

Article Nineteen

If the seaman dies and has no property except his house and has young children, and it is proven that the house came from the money of diving, the captain has to wait until the children reach the age of maturity. Then he will give them the choice between paying the debt to the captain, or diving [to satisfy] the debt of their father, or selling the house and paying its value to the diving captain. If it is proven that the house came from [money] other than diving money, the descendants will be given the choice at the age of maturity between selling the house and paying its value to all the debtors, or keeping the house and guaranteeing payment of the father's debt.

Article Twenty

It is not allowed for the diving captain to pay seamen joining him on the [system] of one-third share more than the specified government increase. He has no right to delay [payment] of the third. It should be paid at the end of the diving season.

Article Twenty-one

If a captain gave a seaman a new note [promising] one-third of the share and another captain joined him, the first [captain] has no right to regain the seaman until the money of the new captain is depleted, unless the first captain has a good excuse to regain [the seaman].

Article Twenty-two

If a captain was unable [to go] diving after the seaman joined him on the [system] of one-third share, the captain has the right to send the seaman diving with whomever he chooses, or give a note [promising] one-third of the share. The captain that is unable to go diving has no rights [on the seaman] until the money of the seaman's new captain is depleted. The new captain has to pay the unable captain one-third of the seaman['s share].

Article Twenty-three

The seaman who joins [a crew] on the [system] of one-third and a leftover occurred from his earnings, and after paying one-third to the first captain, he has to pay one-fourth of the leftover to the unable captain. But if he [the seaman] was paid five rupees of the advance, all the leftovers are for the seaman.

Article Twenty-four

The [financially] weak captain who enlists seamen on the [system] of one-third and pays them [in advance] from 10 to 15 rupees and if he does not get his money by the end of the earning season, the seamen have no right to ask in the coming year for the advance according to the government regulation. They have to be satisfied with last year's advance or repay the advance they have.

Article Twenty-five

If a seaman was not able to dive with the big ships and was able to ride with the small ones or with the Khamamis* on the system of one-third, then one-third goes to his captain if there was one or captains if they were more.

Article Twenty-six

If a seaman accepted a note on the one-third [system] and does not go diving without legitimate reason, then he has to pay the penalty suitable to his circumstances. In the case of disagreement, the ruler will be the final judge.

Article Twenty-seven

If a diver takes to the sea alone [*azzal*] and had taken an advance, no matter how little it may be, he has no right to the fifth except with the agreement and consent of a captain. If he has not taken an advance, he has the right to half of the fifth. And if the loner is indebted to another captain, the loner will have ten percent of the leftover and the rest will go to satisfy the loan.

Article Twenty-eight

If a captain rented a ship on the [system] of half of the fifth and took on an *azzal* [loner] with him, he has one-fourth of the fifth, except if he has a condition [stating] one-half of the fifth; then he has that.

Article Twenty-nine

If a *tabab* [a child usually between seven to ten years old in training to become a diver] dives *rawasi* [dives without assistance] and God was generous, his captain will have one-half of the fifth and the share of the cost of food [for the *tabab*].

If the *tabab* dives with a rock, *hajar* [with assistance], his captain will get one-half of the fifth and one share of *radhif* [children usually not exceeding fourteen years of age in training to become divers] and the cost of food [for the *tabab*]. And if the *tabab* dives *aydah* [with assistance], then he will pay the share of a *seib* [those who pull the divers up] in addition to half of the fifth and the cost of his food.†

Khamamis is a class of divers who do not belong to the diving system and who divide the profits by shares of fifths.

†*Rawasi, hajari, aydah* are different techniques of diving.

Article Thirty

If a captain took a ship and spent on it what is essential [to its maintenance] and this expenditure was more than the ship's earnings, the addition will stay as a debt on the owner of the ship in the coming season to be paid to the captain. But if the owner sold the ship, then he has to pay the debt from the [sale] price. If the ship sinks, the captain will have nothing. But if it broke and can be repaired, the debt stays as it is.

Article Thirty-one

If a captain rents a ship for a fixed [amount] of money, then everything spent on the ship will be counted toward the rental. And the captain has to itemize the expenses in a detailed bill.

Article Thirty-two

Every seaman who is employed in government [services] or the oil company is obliged to pay to the chief of divers [*maamour al-ghawasin*] fifteen percent of his monthly salary.

Article Thirty-three

For every seaman who is employed by other than the government or the oil companies, the captain then has the choice between compensation [*facil*] or the seaman.

Article Thirty-four

[In the case of] every merchant who advances a loan to a diving captain [in anticipation of the] diving harvest and the captain was not able to gain enough to make payment, ... the merchant has no right to demand payment from property. But he takes all the seamen and the ships. And if this does not satisfy all the loan, he then can take property, with the exception of the captain's private dwelling.

Article Thirty-five

If a diving captain borrowed from somebody and uses his property or his house as security in a legal contract and the captain is unable to pay, then the debtor can sell whatever property was put up as security, and the captain has no right to direct the debtor to the seaman or the ships.

Article Thirty-six

Everyone who gives to [lends] the diving captain is obligated to provide all the money [to outfit the ship] and provide food on the sea and land [for the crew] and to pay the captain what he owes on the seamen's account. [The lender is also obliged to pay] the thirds to the crew on [the system of] one third, without interest. The captain is obligated to surrender to the lender all that is purchased and will not hide from him anything. If he hides anything, then he has no right to ask for the remainder of the account and the thirds and a punishment will be inflicted on him.

Article Thirty-seven

Anybody who wants to demand payment of a debt from a captain should do it immediately after *Qafal* [close of the season]. If a month elapses since *Qafal* before the debtor requests payment, then he forfeits his right for this year. The debtor has the right to make his demand next year in accordance with this article . . . .

Article Thirty-eight

It is forbidden for the diving captain to make a condition with a *tawash* [pearl merchant] when selling [in which] some money [is gained] for the captain himself or any of his relatives. [If it] becomes evident that he has taken some [money] this will be taken from him and will be added to the total [income]. It is not allowed for the captain to make an income from pearling [additional] to his share.

Article Thirty-nine

The diving captain is obligated to inform the seamen of the value upon the completion of sale.

Article Forty

Every captain who lends [advances] money to the seaman on *Khanchiya* or on *raddah* after the issuing of this law, all that is left by the end of the two seasons will be considered as cancelled.*

Khanchiya is the name of diving before the official season. It occurs in early spring, around April, and is usually done by a few small ships operating close to the coast. *Reddah* is return to diving after the close of the official season, usually in the fall, around October. Like *Khanchiya,* it is participated in by a few small boats operating close to the coast. Al-Shamlan, *History of Pearling,* pp. 273–74.

Article Forty-one

If a seaman owed a captain a remainder of Khanchiya or raddah before the issuing of this law, its settlement is with the ruler. And if a seaman rides with a captain whom he owed previously and a leftover occurs [after taking the shares] then the captain receives payment of his old debt [from the leftover].

Article Forty-two

If a seaman has in his hand a note on the [system] of one-third and a *tawashi* or *Qatta* [merchant] or others took the seaman [in his service] during the diving season, then the one who included the seaman [in his crew] has to pay the levied penalty. And if he included the seaman without a paper, then the blame is on him and he will pay the levied penalty.

Article Forty-three

If a merchant captain took a seaman on a journey going to Zanzibar or Malabar and fifteen days passed from the diving [season] and this seaman does not arrive, then the merchant captain has to pay the levied penalty to the diving captain. The diving captain has the choice between receiving the levied penalty or taking the seaman. If the seaman is late [the same period] for the second trip, the judgment will be the same.

Article Forty-four

It is obligatory for the captain of a merchant ship on his second trip to ask the diving seaman to have in writing permission from his diving captain to join [the merchant crew]. If the merchant captain signs the seaman without the written [permission] and the season of diving begins and the seaman does not arrive, and the [pearling] ship departs, then the merchant captain has to pay to the diving captain one and a half times the amount of compensation decided by the government. The merchant captain will be reprimanded by the ruler. But if the [diving] captain did not go diving, the merchant captain in this case is obligated to pay the penalty which is paid by the other seamen [of the diving crew] who do not go diving.

Article Forty-five

If a seaman arrives in the season of diving and his merchant captain wants to send him to Basra for unloading of cargo, he has no right to do so.

Article Forty-six

If the seaman was delayed fifteen days because of travelling [with a merchant vessel] and his captain did not go diving, then the captain has a choice of either taking the seaman or taking half of the advance paid by the merchant captain.

Article Forty-seven

It is not allowed for the lender to complain about a seaman who has taken the advance from his captain, but he is obligated to take the complaint earlier to the ruler.

Article Forty-eight

If a seaman stayed behind fifteen days and was of the diving seaman who are supposed to join [the crew] after the first [group] his captain has the choice between taking him or taking the compensation on an average basis. This is paid by the merchant captain.

Article Forty-nine

If a seaman signed a note on the one-third [system] and then took a ship [as a captain], one-third of the harvest of *Qalatiyah* [Sheikh's share] and the fifty or its half, whether the seaman was a seaman or a captain, will be taken from him.

Article Fifty

It is forbidden for any captain to sign up a seaman [who belongs] to other captains unless the seaman has in his hands a book from the accountant of diving in which what he owes and what is owed to him is recorded. Both the captain and the seaman have to appear before the accountant to change the registration.

Article Fifty-one

The Shura Council executes this order: issued 22 Rabia al-Thani; the year 1359 hijari, occurring 29 May 1940.

Signed:

The Ruler of Kuwait	The President of the Shura
Ahmed al-Jabir	Council, Abdullah al
al-Sabah	Salim al-Sabah

It was also decided to add to the law of Diving two new Articles.

Article One

If a seaman dies after he leaves to go diving, even if it was a short period, a complete share will be allocated as if he were alive to the end of the season.

Article Two

If a captain were delayed from going to diving and his seamen want to go with the first [group], he either gives them an advance and they will be delayed with him or he gives them an advance and sends them with the advance [group]. If the captain is unable to do so, he will give the seamen a note on the one-third [system].

Taken from the minutes of the Shura Council's meeting of Tuesday, 6 of Jamadi the First, 1359.

Appendix 2

Councils of Ministers of Kuwait, 1962 to 1981

1. Royal Decree of January 17, 1962, concerning ministerial assignments:
   Jabir al-Ahmad al-Jabir al-Sabah, Finance and Economy
   Jabir al-'Ali al-Salim al-Sabah, Electricity and Water
   Humud al-Zaid al-Khalid, Justice
   Khalid 'Abdullah al-Salim al-Sabah, Customs and Ports
   Salim al-'Ali al-Salim al-Sabah, Public Works
   Sa'ad 'Abdullah al-Salim al-Sabah, Interior
   Sabah al-Ahmad al-Jabir al-Sabah, Guidance and News
   Sabah al-Salim al-Sabah, Foreign Affairs
   Abdul 'Aziz Hamad al-Saqar, Public Health
   Abdullah al-Jabir al-Sabah, Education
   Mubarak al-Hamad al-Sabah, Pious Endowments
   Mubarak Abdullah al-Ahmad al-Sabah, Post, Telegraph and Telephone
   Muhammad Ahmad al-Jabir al-Sabah, Defence
   Muhammad Yusif al-Nisf, Social Affairs and Labour
   Sabah al-Salim al-Sabah, Crown Prince and Prime Minister

2. Royal Decree of March 13, 1964, concerning changes in ministerial assignments:
   Jabir al-'Ali al-Salim, Guidance and News
   Khalid al-Mas'ud al-Fuhayd, Electricity and Water
   Yusif al-Sayed Hashim al-Rifa'i, Post, Telegraph and Telephone

3. Royal Decree of December 6, 1964, concerning ministerial assignments:
   Jabir al-Ahmad al-Jabir, Commerce and Industry
   Jabir al-'Ali al-Salim, Guidance and News
   Khalifah al-Khalid al-Ghunaim, Commerce
   Khalid al-Ahmad al-Jassar, Pious Endowments
   Khalid al-Mas'ud al-Fuhayd, Education
   Sa'ad al-Abdullah al-Salim, Interior and Defence
   Sabah al-Ahmad al-Jabir, Foreign Affairs

173

Abdul Latif Muhammad al-Thunayan, Public Works
Abdul 'Aziz Husayn, Minister of State for Cabinet Affairs
Humud al-Yusif al-Nisf, Public Health
Abdul 'Aziz Muhammad al-Shay'i, Electricity and Water
Muhammad al-Ahmad al-Ghanim, Justice
Yusif al-Sayid Hashim al-Rifa'i, Post, Telegraph and Telephone
Abdullah al-Mishari al-Rowdan, Social Affairs and Labour
Sabah al-Salim al-Sabah, Crown Prince and Prime Minister

4. Royal Decree January 3, 1965:
Jabir al-Ahmad al-Jabir, Finance and Industry and Commerce
Jabir al-'Ali al-Salim, Guidance and News
Khalid Ahmad al-Jassar, Justice
Khalid al-Mas'ud al-Fuhayd, Education
Khalid al-'Isa al-Salih, Public Works
Sa'ad al-Abdullah al-Salim, Interior and Defence
Sabah al-Ahmad al-Jabir, Foreign Affairs
Salih 'Abd al-Malik al-Salih, Post, Telegraph and Telephone
Abdul 'Aziz Abdullah al-Sara'awi, Social Affairs and Labour
Abdullah al-Mishari al-Rowdan, Pious Endowments
Abdullah Ahmad al-Sumait, Electricity and Water
Abdul 'Aziz Ibrahim al-Fulaij, Public Health
Yusef al-Sayid Hasim al-Rifa'i, Minister of State for Cabinet Affairs
Sabah al-Salim al-Sabah, Prime Minister

5. Royal Decree of December 4, 1965:
Jabir al-'Ali al-Salim, Guidance and News
Khalid al-Ahmad al-Jassar, Justice
Khalid al-Mas'ud al-Fuhayd, Education
Khalid al-'Isa al-Salih, Public Works
Sa'ad al-Abdullah al-Salim, Interior and Defence
Sabah al-Ahmad al-Jabir, Finance and Oil (Acting), Foreign Affairs
Salih Abdul Malik al-Salih, Post, Telegraph and Telephone
Abdul 'Aziz Abdullah al-Sara'awi, Social Affairs and Labour
Abdullah al-Jabir, Commerce and Industry
Abdullah al-Mishari al-Rowdan, Pious Endowments and Islamic Affairs
Abdullah Ahmad al-Sumait, Electricity and Water
Yusif al-Sayid Hashim al-Rifa'i, Minister of State for Cabinet Affairs
Jabir al-Ahmad al-Jabir, Crown Prince and Prime Minister

6. Royal Decree of February 4, 1967:
Jabir al-'Ali al-Salim, Guidance and News
Khalid Ahmad al-Jassar, Justice
Khalid al-'Isa al-Salih, Public Works
Khalid Ahmad Jasim al-Mudhaf, Social Affairs and Labour
Sa'ad al-Abdullah al-Salim, Interior and Defence

Sabah al-Ahmad al-Jabir, Foreign Affairs
Salih Abdul Malik al-Salih, Education and Post, Telegraph and Telephone
  (Acting)
Abdullah al-Jabir, Commerce and Industry
Abdullah al-Mishari al-Rowdan, Pious Endowments and Islamic Affairs
Abdullah Ahmad al-Sumait, Electricity and Water
Abdul Rahman Salim al-'Atiqi, Finance and Oil
Abdul 'Aziz Ibrahim al-Fulaij, Public Health
Yusif al-Sayid Hashim al-Rifa'i, Minister of State for Cabinet Affairs
Jabir al-Ahmad al-Jabir, Crown Prince and Prime Minister

7. Royal Decree of April 30, 1967:
   Abdul 'Aziz Abdullah al-Sara'awi, Post, Telegraph and Telephone

8. Royal Decree of February 2, 1971:
   Jasim Khalid Dawud al-Marzuq, Justice and Education (Acting)
   Hamad Mubarak al-'Aiyar, Social Affairs and Labour
   Humud Yusif al-Nisef, Public Works
   Khalid Sulayman al-Adasani, Commerce and Industry
   Rashid Abdullah al-Farhan, Pious Endowments and Islamic Affairs
   Sa'ad al-Abdullah al-Sabah, Interior and Defence
   Sabah al-Ahmad al-Jabir, Foreign Affairs and Information (Acting)
   Abdul Rahman Salim al-'Atiqi, Finance and Oil
   Abdul Razzaq Mishari al-'Adawani, Public Health
   Abdul 'Aziz Husayn, Minister of State for Cabinet Affairs
   Abdul 'Aziz Abdullah al-Sara'awi, Post, Telegraph and Telephone, and
     Electricity and Water (Acting)

9. Royal Decree of February 15, 1971:
   Jasim Khalid Dawud al-Marzuq, Education
   Mahmud Ahmad Abdul Latif al-Hamad, Justice
   Abdullah Yusif al-Ghanim, Electricity and Water

10. Royal Decree of February 9, 1975:
    Jabir al-'Ali al-Salim al-Sabah, Information and Deputy Prime Minister
    Jasim Khalid al-Dawud al-Marzuq, Education
    Hamad Mubarak al-'Aiyar, Housing
    Ahmad Yusif al-Nisf, Public Works
    Salim Sabah al-Salim al-Sabah, Social Affairs and Labour
    Saad al-Abdullah al-Salim al-Sabah, Interior and Defence
    Sulayman Humud al-Zaid al-Khalid, Communications
    Sabah al-Ahmad al-Jabir al-Sabah, Foreign Affairs
    Abdul Rahman Salim al-'Atiqi, Finance
    Abdul Rahman Abdullah al-'Awadi, Public Health
    Abdul 'Aziz Husayn, Minister of State for Cabinet Affairs
    Abdullah Yusif Ahmad al-Ghanim, Electricity and Water

Abdul Muttalib Abdul Husayn al-Kazimi, Oil
Abdul Wahhab Yusif al-Nafisi, Commerce and Industry
Jabir al-Ahmad al-Jabir, Crown Prince and Prime Minister

11. Royal Decree of September 6, 1976:
Jabir al-'Ali al-Salim al-Sabah, Deputy Prime Minister and Information
Jasim Khalid al-Dawud al-Marzuq, Education
Hamad Mubarak al-'Aiyar, Housing
Humud Yusif al-Nisf, Public Works
Salim Sabah al-Salim al-Sabah, Social Affairs and Labour
Sa'ad al-Abdullah al-Salim al-Sabah, Interior and Defence
Salman al-Duaych al-Sabah, Minister of State for Administrative and
    Legal Affairs
Sulayman Humud al-Zaid al-Khalid, Communications
Sabah al-Ahmad al-Jabir al-Sabah, Foreign Affairs
Abdul Rahman Salim al-'Atiqi, Finance
Abdul Rahman Abdullah al-'Awadi, Public Health
Abdul 'Aziz Husayn, Minister of State for Cabinet Affairs
Abdullah Ibrahim al-Mufarrij, Justice
Abdullah Yusif Ahmad al-Ghanim, Electricity and Water
Abdul Muttalib Abdul al-Husayn al-Kazimi, Oil
Abdul Wahhab Yusif al-Nafisi, Commerce and Industry
Muhammad Yusif al-Adasani, Planning
Yusif Jasim al-Haji, Pious Endowments and Islamic Affairs

12. Royal Decree of February 1981:
Subah al-Ahmad al-Jabir, Deputy Prime Minister, Foreign Affairs and
    Information (Acting)
Ya'qub Yusif al-Ghnaym, Education
Jasim Khalid al-Marzuq, Industry and Commerce
'Isa Muhammad Ibrahim, Communications
Abd Allah al-Dakhil al-Rashid, Public Works
Abd al-Latif Yusif al-Hamad, Finance and Planning
Ahmad Sa'ad al-Jasir, Endowments and Islamic Affairs
Nawwaf al-Ahmad al-Jabir, Interior
Salim al-Sabah al-Salim, Defense
Ali al-Khalifah al-'Atdbi, Oil
Abd al-Rahman Abd Allah al-Iwadhi, Public Health
Abd al-Aziz Husayn, Minister of State for Cabinet Affairs
Salman al-Di'ayj al-Salman al-Subah, Justice and Administrative and
    Legal Affairs
Hamad Isa al-Rujayb, Housing and Social Affairs and Labour
Khalaf Ahmad al-Khalaf, Electricity and Water

cNotes to the Chapters

INTRODUCTION

1. Samir Amin, *Unequal Development: An Essay on the Social Formations of Peripheral Capitalism* (New York: Monthly Review Press, 1976), pp. 287–92.

2. Fernando Henrique Cardoso, "Dependency and Development in Latin America," *New Left Review* 74 (July–August 1972):85.

3. Nicos Poulantzas, "Internationalisation of Capitalist Relations and the Nation-State," *Economy and Society* 3, no. 2 (May 1974):146–48.

4. André Gunder Frank, "The Development of Underdevelopment," in James D. Cockcroft, André Gunder Frank and Dale L. Johnson, *Dependence and Underdevelopment: Latin America's Political Economy* (Garden City: Anchor Books, 1972), pp. 3–17.

5. André Gunder Frank, *Capitalism and Underdevelopment in Latin America: Historical Studies of Chile and Brazil* (New York: Monthly Review Press, 1967), pp. 6–14.

6. T. Dos Santos, "The Crisis of Dependency Theory and the Problem of Dependence in Latin America," in *Underdevelopment and Development,* edited by H. Bernstein (Hardmondsworth: Penguin, 1973), p. 73.

7. See, for example, Frank's argument on "The Myth of Feudalism in Brazilian Agriculture," in *Capitalism and Underdevelopment,* pp. 221–77, and his argument in "The Development of Underdevelopment," in *Dependence and Underdevelopment,* pp. 3–17.

8. C. Meillassoux, "From Reproduction to Production," *Economy and Society* 1, no. 1 (1972):102–103.

9. Colin Leys, *Underdevelopment in Kenya: The Political Economy of Neo-Colonialism, 1964–1971* (London: Heinemann, 1975), p. 20.

10. Philip J. O'Brien, "A Critique of Latin American Theories of Dependency," in Ivar Oxaal, Tony Barnett and David Booth, eds., *Beyond the Sociology of Development* (London: Routledge and Kegan Paul, 1975).

11. Ian Roxborough, "Dependency Theory in the Sociology of Development: Some Theoretical Problems," *The West African Journal of Sociology and Political Science* 1, no. 2 (January 1976):120.

12. Samir Amin, "Self-Reliance and the New International Economic Order," *Monthly Review* 29 (July–August 1977):2.

1—THE ORIGINS AND STRUCTURAL DEVELOPMENT OF KUWAIT

1. Quoted in Abdul Jabbar al-Rawi, *Al Badiyah* (The Desert), 3rd ed. (Baghdad: n.p., 1972), pp. 267–68.

2. Philip K. Hitti, *History of the Arabs,* 8th ed. (London: Macmillan, 1964), p. 25.

3. There are no written records of the history of the Bani Utub. The history, preserved in local tradition, was first recorded by the Kuwaiti historian Abd al-Aziz al-Rushaid in 1926, *Tarikh al-Kuwayt (The History of Kuwait)* (Beirut: Dar Mahaahat al-Hayat, n.d.). This tradition has been supplemented and modified by subsequent histories. The account related here is generally substantiated by the histories, unless otherwise noted. Ahmad Abu Hakima, *History of Eastern Arabia —1750—1800: The Rise and Development of Bahrain and Kuwait* (Beirut: Khayats, 1965), pp. 48–51, provides an examination of the various traditions.

4. Al-Rushaid, *History of Kuwait,* p. 32, provides a detailed description of the factions involved in the conflict. It is noteworthy that George N. Curzon, *Persia and the Persian Question* (New York: Barnes & Noble, 1966) 2:268–329, notes several migrations of Arabian tribes into southwestern Persia in the same period. The period appears to have been one of substantial emigration from Central Arabia, then, and may have been the result of drought as observed by al-Rushaid, Curzon, and H. R. P. Dickson, *Kuwait and Her Neighbours* (London: Allen and Unwin, 1956), p. 26, and Abu Hakima, *History of Eastern Arabia,* p. 42.

5. Husayn Khalaf al-Shaykh Khazal, *Tarikh al-Kuwayt al-Siyasi* (The Political History of Kuwait) (Beirut: Matabu Dar al-Kutub, 1962) 1:41. The word *Ahl* (pronounced Aal) means family of or people of and in the tribal context generally denotes a lineage. *Al,* on the other hand is the article "the," and generally denotes the immediate descendants of a person.

6. Yusuf Bin Isa al-Qinaie, *Safahat min Tarikh al-Kuwayt* (Pages from the History of Kuwait), 4th ed. (Kuwait: Government Printing House, 1968), p. 9.

7. Dickson, *Kuwait and Her Neighbors,* pp. 26, 401, identifies the al-Zayyid, a family known for the number of sheep it owned (today in Kuwait known as al-Ghanim) as joining the Bani Utub in Qatar. It may be that it was in Qatar or one of the other ports that the Baharina (master shipwrights of the Arab Gulf) first joined the Bani Utub, thus providing the technical basis for Kuwait's subsequent merchant economy, discussed later in the chapter. See, also, Abu Hakima, *History of Eastern Arabia,* p. 51, who attributes the knowledge of seafaring to their period in Qatar or al-Hasa.

8. J. G. Lorimer's monumental work, synthesizing all available British records of the area, *Gazetteer of the Persian Gulf, Oman and Central Arabia* (Shannon: Irish University Press, 1970), first issued by the Government of India in two volumes, 1908 and 1915, respectively, for official use, and only made available to the public in the early fifties, in vol. 1, pt. 1B, p. 1006, reports that "in 1820 was represented as containing an armed population of 5,000 to 7,000 men, of whom only a few hundred were 'Utub by race."

9. Al-Qinaie, *Pages from the History of Kuwait,* p. 9. Sayf Marzouk al-Shamlan, *Min Tarikh al-Kuwayt* (From the History of Kuwait) (Cairo: Matbat Nahdhat Misr, 1959), p. 109, includes al-Zayyid (who joined the Bani Utub in Qatar), Ahl-Rumi, Ahl-Sayf and Ahl-Bin Ali among the earliest settlers.

10. Kuwait Chamber of Commerce and Industry, *Dalil al-Kuwayt* (Guide to Kuwait) (Kuwait: Chamber of Commerce and Industry, October 1965), p. 145. The accuracy of Niebuhr's observations cannot be assessed as there are no other figures

available until a later period. Even if he overestimated the population or the number of boats by 100 percent, however, it still indicates a substantial settlement in a relatively short period of time.

11. Arnold T. Wilson, *The Persian Gulf: An Historical Sketch from the Earliest Times to the Beginning of the Twentieth Century* (London: Allen & Unwin, 1928), p. 1.

12. This tradition is also reported by Husayn Sulaiman Mahmoud, *al-Kuwayt: Madhiha wa Hadhruha* (Kuwait: Its Past and Present) (Baghdad: al-Ahliyah Bookshop, 1968), p. 149. One of the earliest accounts of the Bani Utub in English also reports this: Francis Warden, "Historical Sketch of the Uttoobee Tribe of Arabs (Bahrein) from the year 1716 to the year 1817," *Bombay Selections* (Bombay, XXIV, 1856) and reproduced in *History of Kuwait*, edited by Ahmad Abu Hakima (Kuwait: Kuwait Government Press, 1970), vol. 1, pt. 2, pp. 158–70.

13. Zahra Freeth and Victor Winstone, *Kuwait: Prospect and Reality* (London: Allen & Unwin, 1972), p. 57.

14. Mohammed Mahjub, *al-Hijrah wa al-Taghayyur al-Binai fi al-Mujtama al-Kuwayti* (Migration and Structural Change in Kuwait Society) (Kuwait: Wakalat al-Mutboaat, n.d.), pp. 87–118.

15. The books of Sayf Marzouk al-Shamlan, *Tarikh al-Ghaus ala al-Lulu fi al-Kuwayt wa- al-Khalij al-Arabi* (History of Pearling in Kuwait and the Arab Gulf) (Kuwait: Government of Kuwait, 1975), and Adil Muhammad al-Ahd al-Mughni, *al-Iqtisad al-Kuwayti al-Qadim* (Traditional Kuwaiti Economy) (Kuwait, 1977), taken together reveal the social, technical, and economic organization of Kuwait's pre-oil economy. In particular, they reveal the unique relationship of tribal groups exchanging their surplus as autonomous producers (agriculture, animal husbandry, fishing), tribal groups as interdependent units in a division of labor (blacksmiths, shipwrights, and producers of tools of fishing, etc.) and tribal groups supplying what was essentially a form of wage labor (divers, seafarers).

16. There is actually very little to document the Sabah's role in the caravan trade. Several Kuwaiti historians refer to it only tangentially. See al-Rushaid, *History of Kuwait*, pp. 54, 121. Nevertheless, the strength of this is indicated in the accounts of Dr. Edward Ives who visited the Kharij Island in March 1758 and made direct contact with Sabah I to arrange desert transport to Aleppo. The Shaikh was able to guarantee safe transport to Aleppo, indicating that "the Arabs of the desert route from Kuwait to Aleppo were on good terms with the Shaikh." Abu Hakima, *History of Eastern Arabia*, further concludes that "the wealth of the Shaikh ... may be judged by his refusal of the Baron's offer of 1,000 piastres when he had asked for 2,000, despite the fact that bargaining was not undesirable" (p. 56).

17. Abd al-Aziz Hysayn, *al-Mujtama al-Arabi bil Kuwayt* (Arab Society in Kuwait) (Cairo: Institute for Higher Arab Studies, 1960), p. 55.

18. According to the historical tradition maintained by al-Khalifah, the ruling house of Bahrein to the present, it was the question of succession that precipitated the migration of al-Khalifah, who expected to succeed Sabah I. See Abu Hakima, *History of Eastern Arabia*, p. 66.

19. "Report on the Commerce of Arabia and Persia by Samuel Manesty and Harford Jones, 1790," p. 32, reproduced in Abu Hakima, *History of Kuwait*, vol. 1, pt. 2, pp. 21–82. This volume is a compilation of British documents and European literature (principally accounts of travellers to the area) relevant to Kuwait available to about 1830.

20. Isa al-Qatami, *Dalil al-Muhtar fi ilm al-Bihar* (Guide for the Confused on the Science of Navigation), 4th ed. (Kuwait: Government of Kuwait Press, 1976), p. 200.

180   NOTES

21. The variation in estimates of the size is quite large, as the table below indicates:

Year	Number of Boats	Source
1833	1,500	Mahmoud, *Kuwait: Its Past and Present*, p. 43.
1907	461	Lorimer, *Gazetteer*, vol. 1, pt. 2, p. 2259.
1907	1,000	*Loghat el-Arab* (Baghdad) 7 (December 1913):320.
1912	1,500	*Loghat el-Arab* (Baghdad) 7 (December 1913:320.
1913	812	al-Shamlan, *History of Pearling*, p. 262.

Part of the problem of determining the size is the lack of records over the period and the consequent dependence upon ad hoc estimates. A large source of error in such estimates is what craft are actually being counted among the fleet — i.e., whether the small boats pearling in nearby waters are included or not.

22. Abu Hakima, *History of Eastern Arabia*, p. 180.

23. See al-Qinaie, *Pages from the History of Kuwait*, pp. 60–62, who gives details of the major families and private fortunes accumulated in both commerce and pearl marketing. Also, al-Shamlan, *History of Pearling*, p. 281, who explains the difference in operations between the big pearl merchants and the petty merchants.

24. Badr al-Din Abbas al-Khususi, *Dirasat fi Tarikh al-Kuwayt al-Ijtimai wa al-Iqtisadi: 1913–1961* (Studies in the Social and Economic History of Kuwait: 1913–1961) (Kuwait: Sharikat al-Matbuat lil Tawzi wa al-Nashr, 1972), p. 127; al-Shamlan, *From the History of Kuwait*, p. 117; al-Qanie, *Pages from the History of Kuwait*, p. 29.

2—BRITISH GULF POLICY AND KUWAIT IN THE NINETEENTH CENTURY

1. Abu Hakima, *History of Eastern Arabia*, p. 43.

2. Lorimer, *Gazetteer*, vol. 1, pt. 1A, p. 10.

3. J. B. Kelly, *Britain and the Persian Gulf, 1795–1880* (Oxford: Clarendon Press, 1968), pp. 260–89.

4. "Report on the Commerce of Arabia...," Abu Hakima, *History of Kuwait*, vol. 1, pt. 2, p. 25.

5. For the text of the treaty see C. U. Aitchison, *Collection of Treaties, Engagements and Sanads Relating to India and Neighbouring Countries* (Calcutta, 1909) 12:172–76.

6. *Iraq: A Study in Political Development* (New York: Macmillan, 1938), p. 33.

7. For an excellent study of British policy in the Gulf between 1894 and 1914, see Briton C. Busch, *Britain and the Persian Gulf, 1894–1914* (Berkeley: University of California, 1967).

8. George N. Curzon, *Persia and the Persian Question* (New York: Barnes & Noble, 1966) 1:pp. 4–5.

9. *Mesopotamia (Iraq), 1600–1914: A Study in British Foreign Affairs* (Baghdad: al-Maaref Press, 1957), p. 170. See also Ravinder Kumar, *India and the Persian Gulf Region, 1858–1907: A Study in British Imperial Policy* (New York: Asia Publishing House, 1965) for a comprehensive study of the relationship between Britain's Indian empire and Gulf policy.

10. The political expatriates were Shaikh Thuwaini and Mustafa Agha who cooperated in an abortive attempt to wrest Basra from Suleiman Pasha. See Stephen Hemsley Longrigg, *Four Centuries of Modern Iraq* (Oxford: Clarendon Press, 1925), pp. 204–206.

11. The complete texts of these letters are reproduced in Abu Hakima, *History of Kuwait,* vol. 1, pt. 2, pp. 19–20.

12. Abu Hakima, *History of Eastern Arabia,* pp. 97–99.

13. Latouche and Manesty, November 6, 1784, in Abu Hakima, *History of Kuwait,* vol. 1, pt. 2, p. 18.

14. *History of Eastern Arabia,* p. 123.

15. Mustapha Abd al-Qadir al-Najjar, *al-Tarikh al-Siyasi li'Ilaqat al-Iraq al-Dawliyah bi al-Khalij al-Arabi* (The Political History of Iraqi International Relations with the States of the Arab Gulf) (Basra: Basra University Press, 1975), pp. 46–47.

16. In 1899, the revenues of the Fao estates alone were estimated at 6,000 pounds annually. Government of India to Lord G. Hamilton, February 12, 1899, Foreign Office Confidential Print: Correspondence Respecting Affairs at Koweit, 1896–1905, first printed for Foreign Office use only in 1900, and only recently made available to the public under the title, *The Affairs of Kuwait, 1896–1904,* 2 vols., edited by Robin Bidwell (London: Frank Cass, 1971), vol. 1, pt. 1, pp. 39–40.

17. See Abdul Aziz Suleiman Nawar, *Tarikh al-Iraqi al-Hadith* (The History of Modern Iraq) (Cairo: Dar al-Katab al-Arabi, 1968), pp. 233–36, who examines British efforts to forestall developing ties between Ottoman Iraq and Kuwait.

18. Memorandum by Mr. Stavrides, June 30, 1896, *The Affairs of Kuwait,* vol. 1, pt. 1, pp. 1–2.

19. *Ibid.,* p. 2.

20. This correspondence, covering the period from July 1896 to January 1899, is compiled in *The Affairs of Kuwait,* vol. 1, pt. 1, pp. 1–36.

21. The disagreement between the Home Office and the India Office over Gulf affairs was one of the principal themes of Busch's study, *Britain and the Persian Gulf, 1894–1914* (Berkeley: University of California Press, 1967). After an intensive examination of this era, he concluded that "the development of the British Gulf position was not accomplished without friction — sometimes severe friction — between Home and Indian authorities. In this controversy, India took a forward line in most instances, occasionally even initiating policy without Home approval, at least until 1905" (p. 387). It is not without some precedent, then, to suggest that Colonel Wilson may have taken considerable initiative in encouraging Mubarak's coup, and that his actions would have been concealed in the official correspondence.

22. Government of India to Hamilton, February 24, 1897, *The Affairs of Kuwait,* vol. 1, pt. 1, p. 3; and Marquis of Salisbury to Currie, July 17, 1897, *ibid.,* p. 12.

23. Baker to Drummond, August 4, 1896, *ibid.,* pp. 16–17.

24. Moubray to Drummond, July 7, 1897, *ibid.,* pp. 15–16.

25. Moubray to Meade, November 7, 1897, and Meade to Government of India, November 12, 1897, *ibid.,* p. 23.

26. Foreign Office to India Office, November 25, 1897, *ibid.,* p. 22.

27. Lock to Government of India, December 22, 1897, *ibid.,* pp. 24–26, first raises this issue, and it is the predominant theme of correspondence through March, 1898, pp. 26–28. It remained an issue of British policy in the Gulf throughout the early twentieth century. However, there was never real danger of Russian competition to British hegemony in the Gulf in this period, as pointed out by T. Hungerford Holdich, *The Indian Borderland, 1880–1900* (London: Methuen, 1901), pp. 223–24. The issue, then, appears more a rationale for turning the Gulf into a private British lake than a cause of it, the *raison d'être* of which was the growth of Russian influence in Persia and the Ottoman Empire.

28. *Ibid.*, pp. 27–28.

29. *Ibid.*, pp. 30–31.

30. See Meade's report to Government of India, January 30, 1899, on conclusion of the agreement, *The Affairs of Kuwait,* vol. 1, pt. 1, pp. 47–50.

31. Complete text of Agreement available in Lorimer, *Gazetteer,* vol. 1, pt. 1B, pp. 1048–49.

32. Complete text of letter available in *ibid.,* pp. 1049–50.

33. Foreign Office to India Office, February 14, 1899, *The Affairs of Kuwait,* vol. 1, pt. 1, p. 41.

34. Wratislaw to Melvill, February 2, 1899, *ibid.,* p. 53.

35. Busch, *Britain and the Persian Gulf,* pp. 187–234.

36. This correspondence is available in *The Affairs of Kuwait,* vol. 1, pts. 2 and 3.

3—THE UNDERDEVELOPMENT OF KUWAIT

1. For an examination of the structure of taxation under Mubarak, see al-Mughni, pp. 121–22, who estimates that about 60 percent of Mubarak's income came from taxes. See also Lorimer, *Gazetteer,* vol. 1, pt. 1B, pp. 1047–48, and vol. 2, pt. 2B, p. 1076.

2. See Lorimer, *Gazetteer,* vol. 2, pt. 2B, pp. 1056–58, for tables on Kuwait's imports and re-exports in 1905–1906 and the means of transport.

3. There is no indication of the nature of the concessions. Al-Rushaid's account stresses Mubarak's guarantee to respect the personal authority and integrity of the pearl merchants. Also see al-Shamlan, *From the History of Kuwait,* pp. 151–52.

4. Text of lettter from Sir Percy Cox, British Political Resident in the Gulf, to Mubarak, in Khazal, *Political History of Kuwait,* vol. 2, p. 155.

5. Jahrah was the only center of sedentary agriculture in Kuwait where any surplus was realized. About twenty miles west of Kuwait City, the village in 1904 had eighty-six permanent dwellings which accommodated about five hundred inhabitants. They lived as tenant farmers tilling the land owned by the sheikh or rich town merchants. The organization of production, then, was essentially feudal. Only about 30 tons of surplus grain were realized annually and exported to Kuwait City. See Lorimer, *Gazetteer,* vol. 2, pt. 2A, pp. 1896–1898.

6. Najat Abdul Qadir al-Jasim, *al-Tatawur al-Siyasi wa-al-Iqtisadi lil Kuwayt bayn al-Harbayn, 1914–1939* (The Political and Economic Development of Kuwait Between Two World Wars, 1914–1939) (Cairo: al-Matbaah al-Fanniyah al-Haditha, 1973), p. 206.

7. Fatima Husayn Yusif al-Abdul Razzak, *al-Miyah wa al-Sukan fi al-Kuwayt* (Water and Population in Kuwait) (Kuwait: n.p., 1974), p. 178.

8. Mohammed Mahjub, *Muqaddimah li-dirasat al-Mujtamaat al-Badawiyah* (Introduction to the Study of Bedouin Societies), (Kuwait: Wakalat al-Mutboaat, 1974), p. 110. A British Trade Report for 1937–38 estimated the population at that time at 60,000. Political Agent, Kuwait, Trade Report for Kuwait, 1937–38, F. O. File #L/P&S/12/3743, p. 4.

9. Al-Qatami, *Guide on Navigation,* p. 200, one of the foremost authorities on sea industries in Kuwait, states that in that year the number of pearling boats in the Kuwait registry was 1,200.

10. See *ibid.*, pp. 222–23, for details of this system.

11. Allan Villiers, *Sons of Sinbad* (New York: Scribner's, 1969), p. 353. Villiers spent two years sailing with the oceangoing fleet and the pearling fleet in Kuwait, 1938–40. In this book, he describes in detail the social, technical, and economic organizations of these industries. Also see Lorimer, *Gazetteer,* vol. 1, pt. 2, pp. 2236–42, for a detailed description of the valuation systems for pearls and some of the methods used by the merchants to minimize the price paid to the captains.

12. Al-Shamlan, *History of Pearling in Kuwait,* p. 319, comments that "this tax is taken by the ruler, who provides nothing in return. In other words, he does nothing to help the diver."

13. This system was not even identified by Lorimer as a distinct system of financing. By 1912, Ruziq Isa, in an article entitled "Maghasat al-Lulu" (The Location of Pearls), published in the Baghdad journal, *Lughat al-Arab* 12, identified the System of Advances as a distinct and indeed dominant one.

14. Mohammad Ghanim al-Rumaihi, *al-Bitrol wa- al-Taghayur al-Ijtimai fi al-Khalij al-Arabi* (Oil and Social Change in the Arab Gulf) (Kuwait: Myussasat al-Wihdah lil Nashr wa- al-Tawzi, 1975), p. 33.

15. Richard Le Baron Bowen, "Pearl Fisheries of the Persian Gulf," in *The Middle East Journal* 5, no. 2 (Spring 1951):173.

16. The *Trade Report for Kuwait, 1937–38,* p. 4, noted that "the Kuwait pearling fleet consists of 700 boats but only 200 to 300 boats put to sea in recent years."

17. Al-Qanaie, *Pages from the History of Kuwait,* p. 69. Even in 1904, according to Lorimer, *Gazetteer,* vol. 2, pt. 2B, p. 1052, this traffic did not exist. See also Alan Villiers, "Some Aspects of the Arab Dhow Trade," *The Middle East Journal* 2, no. 4 (October 1948):399, who noted that in 1939 there were fifty or sixty small dhows in Kuwait engaged in local trade, and "many of them engaged in bringing fresh water" to Kuwait from Basra.

18. "Administration Report of the Political Agency for the Year 1918," Dickson's Private Papers, Middle East Library, St. Antony's College, Oxford.

19. Except for the groves of the ruling family, there is no indication in the records of the ownership by merchant families of palm groves in Iraq prior to the First World War. It appears that this developed in the period between the wars while the British were in occupation of Iraq, although the extent of such holdings is unknown. See Villiers, "Some Aspects of the Arab Dhow Trade," *Middle East Journal* 2, no. 4 (October 1948):401, and *Sons of Sinbad,* p. 399. For a description of al-Sabah property in Iraq see Foreign Office File #R/15/1/510, "Kuwait: Properties of Sheikhs of Kuwait and Mohammerah in Mesopotamia, 1913–1914," and Freeth and Winstone, *Kuwait,* pp. 112–13. By 1938, the British Political Agent estimated that 35 families had "date-gardens of some size in Iraq." G.S. de Gaury to Britconsul, Bushire, March 12, 1939. IOR #L/P&S/12/3894A.

20. Villiers, "Some Aspects of the Arab Dhow Trade," *Middle East Journal* 2, no. 4 (October 1948):401.

21. Villiers, *Sons of Sinbad,* p. 399; see pp. 397–404 for details of the economics of the deep-sea dhow.

22. Villiers, "Some Aspects of the Arab Dhow Trade," *Middle East Journal* 2, no. 4 (October 1948):401–403.

23. The number of crew given in the table indicates one of the smaller oceangoing vessels—about 100 tons. The larger ships carried a much larger crew, including singers and musicians for the entertainment of crew and the captain's business parties in every port.

Villiers' 150-ton ship had a total crew of 36, which included the entertainers. The captain's shares also varied; on Villiers' ship, the captain took five shares. See Villiers, *Sons of Sinbad*, p. 402, and al-Qatami, *Guide on Navigation*, pp. 239–41.

24. See Articles 1 to 3 and 43 to 49 in the Law of the Divers, Appendix 1.

25. By the mid-thirties, the Japanese were entering the Gulf as significant competitors of the British. Of the eighty-five steamers which entered the Port of Kuwait in 1937–38, fifty-seven were British and twenty-one Japanese (the remainder being two German and five Dutch steamers). The *Trade Report for Kuwait, 1937–38* reported: "Japan continued to exploit the Kuwait market as was reported last year. Their goods retained their popularity almost to the exclusion of those of all other nationalities.... The majority of the inhabitants of Kuwait earn little more than suffices to eke out a bare existence. To be readily saleable therefore everything must be of the lowest possible price whatever its quality or lasting properties may be" (p. 2).

26. See Khaldoun H. al-Naqeeb, "Changing Patterns of Social Stratification in the Middle East: Kuwait (1950–1970) as a Case Study," unpublished Ph.D. dissertation (Austin: University of Texas at Austin, 1976), p. 130, and Adil Muhammad al-Abd al Mughni, *al-Iqtisad al-Kiwayti al-Qadim* (Traditional Kuwaiti Economy) (Kuwait: n.p.), p. 132.

27. For the text of draft convention, see J. C. Hurewitz, comp., trans., ed., *The Middle East and North Africa in World Politics: A Documentary Record* (New Haven: Yale University Press, 1975) 1:568–70.

28. See "Note by Sir Andrew Ryan [His Majesty's Minister at Jedda]: Ibn Saud's Attitude towards Kuwait," August 16, 1933, IOR #L/P&S/12/3732.

29. See "Relations Between His Majesty's Government in the United Kingdom and the Sheikh of Koweit, Final Record of a Meeting held at the Foreign Office, on October 5, 1933," IOR #L/P&S/12/3732.

30. See Secretary of State for India to the Political Resident, Persian Gulf, March 9, 1934, IOR #L/P&S/12/3732.

31. See the complete file IOR #L/P&S/12/3732 for the details of these issues from British diplomatic correspondence.

32. See H. R. P. Dickson, "Note on the Shabiba Movement in Iraq: Its Aims and Methods," June 12, 1939, Dickson's Private Papers, Middle East Library, St. Antony's College, Oxford for British reaction to the Arab Nationalist Movement. Also, Political Agent, Kuwait, to Britconsul, Bushire, March 19, 1938, IOR #L/P&S/12/3894A.

33. See Khazal, *Political History of Kuwait*, vol. 5, p. 14, and al-Shamlan, *From the History of Kuwait*, p. 199–200. Al-Shamlan is the grandson of Shamlan Ibn Ali bin Sayf who was a member of the Council, and the author utilized private family records to trace the history of Kuwait, particularly in this turbulent period.

34. Khazal, *Political History of Kuwait*, vol. 5, p. 15, provided the text of the Amir's handwritten letter.

35. Similar opposition movements were under way in other parts of the Gulf—in Bahrain, Dubai, and the Trucial sheikhdoms. By the thirties, the process of underdevelopment of the sheikhdoms of the Gulf had resulted in the poverty of the region, and there was growing opposition to the relations of production created by Britain. See Mohammad Ghanim al-Rumaihi, *Muawiqat al-Tanniyah al-Ijtimaiyah wa-al-Iqtisadiyah, fi Mujtamaat al-Khalij al-Arabi al-Muasirah* (Obstacles to Social and Economic Development in the Contemporary Arab Gulf Societies) (Kuwait: Kadhimah, 1977), pp. 12–14.

36. The British did not want to declare an open protectorate in Kuwait and wanted to preserve their control through the Amir. However, the increasing nationalist elements of the movement and its relationship with Arab nationalism in general and Iraqi Arab nationalist groups in particular, and Sheikh Ahmed's repressive measures threatened to polarize the situation. The Political Agent encouraged the leadership of the most moderate element, the merchant class, and supported concessions to this group. For the details of this period through British diplomatic correspondence, see IOR #L/P&S/12/3894A, "Persian Gulf: Kuwait Disturbances, 1938, and Consequent Administrative Changes: Kuwait Council." Also see al-Jasim, pp. 213–24, where the author examined not only the British records in her study but also the Iraqi newspapers which provided the only outlet for the expression of Kuwaiti opposition in the period.

37. According to al-Jasim, *Kuwait between Two Wars,* p. 225, about 150 families, the "notables" of Kuwait, formed the electorate.

38. Khalid Suleiman al-Adsani, *Nisf 'Am lil Hukm al-Niyabi fi al-Kuwayt* (Half a Year of Parliamentary Rule in Kuwait) published 1947 without further publication information. The author was secretary to the Legislative Council, and in this work gives a detailed account of the Council's formation and functioning during the brief period of its existence. On pp. 5–6, he gives details of British involvement in the Council's formation.

39. Al-Jasim, *Kuwait between Two World Wars,* p. 225. Shiyan al-Ghanim resigned due to family circumstances and was replaced by Muhammad bin Shahin al-Ghanim on the basis of the number of votes.

40. Text of letter from al-Adsani, "Half a Year of Parliamentary Rule," p. 10.

41. Text from *ibid.,* pp. 11–12.

42. "Improvements Introduced by the Kuwait Council Since Its Formation," appended to T. C. Fowle, British Residency, Bushire, to R. T. Peel, India Office, London, November 17, 1938, IOR #L/P&S/12/3894A.

43. Text of letter from al-Adsani, "Half a Year of Parliamentary Rule," pp. 43–44.

44. Al-Adsani notes in *ibid.* that the club, called *Nadi Qutlat al-Shabab al-Watani* (club of the Nationalist Youth Bloc) had 200 members. "The fruit of this bloc was carried through the seeding of nationalist feeling in the hearts of 200 youth who divided themselves into committees and groups to serve the existing movement by propagating the ... Arab spirit among the general public and teaching illiterates the basics of reading and writing ... in free night classes" (pp. 22–23).

45. For details of this confrontation, see H. R. P. Dickson, "An Account of the Political Situation in Kuwait, 1938." *Dickson's Private Papers,* St. Antony's College, Oxford. For a list of the nationalists reported to have fled Kuwait, see appendix to "Kuwait Intelligence Summary for the period from 16th to 31st March, 1939, No. 6 of 1939," IOR #L/P&S/12/3894A.

46. Mubarak to Political Resident in the Gulf, October 27, 1913, in A. H. T. Chisholm, *The First Kuwait Oil Concession: A Record of the Negotiations for the 1934 Agreement* (London: Frank Cass, 1975), p. 89.

4—THE NEW INTEGRATION: THE CONTINUITY OF DEPENDENCY

1. For text of treaty, see Husain M. Albaharna, *The Arabian Gulf States: Their Legal and Political Status and Their International Problems,* 2nd ed., (Beirut: Librairie du Liban, 1974), Appendix XI.

2. *Kuwait Today: A Welfare State* (Kuwait: Ministry of Guidance and Information, n.d.), p. 53.

3. Complete text of Constitution in Abid A. Al-Marayati, ed., *Middle Eastern Constitutions and Electoral Laws* (New York: Praeger, 1968), pp. 200–29.

4. See Appendix 2 for the membership of the successive cabinets.

5. Central Bank of Kuwait, *Economic Report for 1979* (Kuwait: Central Bank of Kuwait, 1980), p. 75.

6. *Kuwait Today,* p. 53.

7. See, for example, Ibrahim Abu-Nab, "The Lamp is Still Burning in the Gulf," *al-Hawadith* (Beirut), January 24, 1975, pp. 30–31, and Abd Allah Fahad al-Nifaisi, *al-Kuwait al-Raay al-Akhar* (Kuwait: Another Opinion) (London: Ta-ha Advertising, 1978), pp. 74–90, who discuss tribal and religious manipulation of elections.

8. The role of the opposition in the National Assembly is fully revealed in the Kuwait weekly newspaper, *al-Taliah,* 1963–76, which was the principal organ for the expression of opposition views. For a concise review of the Assembly's history of opposition, see *Middle East Annual Review, 1977* (Essex: The Middle East Economic Review, 1978), p. 215; also see al-Nifaisi, *Kuwait: Another Opinion.*

9. The increasing size and literacy of the electorate (males twenty-one years and over) was a function of the age structure of the population and the expansion of education initiated in 1954. These will be discussed in other chapters.

10. See, for example, "Charter of the Congress of Democratic Liberals," *al-Rai al-Amm* (Kuwait), June 8, 1974, pp. 17–18. This was one of the four main non-tribal, non-sectarian groups that emerged in the 1975 election, and the Charter reflects generally the main areas of issue of these nascent political parties.

11. *Middle East Annual Review, 1977,* p. 215.

12. See Anthony Sampson, *The Seven Sisters: The Great Oil Companies and the World They Made* (New York: The Viking Press, 1975), pp. 67–68.

13. The International Bank for Reconstruction and Development, *The Economic Development of Kuwait* (Baltimore: The Johns Hopkins Press, 1965), p. 33.

14. *Ibid.,* p. 23.

15. Planning Board, *The First Five Year Development Plan 1967/68–1971/72* (Kuwait: al-Rissala Press, 1968), p. 25.

16. *Al-Taliah* (Kuwait), October 30, 1968, p. 3.

17. *Kuwait—Monthly Bulletin* (Published by the Permanent Mission of the State of Kuwait to the United Nations) 10, no. 2 (September 1973).

18. *Kuwait—Monthly Bulletin* 10, no. 5 (December 1973).

19. *Middle East Annual Review, 1975,* p. 166.

20. *Kuwait—Monthly Bulletin* 11, no. 4 (November 1974).

21. *Middle East Economic Survey* 18, no. 4 (November 15, 1974).

22. A. Al-Hamad, *Some Aspects of the Oil Controversy: An Arab Interpretation* (Kuwait: Kuwait Fund for Arab Economic Development, 1974), p. 6.

23. For a detailed description of Kuwait's economy, see the 1965 IBRD study, *The Economic Development of Kuwait* (already cited); Ragaei El Mallakh, *Economic Development and Regional Cooperation: Kuwait* (Chicago: University of Chicago Press, 1968); and M. W. Khoiya and P. G. Sadler, *The Economy of Kuwait: Development and Role in International Finance* (London: Macmillan, 1979).

24. *Middle East Economic Survey* 19, no. 17 February 13, 1976:1.

25. *Kuwait—Monthly Bulletin* 10, no. 5 (December 1973).

26. Central Bank of Kuwait, *Economic Report for 1976* (Kuwait: Central Bank of Kuwait, 1977), pp. 42–62.

27. *Ibid.*, pp. 94–97.

28. *Ibid.*, p. 61.

29. *Middle East Economic Survey* 19, no. 17 (February 13, 1976).

30. *Economic Report for Kuwait, 1976*, p. 62.

31. *Middle East Economic Review, 1975*, p. 77.

32. *Middle East Economic Survey* 19, no. 17 (February 13, 1976).

33. *Middle East Economic Digest,* April 9, 1976.

34. *Financial Times* (London), February 27, 1978, p. 14.

5—THE TRANSFORMATION OF KUWAIT

1. The original plan was superceded in 1954 by a new plan for the development and expansion of Kuwait City. See, *The Economic Development of Kuwait*, pp. 28–30.

2. The Planning Board, *The First Five Year Development Plan*, 1967/68–1971/72 (Kuwait: al-Rissala Press, 1968), pp. 21–22.

3. *The Economic Development of Kuwait*, p. 4.

4. Fakhry Shehab, "Kuwait: A Super-Affluent Society," *Foreign Affairs* 42, no. 3 (April 1964):469–570.

5. Central Bank of Kuwait, *Economic Report for 1977*, pp. 67–72.

6. "Kuwait," *Financial Times Survey* (London), February 27, 1978, p. 14.

7. In 1961, for example, the IBRD mission noted that about half the inbound tonnage of the Port of Kuwait was material for the construction program. *The Economic Development of Kuwait*, p. 110. For a comprehensive critique of the development of modern Kuwait City, see Saba George Shiber, *The Kuwait Urbanization* (Kuwait: Government Press, 1964).

8. Mahmud Bajat Sinan, *al-Kuwayt: Zahrat al-Khalij al-Arabi* (Kuwait: Blossom of the Arab Gulf) (Beirut: Matabi Dar al-Kashshab, n.d.), p. 174.

9. *The Economic Development of Kuwait*, p. 45.

10. *Annual Statistical Abstract*, 1977, p. 81. Enumeration in 1957 for labor force twelve years and over; in 1975, for labor force fifteen years and over.

11. *Annual Statistical Abstract*, 1976, p. 52.

12. *The Economic Development of Kuwait*, pp. 114–19. Also see El Mallakh, Economic Development, pp. 112–16.

13. Amiri Decree No. 15, December 5, 1959.

14. Razzak, *Water and Population*, pp. 178–79.

15. Sinan, *Blossom of the Gulf*, p. 171.

16. Professional, technical, and related workers constitute the following occupational categories in the census: physical scientists and related technicians; architects, engineers, and related technicians; surveyors, draughtsmen, and technical assistants; aircraft and ships officers; life scientists and related technicians; medical doctors, dentists,

and veterinarians; other medical occupations; statisticians, mathematicians, system analysts, and related technicians; economists; accountants; jurists; teachers; members of religious orders; authors, journalists, and related workers; sculptors, painters, photographers, and related creative artists; composers and performing artists; athletes; sportsmen, and related workers; professional, technical, and related workers N.E.C. Central Statistical Office, *Classification of Occupations, 1975* (Kuwait: Planning Board, 1975).

17. Anon., *A View of Kuwait* (Washington, D.C.: Embassy of the State of Kuwait, n.d.), p. 31.

18. Council of Planning, *Mashru Khitat al-Tanmiyah al-Khamsiyah, 1976/77– 1980/81* (Proposed Five Year Plan 1976/77–1980/81) (Kuwait: Secret Document: 1976), p. 82.

19. See Robert Stephens, *The Arab's New Frontier* (London: Temple Smith, 1976), and Soliman Demir, *The Kuwait Fund and the Political Economy of Arab Regional Development* (New York: Praeger, 1976), for studies of the Kuwait Fund.

20. The *Annual Reports* of the Kuwait Fund for Arab Economic Development provide the details of all projects funded.

21. R. El Mallakh, M. Kadhim, and B. Poulson, *Capital Investment in the Middle East: The Use of Surplus Funds for Regional Development* (New York: Praeger, 1977), pp. 92–93.

22. See Galal A. Amin, *The Modernization of Poverty: A Study in the Political Economy of Growth in Nine Arab Countries, 1945–1970* (Leiden: Brill, 1974).

23. The population policy was outlined in general form in *The First FXIVE Year Plan, 1967/68–1971/72*, pp. 128–133.

24. ASA, 1977: pp. 92, 123–28. The percentages are approximate since the labor force by occupational groups was based on the 1975 census while the government civil servants by occupation groups was based upon a February 1976 census of government employees. This difference introduces some error in the comparison.

25. El Mallakh, *Economic Development and Regional Cooperation*, p. 98.

6—THE POLITICS OF STRATIFICATION: SOCIAL CHANGE AND SOCIAL CONTROL IN THE WELFARE STATE

1. *The Middle East and North Africa*, p. 434.

2. Al-Rumaihi, *Social and Economic Obstacles to Development in the Contemporary Arab Gulf*, p. 16.

3. *Al-Hawadith* (Beirut), January 31, 1975.

4. *Al-Nahar* (Beirut), Febuary 12, 1969.

5. *The Economic Development of Kuwait*, p. 97.

6. For a summary of the recommendations, see Chapter 1 of the missions' report, *The Economic Development of Kuwait*.

7. *Kuwait Today*, p. 87. The composition of the Board was changed in December 1970 to the following: Prime Minister, Minister of State for Cabinet Affairs, Minister of Finance and Oil, Minister of Social Affairs and Labor; Minister of Public Works, Minister of Education, Chairman of the Municipal Council, ten members of different professions from the private sector to be appointed by decree for four years. *Decree Concerning the Planning Board*, December, 1970.

8. Muhammed Ali al-Farra, *al-Tanmiyah al-Iqtisadiyah fi Dawlat al-Kuwayt* (Economic Development and the State of Kuwait) (Kuwait: Jamiat al-Kuwayt, n.d.), p. 195.

9. *The First Five Year Development Plan, 1967/68–1971/72,* pp. 7–10.

10. These objectives are given in terms of the formulation of specific policies, delineated in chapter 6 of *The First Five Year Development Plan.*

11. *Ibid.,* pp. 58–59.

12. *Kuwait Population Census, 1957* (Kuwait: Office of Social Affairs), p. 227. In Arabic.

13. James A. Socknat, "An Inventory and Assessment of Employment-Oriented Human Resources Development Programs in the Gulf Area" (Manama, Bahrein: The Ford Foundation, 1975), Appendices 1–5. Unpublished Report.

14. Proposals of the Five Year Plan, 1976/77–1980/81, p. 16.

15. Mohammed Rumaihi, "The Human Capital in the Gulf: A Way for Lasting Development." Unpublished monograph.

Bibliography

Abu Hakima, Ahmad. 1965. *History of Eastern Arabia —1750—1800: The Rise and Development of Bahrain and Kuwait*. Beirut: Khayats.

Abu Hakima, Ahmad, ed. 1967, 1970. *History of Kuwait*. 2 vols. Kuwait: Kuwait Government Press.

Abu-Nab, Ibrahim. 1975. "The Lamp is Still Burning in the Gulf." *Al-Hawadith* (Beirut), January 24.

Aitchison, C. U. 1909. *Collection of Treaties, Engagements and Sanads Relating to India and Neighboring Countries*. Vol. 12. Calcutta: n.p.

Al-Adsani, Khalid Suleiman. 1947. *Nisf Am lil Hukm al-Niyabi fi al-Kuwayt* (Half a Year of Parliamentary Rule in Kuwait). N.p.

Albaharna, Husain M. 1974. *The Arabian Gulf States: Their Legal and Political Status and Their International Problems*. 2nd ed. Beirut: Librairie du Liban.

Al-Farra, Muhammed Ali. n.d. *Al-Tanmiyah al-Iqtisadiyah fi Dawlat al-Kuwayt* (Economic Development and the State of Kuwait). Kuwait: Jamiat al-Kuwayt.

Al-Hamad, A. 1974. *Some Aspects of the Oil Controversy: An Arab Interpretation*. Kuwait: Kuwait Fund for Arab Economic Development.

Al-Hawadith. Beirut. January 31, 1975.

Al-Jasim, Najat Abdul Qadir. 1973. *Al-Tatawur al-Siyasi wa- al-Iqtisadi lil Kuwayt bayn al-Harbayn, 1914–1939* (The Political and Economic Development of Kuwait between Two World Wars, 1914–1939). Cairo: al-Matbaah al-Fanniyah al-Haditha.

Al-Khususi, Badr al-Din Abbas. 1972. *Dirasat fi Tarikh al-Kuwayt al-Ijtimai wa al-Iqtisadi: 1913–1961* (Studies in the Social and Economic History of Kuwait: 1913–1961). Kuwait: Sharikat al-Matbuat lil Tawzi wa al-Nishr.

Al-Marayati, Abid A., ed. 1968. *Middle Eastern Constitutions and Electoral Laws*. New York: Praeger.

Al-Mughni, Adil Muhammad al-Abd. 1977. *Al-Iqtisad al-Kuwayti al-Qadim* (Traditional Kuwaiti Economy). Kuwait: n.p.

Al-Nahar. Beirut. February 12, 1969.

Al-Najjar, Mustapha Abd al-Qadir. 1975. *Al-Tarikh al-Siyasi li Ilaqat al-Iraq al-Dawliyah bi al-Khalij al-Arabi* (The Political History of Iraqi International Relations with the States of the Arab Gulf). Basra: Basra University Press.

191

Al-Naqeeb, Khaldoun H. 1976. "Changing Patterns of Social Stratification in the Middle East: Kuwait (1950–1970) as a Case Study." Austin: The University of Texas at Austin. Unpublished Ph.D. dissertation.

Al-Nifaisi, Abd Allah Fahad. 1978. *Al-Kuwait al-Raay al-Akhar* (Kuwait: Another Opinion). London: Ta-ha Advertising.

Al-Qatami, Isa. 1976. *Dalil al-Muhtar fi ilm al-Bihar* (The Guide for the Confused on the Science of Navigation), 4th ed. Kuwait: Government of Kuwait Press.

Al-Qinaie, Yusuf Bin Isa. 1968. *Safahat min Tarikh al-Kuwayt* (Pages from the History of Kuwait), 4th ed. Kuwait: Government Printing House.

Al-Rawi, Abdul Jabbar. 1972. *Al Badiyah* (The Desert), 3rd ed. Baghdad: n.p.

Al-Rumaihi, Mohammed Ghanim. 1975. *Al-Bitrol wa- al-Taghayur al-Ijtimai fi al-Khalij al-Arabi* (Oil and Social Change in the Arab Gulf). Kuwait: Muussasat al-Wihdah lil wa- al-Tawzi.

———. 1977. *Muawiqat al-Tanniyah al-Ijtimaiyah wa- al-Iqtisadiyah, fi Mujtamaat al-Khalij al-Arabi al-Muasirah* (Social and Economic Obstacles to Development in the Contemporary Arab Gulf). Kuwaiti Kadhimah Co.

Al-Rushaid, Abd al-Aziz. n.d. *Tarikh al-Kuwayt* (The History of Kuwait). Beirut: Dar Mahaahat al-Hayat.

Al-Shamlan, Sayf Marzouk. 1959. *Min Tarikh al-Kuwayt* (From the History of Kuwait). Cairo: Matbat Nadhat Misr.

———. 1975. *Tarikh al-Ghaus ala al-Lulu fi al-Kuwayt wa- al-Khalij al-Arabi* (History of Pearling in Kuwait and the Arab Gulf). Kuwait: Government of Kuwait.

Al-Taliah. Kuwait. 1963–76.

Amin, Galal A. 1974. *The Modernization of Poverty: A Study in the Political Economy of Growth in Nine Arab Countries, 1945–1970.* Leiden: Brill.

Amin, Samir. 1976. "Self-Reliance and the New International Economic Order." *Monthly Review* 29 (July–August).

———. 1976. *Unusual Development: An Essay on the Social Formations of Peripheral Capitalism.* New York: Monthly Review Press.

Anon. n.d. *A View of Kuwait.* Washington, D.C.: Embassy of the State of Kuwait.

Bidwell, Robin, ed. 1971. *The Affairs of Kuwait, 1896–1905.* 2 vols. London: Frank Cass.

Bowen, Richard Le Baron. 1951. "Pearl Fisheries of the Persian Gulf." *The Middle East Journal* 5, no. 2 (Spring).

Busch, Briton C. 1967. *Britain and the Persian Gulf, 1894–1914.* Berkeley: University of California Press.

Cardoso, Fernando Henrique. 1972. "Dependency and Development in Latin America." *New Left Review* 74 (July–August).

Central Bank of Kuwait. 1975. *Economic Report for 1974*. Kuwait: Central Bank of Kuwait.

———. 1976. *Economic Report for 1975*. Kuwait: Central Bank of Kuwait.

———. 1977. *Economic Report for 1976*. Kuwait: Central Bank of Kuwait.

———. 1978. *Economic Report for 1977*. Kuwait: Central Bank of Kuwait.

———. 1980. *Economic Report for 1979*. Kuwait: Central Bank of Kuwait.

Central Statistical Office. 1975. *Annual Statistical Abstract, 1975*. Kuwait: Planning Board.

———. 1976. *Annual Statistical Abstract, 1976*. Kuwait: Ministry of Planning.

———. 1977. *Annual Statistical Abstract, 1977*. Kuwait: Ministry of Planning.

———. 1975. *Classification of Occupations*. Kuwait: Planning Board.

———. 1968. *Statistical Abstract, 1968*. Kuwait: Planning Board.

———. 1972. *Statistical Abstract, 1972*. Kuwait: Planning Board.

———. 1973. *Statistical Abstract, 1973*. Kuwait: Planning Board.

———. 1974. *Statistical Yearbook of Kuwait*. Kuwait: Planning Board.

"Charter of Democratic Liberals." 1974. *Al-Rai al-Amm* (Kuwait), June 8.

Chisholm, A. H. T. 1975. *The First Kuwait Oil Concession: A Record of the Negotiations for the 1934 Agreement*. London: Frank Cass, 1975.

Council of Planning. 1976. *Mashru Khitat al-Tanmiyah al-Khamsiyah, 1976/77–1980/81* (Proposed Five Year Plan, 1976/77–1980/81). Kuwait: Secret Document.

Curzon, George N. 1966. *Persia and the Persian Question*. 2 vols. New York: Barnes and Noble.

Demir, Soliman. 1976. *The Kuwait Fund and the Political Economy of Arab Regional Development*. New York: Praeger.

Dickson, H. R. P. 1938. "An Account of the Political Situation in Kuwait, 1938." Dickson's Private Papers, St. Antony's College, Oxford.

———. 1956. *Kuwait and Her Neighbours*. London: Allen & Unwin.

Dos Santos, T. 1973. "The Crisis of Dependency Theory and the Problem of Dependence in Latin America." In *Underdevelopment and Development*, edited by H. Bernstein. Harmondsworth: Penguin.

El Mallakh, Ragaei. 1968. *Economic Development and Regional Cooperation: Kuwait*. Chicago: University of Chicago Press.

El Mallakh, R.; M. Kadhim; and B. Poulson. 1977. *Capital Investment in the Middle East: The Use of Surplus Funds for Regional Development*. New York: Praeger.

Foreign Office. 1933. "Relations Between His Majesty's Government in the United Kingdom and the Sheikh of Koweit." With Appendices. IOR #L/P&S/12/3732.

Frank, André Gunder. 1967. *Capitalism and Underdevelopment in Latin America: Historical Studies of Chile and Brazil.* New York: Monthly Review Press.

———. 1972. "The Development of Underdevelopment." In *Dependence and Underdevelopment: Latin America's Political Economy,* edited by James D. Cockcroft, André Gunder Frank, and Dale L. Johnson. Garden City: Anchor Books.

Freeth, Zahra, and Victor Winstone. 1972. *Kuwait: Prospect and Reality.* London: George Allen & Unwin.

Hitti, Philip K. 1964. *History of the Arabs,* 8th ed. London: Macmillan.

Holdich, T. Hungerford. 1901. *The Indian Borderland.* London: Methuen.

Hurewitz, J. C., comp. trans., ed. 1975. *The Middle East and North Africa in World Politics: A Documentary Record.* Vol. 1. New Haven: Yale University Press.

Husayn, abd al-Aziz. 1960. *Al-Mujtama' al-'Arabi bil Kuwait* (Arab Society in Kuwait). Cairo: Institute for Higher Arab Studies.

Ireland, Philip. 1938. *Iraq: A Study in Political Development.* New York: Macmillan.

Isa Ruziq. 1912. "Maghasat al-Lulu" (The Location of Pearls). *Lughat al-Arab* 12 (May).

The International Bank for Reconstruction and Development. 1965. *The Economic Development of Kuwait.* Baltimore: Johns Hopkins University Press.

Kelly, J. B. 1968. *Britain and the Persian Gulf: 1795–1880.* Oxford: Clarendon Press.

Khazal, Husayn Khalaf al-Shaykh. 1962–1970. *Tarikh al-Kuwayt al-Siyasi* (The Political History of Kuwait), 5 vols. Beirut: Matabu Dar al-Kutub.

Khoiya, M. W., and P. G. Sadler. 1979. *The Economy of Kuwait: Development and Role in International Finance.* London: Macmillan.

Kumar, Ravinder. 1965. *India and the Persian Gulf Region, 1958–1907: A Study in British Imperial Policy.* New York: Asia Publishing House.

Kuwait Chamber of Commerce and Industry. 1965. *Dalil al-Kuwayt* (Guide to Kuwait). Kuwait: Chamber of Commerce and Industry.

Kuwait—Monthly Bulletin 10, no. 2 (September), 10, no. 5 (December). 1973. New York: Permanent Mission of the State of Kuwait to the United Nations.

———. 11, no. 4 (November). 1974. New York: Permanent Mission of the State of Kuwait to the United Nations.

Kuwait Population Census, 1957. 1958. Kuwait: Office of Social Affairs.

Kuwait Today: A Welfare State. n.d. Kuwait: Ministry of Guidance and Information.

Leys, Colin. 1975. *Underdevelopment in Kenya: The Political Economy of Neo-Colonialism, 1964–1971.* London: Heinemann.

Loghat el-Arab. Baghdad. 7 (December 1913).

Longrigg, Stephen Hemsley. 1925. *Four Centuries of Modern Iraq.* Oxford: Clarendon Press.

Lorimer, J. F. 1970. *Gazetteer of the Persian Gulf, Oman and Central Arabia.* 2 vols. Shannon: Irish University Press.

Mahjub, Mohammed. n.d. *Al-Hijrah wa- al-Taghayyur al-Binai fi al-Mujtama al-Kuwayti* (Migration and Structural Change in Kuwaiti Society). Kuwait: Wakalat al-Mutboaat.

———. 1974. *Muqadimmah lidirasat al-Mujtamaat al-Badawiyah* (Introduction of Bedouin Societies). Kuwait: Wakalat al-Mutboaat.

Mahmoud, Husayn Sulaiman. 1968. *Al-Kuwayt: Madhiha wa Hadhruha* (Kuwait: Its Past and Present). Baghdad: al-Ahliyah Bookshop.

Manesty, Samuel, and Harford Jones. 1790. "Report on the Commerce of Arabia and Persia." In *History of Kuwait,* edited by Ahmad Abu Hakima, 2 vols. Kuwait: Kuwait Government Press.

Meillassoux, C. 1972. "From Reproduction to Production." *Economy and Society* 1, no. 1.

Middle East and North Africa, 1973–74. 1973. London: Europa Publications.

Middle East Annual Review. 1977. 1978. Essex: The Middle East Economic Review.

Middle East Annual Review. 1975. Essex: The Middle East Economic Review.

Middle East Economic Digest. Beirut. April 9, 1976.

Middle East Economic Survey. 1974. 18, no. 4 (November 15).

———. 1976. 19, no. 17 (February 13).

———. 1976. 19, no. 30 (May 17)

Nawar, Aziz Suleiman. 1968. *Tarikh al-Iraqi al-Hadith* (The History of Modern Iraq). Cairo: Dar al-Katab al-Arabi.

New York Times. April 16, May 16, October 16, October 18, October 22, 1973; March 14, November 11, 1974.

Planning Board. 1968. *The First Five Year Development Plan, 1967/68–1971/72.* Kuwait: al-Rissala Press.

Political Agent, Kuwait. 1914. "Kuwait: Properties of Sheikhs of Kuwait and Mohammerah in Mesopotamia, 1913–1914." F.O. File # R/15/1/510.

———. 1938. "Persian Gulf: Kuwait Disturbances, 1938, and Consequent Administrative Changes: Kuwait Council." IOR #L/P&S/12/3894A.

———. 1938. "Trade Report for Kuwait, 1937–38." F.O. File # L/P&S/12/3743.

Poulantzas, Nicos. 1974. "Internationalization of Capitalist Relations and the Nation-State." *Economy and Society* 3, no. 2. (May).

Razzak, Fatima Husayn al-Abdul. 1974. *Al-Miyah wa al-Sukan fi al-Kuwayt* (Water and Population in Kuwait). Kuwait: n.p.

Roxborough, Ian. 1976. "Dependency Theory in the Sociology of Development." *The West African Journal of Sociology and Political Science* 1, no. 2 (January).

Rumaihi, Mohammed. 1975. "The Human Capital in the Gulf: A Way for Lasting Development." Unpublished monograph.

Ryan, Sir Andrew. 1933. "Iban Saud's Attitude Towards Kuwait. August 16. IOR #L/P&S/12/3732.

Saleh, Zaki. 1957. *Mesopotamia (Iraq), 1600–1914: A Study in British Foreign Affairs*. Baghdad: al-Maaref Press.

Sampson, Anthony. 1975. *The Seven Sisters: The Great Oil Companies and the World They Made*. New York: Viking.

Secretary of State for India to the Political Resident, Persian Gulf. March 9, 1937. IOR #1/P&S/12/3732.

Shehab, Fakhry. 1964. "Kuwait: A Super-Affluent Society." *Foreign Affairs* 42, no. 3 (April).

Shiber, Saba George. 1964. *The Kuwait Urbanization*. Kuwait: Government Press.

Sinan, Mahmud, Bajat. n.d. *Al-Kuwayt: Zahrat al-Khalij al-Arabi* (Kuwait: Blossom of the Arab Gulf). Beirut: Matabi Dar al-Kashshab.

Socknat, James A. 1975. "An Inventory and Assessment of Employment-Oriented Human Resources Development Programs in the Gulf Area." Manama, Bahrein: The Ford Foundation. Unpublished.

Stephens, Robert. 1976. *The Arabs' New Frontier.* London: Temple Smith.

Villiers, Alan. 1948. "Some Aspects of the Arab Dhow Trade." *The Middle East Journal* 2, no. 4 (October).

―――. 1969. *Sons of Sinbad*. New York: Scribner's.

Warden, Francis. 1856. "Historical Sketch of the Uttoobee Tribe of Arabs (Bahrein) from the year 1716 to the year 1817." In *History of Kuwait,* edited by Ahmad Abu Hakima, 2 vols. Kuwait: Kuwait Government Press, 1970.

Wilson, Arnold T. 1928. *The Persian Gulf: An Historical Sketch from the Earliest Times to the Beginning of the Twentieth Century*. London: Allen & Unwin.

Index

Abd al-Aziz, Husayn, 32, 36
Abdullah, Sheikh (1762–1812), 35, 42, 43
Abdullah, Sheikh (1866–1892), 35, 45
Abdullah al-Salim, Sheikh (1950–1965), 72, 76, 82
Abu Hakima, Ahmad, 30, 37, 43
Agriculture, 22, 25, 60, 113
Agricultural Institute, 139
Ahl Musallam, rulers of Qatar, 20
Ahmed al-Jabir, Sheikh, and Uqair Conference, 70, 71; and Consultative Council, 72; and People's Legislative Council, 76; and oil negotiations, 78; death of, 81; and Arab nationalism, 185n.36
Al-Adsani, and People's Legislative Council, 77
Jabir al-Ahmad al-Sabah, prime minister: and foreign investment policy, 98; and oil pricing, 90–91
Al Awazim, tribe, 25
Al Ghanim, Shiyan, resignation of, 185n.39
Al-Ghanim, Muhammad bin Shahin, 185n.39
Al-Ibrahim, Yusuf ibn Abdullah, and Mubarak, 47
Al-Jalaahmeh, pearl merchants, 22, 28
Al-Khalifah, 22; migration of, 28–29, 179n.18; capture of Bahrain, 29
Al-Kuwayt, Dalil, 43
Al-Maadaw, Utbi tribe, 22
Al-Qinaie: and Bani Utub, 21; and Kuwait City, 22; and pearl divers, 34
Al-Qutlah al-Wataniyah (The National Bloc), 73
Al-Rashaida, tribe, 25
Al-Rushaid, Abd al-Aziz: and boat building, 24; and Kuwait City, 22; and Mubarak, 55; and pearling, 58; and occupation of Basra, 59

Al-Sabah, Salem, Kuwaiti Ambassador to the United States, 90
Al-Sabah, Utbi tribe, 22
Al-Saud, Abd al-Aziz, future ruler of Saudi Arabia, 50–51
Al-Shamlan, Sayf Marzouk, and Sabah family, 27, 35, 184n.33
Al-Taliah, Kuwaiti newspaper, 89
Amin, Samir: *Accumulation on a World Scale,* 7; and capitalism, 3, 8
Anglo-Turkish Convention of 1913, 69
Animal husbandry, 60
Anizah tribe, and Bani Utub emigration, 20
Anti-British sentiment. *See* Arab nationalism
Arabia, Central, Wahabi unification of, 22
Arabia, Saudi. *See* Saudi Arabia
Arabian tribes, migrations of, 178n.4
Arab-Israeli war, 89, 90, 95, 144
Arab League, and U.N., 82
Arab nationalism, 8, 56, 69, 77, 123, 151, 184n.35; and American intervention, 144; goals of, 125; in Iraq, 71; and National Assembly, 154; suppression of, 153
Arab Planning Institute, 139
Arms flow, 52–53

Baharina, boat builders, 24, 26, 178n.7
Bahrain, pearl banks, 28, 29
Bandar Abbas, Persian port, 37
Bani Kaab Arabs, 44, 45
Bani Khalid tribes, 21, 27
Bani Utub: as boat captains, 26; emigration of, 20–22; history of, 178n.3; independence of, 27; in Kuwait, 22–24, 37; merchants, 47, 55, 56–58, 59; in Qatar, 178n.7
Banking, 98

197

KUWAIT

was composed in 10-point VIP Times Roman and leaded two points
by Partners Composition,
with display type in foundry hand-set Legend
by J. M. Bundscho, Inc.;
printed by sheet-fed offset on 50-pound acid-free Glatfelter Antique Cream,
Smythe-sewn and bound over boards in Joanna Arrestox C,
by Maple-Vail Manufacturing Group, Inc.;
and published by

SYRACUSE UNIVERSITY PRESS
SYRACUSE, NEW YORK 13210